Masculinity Beyond the Metropolis

Masculinity Beyond the Metropolis

Jane Kenway, Anna Kraack, Anna Hickey-Moody

First published 2006 by
PALGRAVE MACMILLAN
Houndmills, Basingstoke, Hampshire RG21 6XS and
175 Fifth Avenue, New York, N.Y. 10010
Companies and representatives throughout the world

PALGRAVE MACMILLAN is the global academic imprint of the Palgrave Macmillan division of St. Martin's Press, LLC and of Palgrave Macmillan Ltd. Macmillan® is a registered trademark in the United States, United Kingdom and other countries. Palgrave is a registered trademark in the European Union and other countries.

ISBN-13: 978-1-4039-3932-6 hardback
ISBN-10: 1-4039-3932-2   hardback

This book is printed on paper suitable for recycling and made from fully managed and sustained forest sources.

A catalogue record for this book is available from the British Library.

Library of Congress Cataloging-in-Publication Data

Kenway, Jane.
    Masculinity beyond the metropolis / Jane Kenway, Anna Kraack, Anna Hickey-Moody.
        p. cm.
    Includes bibliographical references and index.
    ISBN 1-4039-3932-2 (cloth)
    1. Masculinity. 2. Rural youth. 3. Rural development–Sociological aspects. 4. Social change. I. Kraack, Anna, 1974– II. Hickey-Moody, Anna, 1977– III. Title.

HQ1090.K465   2006
305.3109173′4–dc22

                                                            2006041162

10   9   8   7   6   5   4   3   2   1
15   14   13   12   11   10   09   08   07   06

Printed and bound in Great Britain by
Antony Rowe Ltd, Chippenham and Eastbourne

Jane dedicates this book to
Joan Fox and Lindsay Fitzclarence,
whose generosity knows no bounds

Contents

Acknowledgements

We express our appreciation to the Australian Research Council, which funded this project through a Discovery Research Grant, and to the University of South Australia and Monash University, which also provided funding and institutional support. We also offer our genuine and warm thanks to all those people who took part in the ethnographic research in participating towns and who so freely shared their perspectives with us. We particularly thank the young people who participated in the extensive interview programme and the school staff who assisted us to organize the research in their schools and towns. We hope that you all feel the text does you and your town justice. We are especially greatful to Lindsay Fitzclarence for his unsparing intellectual input at every stage of the project from its inception to conclusion; Joan Fox for her careful reading and tidying over several drafts and for her contribution to our thumbnail sketches; Charlie Fox for his valuable criticisms on Chapter 5; and Vashti Kenway for her gracious unpaid research assistance at crucial moments. Hannah Walker and Jeremy Mackinnon worked as research assistants on this project for a period and we thank them for their insightful input. We also thank Trudi Brunton for her help with the final formatting. We also thank Peter Lang for agreeing to allow us to use selections of text from Singh, Kenway and Apple (2005) and to Routledge for agreeing to allow us to reprint sections from Kenway and Kraak (2004). Anna Kraack wishes to thank Eleanor Doig for her ongoing care and encouragement, particularly when she was in the field for long periods of time. Jane and Anna Kraack also give thanks to Anna's trusty car which, remarkably, given its antediluvian status, took them to far-flung parts of Australia without breaking down. Anna Hickey-Moody would like to say thank you to her (Big) Little Brother B and to Eszeki: the men who have taught her about boys outside cities, and especially to Pen for being her best mate. Collectively we also thank all those colleagues, friends and family who have engaged us in rich, feisty and generative conversations on the topic of this book and whose love and company continue to sustain us. Finally, we thank Briar Towers, commissioning editor for Palgrave Macmillan, whose suggestions for the shape of the book and whose faith in the project began its road to print.

Introduction

Nine point one million Americans tuned in to watch tales of straightforward country males and two young, flashy and faddish city women in Fox's 'reality TV' series, *The Simple Life #2* (2004). The stories that glued American viewers to their screens were also closely followed by audiences in Asia, Europe, the United Kingdom and Australia – along with many other countries connected by the global web of TV broadcasting. For the viewing pleasure of this global audience, regional American communities and their masculinities were commodified and caricatured as Paris Hilton and Nicole Ritchie, glamour girls from the metropolis of California, try to live *The Simple Life* and engage with those who are presented as simple people.

One typical, 'simple' country male is Bob Click, the restrained ranch man and loyal husband who tries hard not to be derailed from his quiet and friendly small-town life by these slick city girls' calls for his transformation. Bob doesn't talk about his sex life to strangers (what kind of proud married man would?) and neither is he inclined to accept these young women's suggestions about possible ways of 'glamming it up'. Some naive younger country males, however, are beguiled by these women's highly honed charms and their titillating talk. Fired from three of their four jobs in the first series of *The Simple Life*, Paris and Nicole manage to hold down only their unskilled positions pumping gas at a local service station. The boys working at the station, Anthony, Chops and Buffalo, seem to think there is something pretty exciting about having two shiny looking girls pump gas. Scattered across Series 1 and 2, many other young men are drawn to the glitz and glamour of

1

these wealthy young women from the city. In *The Simple Life*, country males are slow thinkers, and talkers, and young country men are easily impressed by city women and city ways. They are naive about the complex workings of the world beyond them and cognitively ill equipped to deal with it. They are contrasted to the slow, quiet and reflective older men, also depicted as typical inhabitants of the US countryside. The older, established country man is calm, conservative and, above all, a family man – a man who tries to live out his values in a consistent and dependable fashion. But who believes the partial and stereotypical representations of masculinity and rural America in *The Simple Life*?

Out-of-the-way places and their people have long held sway in the popular imagination via notions of, for example, the backwater, the sticks, the middle of nowhere, the boondocks, the frontier, the outback, the heartlands, the badlands or the rural/coastal/mountain idyll. By way of various print, electronic and digital media, programmes such as *The Simple Life*, these places are represented and come to be understood in particular ways; they are allocated identities often as the devalued or valued other of the city. Perhaps they come to be seen as diehard traditional and slow moving, inhabited by good-hearted and unpretentious, if somewhat unsophisticated, people. The popular British radio programme *The Archers* (BBC Radio 4) is an example; although it has relatively recently updated its spatial fictions. Some such places may also be represented as dangerous and hostile to 'outsiders' (even within); peopled by backward, prejudiced and violent 'rednecks'; as is the case in the classic film *Deliverance* (1972) and the Oscar winning *Boys Don't Cry* (1998). In some road movies the camera barely registers their existence, they become a blur (beside the road/beside the point), contrasted with the sharp focus on the highway ahead to the places that matter. But out of the way places have also come to stand for a regretfully lost past and a possible place of escape for stressed-out, hyper-competitive and environmentally overstimulated city dwellers. Here, places beyond the metropolis are nostalgically contrasted with city life and seen as uncomplicated, safe, community-minded, clean, green and grounded in nature. Such images have helped to produce the 'sea change' or 'tree change' moves of disillusioned city dwellers to the coast or the country. The popular imagination of life outside the metropolis has also been fuelled by media-marketed images of lifestyles (particularly subcultural style), lifestyle goods and tourist destinations. An example is the 'timeless' surfing film *Endless Summer* (1966). This documentary-style eulogy to surf culture showcases idyllic coastlines, surfing subcultures and the lifestyle goods associated with them.

Print, TV and web-based news stories and documentaries tell also of tradition and change beyond the metropolis. They often chronicle the impact of economic and cultural globalization. They illustrate, among other things, how the global impacts on the local and how the local retaliates. For example, current affairs shows and documentaries often tell stories of the 'rural drain'; of capital flight, of places left economically desolate after many businesses and people have fled to the cities. Such stories etch images of ghost economies supporting left-behind 'battler', and some times backlash, communities. Other documentaries show the ways in which global signs and corporate cultures invade localities and drain local businesses of life and livelihood. Further, news bulletins beam around the globe images of the countryside fighting back, drawing attention to itself and its issues; for instance, the Belgian farmers' angry march on Paris (Tyler 1999). Rural rebound/renewal stories are part of this genre.

Such representations often, in one way or another, tap into the national psyche of such countries as the United States (small-town America), England (the countryside) and Australia (the bush), producing new and reproducing old myths and stereotypes and sociospatial divisions. They help to generate such things as longing and belonging, fear and desire, separation and distinction. They speak to cultural anxieties as well as aspirations. They may steer actual or imagined movements of people in and out of place, and illustrate and influence local and other perceptions of the historical and current links between place, change, masculinity and gender dynamics. Each set of representations we have mentioned invokes images of manhood; the laconic 'true blue' Aussie bloke in *Crocodile Dundee* (1986), the Southern Man in New Zealand beer advertisements, the fox hunter in the streets of London for instance. Overall 'the power of the symbolic to occlude the realities of the mundane' (Finkelstein and Bourke 2001: 48) means that the lines between the authentic and the fictional countryside and the authentic and the fictional non-urban male are difficult to draw.

This book is about such imaginings and places. Its central concern is places outside of densely populated cities; places that are variously marginalized, stigmatized, pitied and patronized, romanticized and exoticized in such textual forms. It tells of the males who live in such places and the complex range of masculinities that now emerge beyond the metropolis. It is about spatially marginalized masculinities in so-called developed, Western nations. These out of the way places include, for example, remote coastlines, the bush, the 'outback' and small country towns. We show how such places have been reconfigured by the social, cultural and geographical shifts associated with globalizing processes. And we show how this impacts on males', particularly young males', identities and identifications, lives and livelihoods and relationships – how they and their communities are increasingly caught up in, sometimes uprooted by, and may also attempt to stand apart from, globalization.

Throughout this book we draw on, and energize, two bodies of interdisciplinary literature: that on masculinities – particularly youthful masculinities – and that on globalization. Masculinity studies and globalization studies are bourgeoning fields of research. Indeed, since the 1980s there has been a rapid growth, across the disciplines and in interdisciplinary inquiry, in both fields. Surprisingly, such literatures are rarely brought together. The literature on globalization has scant understanding of masculinity and, correspondingly, the masculinity literature has only a little understanding of globalization (Chapter 1). In studying masculinity and globalization as one, we bring a new line of analysis to scholarship on both masculinity and globalization. Further, in focusing on out of the way places we challenge metrocentric studies of both masculinity and globalization. We also challenge studies that homogenize such places and the people within them.

In an unequal dialogue with the multifarious forces and figuring, signals and signs of globalization (Chapter 1), many non-metropolitan places have become economically, culturally and geographically volatile. But how and why this happens, with consequences for what and for whom, varies between and within such places. We will show this. The volatile 'globalizing local' reconfigures local industries, workplaces and ways of being a worker (Chapter 3). It alters the identities of place, place/place relations and identifications with place (Chapter 4). It adjusts and 'updates' existing geographies of injustice (Chapter 5). It destabilizes the conventional links between knowledge, value and the self (Chapter 6). And it redefines the relationships between leisure, pleasure and generation (Chapter 7). All such matters are fundamental makers and markers of masculine identity. We will explain how such global–local volatility intersects with fabrications of masculinity across these central coordinates of young men's lives.

As all this suggests, in altering places globalization puts male (and other) identities and relationships under the pressure *of* change and under pressure *to* change. Habit and history collide with such pressure as traditional expressions of masculinity confront more open, and sometimes more appealing or more threatening, identity possibilities. The manner in which such collisions are worked through in young men's lives is a focus here, as gender and generation wrangle and as gender fundamentalism meets gender complexity. We are concerned with young males' everyday/night experiences of, and engagements with, various aspects of globalization in place. And we are also concerned with the specific ways that various groupings of boys/young men in locations that are poles apart negotiate the different global processes they come to grips with, through necessity or choice; or the choices of necessity.

We deploy ethnography to pursue our inquiries. Our ethnographic methods are linked to ideas associated with global ethnographies. We call our approach 'place-based global ethnography' and justify and explain it in Chapter 2. This approach has been tailored to studying the production of masculine identities in and through globalizing localities. It allows for a comprehensive consideration of the ways in which young males shape themselves and are shaped through their relationship to the 'globalizing local' as it is manifest in changing patterns of work and leisure, perceptions of place, worthwhile knowledge and spatial geometries of injustice. Our approach allows us to create a holistic picture of young males' lives. This contrasts with the methodological practices associated with a number of ethnographic studies of masculinity that focus on a specific aspect of young males' lives, such as work, sport, popular culture or schooling, to the exclusion of others. While often fascinating, such studies offer a somewhat distorted perspective of their lives as a whole. Our approach allows us to provide a more complex and nuanced account. Further, in terms of globalization, we consider how its intersecting economic and cultural dynamics are lived out together *in situ*. We illustrate that out of the way places are complex and linked to global forces, connections and imaginings – including the imaginings produced through various media texts.

Places beyond the metropolis

We deploy the 'metropolis' as a collective noun to represent the first-world Western cities and peoples that we *look beyond*. Derived from the Greek 'meter', or mother, and the Indo-European 'polis' (city), 'metropolis' literally means 'mother city'. More conventionally the metropolis is associated with big-city life; with vibrant trade, culture and lifestyle. It is highly textured and aestheticized and teaming with sonic and sensory resonances. It exudes atmosphere, confidence, sophistication and significance. It has size and speed on its side and worldwide connections. It is imbued with the magnetic appeal of accessibility, possibility and hospitality to difference. Of course this metropolis is a somewhat fantastic formulation which resembles the city only in part. The less-alluring metropolis is congested, conflicted, polluted, divided and dangerous, and is usually also attached to an endlessly bland sub-urban sprawl.

The modest towns that we are concerned with are outside and some distance from the major population centres of the cities and have a very different character.[1] They are small in size and population and are not immediately accessible or necessarily magnetic; at least not in the way of the modern metropolis. From without they may appear isolated and closed, while from within they may feel neither or both. Their links to the rest of the world are not readily apparent; in fact they may seem worlds apart in time as well as space. They have much less speed and noise and more open space – more fresh air, more sky, more 'nature'. They tend to exude a more 'humble ontology' (Knopp 2004). Such towns arise everywhere in regions outside the city; in the middle of deserts, prairies and long belts of flatland, they flank peaceful or wind-whipped coastlines. They have been built in forests, hills and moun-tains, amidst rocky outcrops, adjacent to lakes and rivers, and along river valleys. Their economies have usually emerged specifically from their natural assets, their geography. In all such places, pockets of people share the economic imperative to make the specificities of their loca-tion fulfil their economic and social needs. Their economies have his-torically been finely tuned to harnessing nature through culture. The options they make available to local people and outsiders are in many ways enriched, but also limited by their geography.

Our ethnographies were conducted in four diverse and dynamic glob-alizing places in Australia. While in some ways their spatial stories are unique, in other ways they are resonant with meaning for like places elsewhere. Certainly their economic biographies are like other places with similar economic bases in comparable Western countries. The eco-nomic bases of the places that we are concerned with here are forestry, fishing, mining (coal, opal) and viti- and horticulture. Under the imper-atives of global economies, environmental pressures and global cultural forms, each place is having to rethink and reconfigure its economic base, its view of sustainable living, its sense of place and what this means for local identities and identifications. All out of the way places around the Western world are similarly having to rethink themselves.

Thumbnail sketches

Coober Pedy, with a multicultural population of 3062 (ABS 2001a) in the northern desert of the state of South Australia, is hot, dry and barren. Aborigines, who passed through on their seasonal migrations in the past, can still be found there, some still migratory, some living on the outskirts of the town and some within it. Since the discovery of the opals, however, Coober Pedy has become a frontier town, a harsh desert town that is a centre for mining as an industry and a destination for tourists and backpackers. They share the underground dwellings, 'dugouts', made necessary by the rigours of the climate. Silver and white pipes cover the hills and streetscape and are the only visible markers of the life beneath. These pipes are the ventilation shafts that bring fresh air to the 'dugouts'. The oppressive desert climate has forced the residents underground, to the cool stable temperatures below ground. Yet, Coober Pedy cannot escape the desert; it is around every corner, at the end of every street, filling each vista with wide-open 'space'. There are no greens, no yellows, no purples here; instead, only one tree, the faded reds of the desert and the blue enormous sky. Coober Pedy feels as if it could be taken back by nature at any time, especially when the dust storms roll in to cover the town with desert debris. It has one main street, packed with cafes and opal shops and the rest of the town is dotted with metal corpses, the empty shells of cars, trucks and tractors, left where they last broke down. Tidy surfaces don't matter much here, as most local life is lived below ground. This, however, is not a new dumping ground. Past governments have used surrounding lands to test nuclear bombs, and now to dump toxic waste. And the international film industry, there to capture on celluloid the strange beauty of the stark landscapes, leaves behind its 'Hollywood trash'. Coober Pedy has aura, its severity is diminished by the strength of the dreams it provokes. It survives because it still holds promise for the miner and fascination for the tourist and the media with its remoteness, its harshness, the mystery of its muted red colours and the range of folk; miners, misfits, wanderers and travellers from all over the globe who have made it their stopping place.

Eden, set between the Pacific Ocean and the foothills of the Australian Alps on the Southern coast of New South Wales (NSW) has a population of approximately 3157 (ABS 2001d). It boasts the peace and serenity of the original Garden, for it is in a beautiful location. Built on Two Fold Bay, it has a fine natural harbour, accessible beaches and naturally forested hills abundant with wildlife. Many homes have views of the ocean and, when the sun sets behind the boats, it has the atmosphere of a Greek fishing village. However, the town has not historically been focused on its aesthetics for Eden's main industries are fishing and forestry, and there are some ugly deforested hills that give witness to the latter occupation. And the Heinz cannery has closed. It no longer employs the many local people it once did. Yet logging and fishing go on, and the energy they still require is symbolized by the huge petrol tanks on the hill overlooking the harbour. But environmental regulation has set severe limits to growth and these industries are thus capped and appear at a standstill. The local school and a major sporting complex sit beside the sea on some of the finest real estate. A cemetery lines the foreshore of the best beach in town, possibly with no connection to the fact that many people retire here. They came for the peace and quiet, for the natural beauty of the place; the main street has no brand name stores. Eden looks well cared for and comfortable. Tourism could flourish here. There is an annual whale festival, dolphins' sleek bodies skim the bay waters. Eden is unique. It is certainly unlike nearby Merimbula: a 'tinsel town' to conservative Eden, but a highlight of the Sapphire Coast to promoters of tourism. Eden simply has a down-market holiday industry involving beach activities and leisure fishing.

Morwell, a deindustrializing town of 13,527 (ABS 2001c) people, is situated in the middle of the Latrobe Valley, a two-hour drive from Melbourne, the state of Victoria's capital city. Morwell is a 'power town'; its main source of employment and income has traditionally been from the provision of coal-generated electricity via government-owned power stations. In the 1990s the four local power stations were downsized and sold to private, including foreign, investors. Morwell's power industry now competes for trade in Australia's national electricity market, but its greenhouse gas emissions mean that its future is constantly threatened as the pressure for clean sources of energy increases. The widespread unemployment that was associated with 'industry restructuring' had devastating effects that resulted in many local businesses and shops closing, the loss of services, and many people leaving the area. Morwell has little prospect of a tourist industry, although it is on the major highway to the Gippsland Lakes and the Strezlecki Ranges; places teaming with mountaineers and bush walkers. Because of Morwell's beginnings as a government-owned industrial centre, its many state-owned houses express its past personality; the same shape, the same materials. Individuality is difficult to express, optimism hard to discover now that the deep open-cut mines no longer support a clear and hopeful future. Once, the bustling town centre exemplified such a future. Now

1
Globalization, Place and Masculinities

The small town of Ashland in North America was once a quiet, leafy, green, out of the way location. A country-loving visitor described it as a perfect example of small-town America, a spot that had a 'sense of unique place' and a feeling of 'what makes my town different' (*Store Wars* 2001). That was before Wal-Mart came to town. Space and place were reconfigured around the global sign of the world's largest retail outlet, as Wal-Mart built new roads and reconstructed the face of consumption in Ashland. When Wal-Mart set up shop in Ashland, it squeezed out the flows of capital that used to be directed towards local businesses.

Wal-Mart's track record of bleeding dry the economic ecology of country towns (The *Guardian* 4/10/04) suggests that sustaining many small-town businesses in the shadow of this corporate giant is unlikely. Wal-Mart alters the flows of people, commodities, traffic and finances. It leads residents to reconfigure their connections to and their understandings of spaces and places. This is illustrated in the documentary film text *Walmart: The High Cost of Low Price* (2005). Different people respond differently. For some, Wal-Mart is appropriating their place and also public space, stealing farmlands and open spaces in all states of the United States. According to such 'sprawl-buster' activist groups as 'Protect our Small Town' and 'Citizens against the Wal', it's a global cancer corroding the face of place (Lippard 1997). Wal-Mart is a source of opportunity for others, many local people find work there for example. Such diverse kinds of engagement (including Wal-Mart women-workers' protests about their working conditions) constitute different relations to the same space. For Wal-Mart, the appealing nature of Ashland as a location for a new store was the distance between it and the nearest existent Wal-Mart outlet: a sizeable 10 km. Well, sizeable in Wal-Mart's terms.

Store Wars and other media stories about Wal-Mart alert us to some of the ways in which corporately driven global economies reconfigure out of the way places and the life and livelihoods of their people. Such stories are a reminder of the analytical importance of theories that help us to comprehend the contemporary relationship between globalization, place and identities. The purpose of this chapter is to introduce the theoretical resources that inform this book and that will be elaborated and developed in subsequent chapters. We begin with a discussion of different theories of globalization, focusing first on conceptualizations of big trends and patterns, and then on those perspectives that concentrate on globalization's particularities. Both viewpoints are vital to understanding places beyond the metropolis. The second part of the chapter identifies different understandings of the relationship between globalization, place and identity, then the third part considers studies of globalization and masculinity. Our purpose is to offer a conceptual framework that allows for a situated analysis of large-scale economic and cultural shifts and influences, their social and cultural manifestations in place, and their implications for identity and masculinity. This framework allows many apparently disparate changes and issues to be understood together.

Globalization: angles of vision[1]

Analysts face serious problems when trying to pin down the key features of contemporary times. However, most, across a range of theoretical and disciplinary orientations, agree on the necessity of adopting a global analytic. Predictably, what this means is explored and contested at length in the literature, which reveals a dazzling array of descriptions, theories, concepts and ideological standpoints. Indeed, there is a deluge of popular and academic literature that seeks to define globalization, to explain its genesis and to clarify the complexities of the economic, political, cultural and social contours of globalizing processes. Some focus on one such aspect and some consider different aspects in combination. Indeed, there has been such a proliferation of literature on globalization that it has emerged as a field of study in its own right (e.g., Cohen and Kennedy 2000). This field is increasingly multi- and interdisciplinary and theoretically eclectic (Benyon and Dunkerley 2000). While it is difficult to generalize across such a diverse body of literature, one must, nonetheless, try to find a meaningful way to make sense of it.

One way of categorizing the globalization literature divides it into two sets – that which focuses on 'globalization from above' and that which focuses on 'globalization from below' (Falk 1999). We find this a useful, but problematic categorization. It is useful because it offers some ready points of entry into what is an intricate set of ideas about an intricate set of processes. It is problematic, however, because it represents in layers, what are dynamic processes involving multiple, convoluted and uneven trajectories. It thus obscures the manner in which many apparently disparate changes come together. More specifically, it provides no way to portray the dense relationship that exists between the big material and structural shifts and patterns associated with globalization and everyday life. A further difficulty is that due to the multiple and changing foci of their work, some globalization scholars do not fit easily into one set or the other. Nonetheless, for the purposes of this book, we will use it as a starting heuristic device. In so doing, we will draw from key thinkers in sociology, cultural studies and cultural geography and from those who work across these disciplinary boundaries.

Globalization from above

Studies of 'globalization from above' focus on the big picture and describe the major trends and patterns associated with globalization. They usually offer an eagle's eye view of such global trends as internationalization, liberalization, universalization, Westernization and deterritorialization (Scholte 2000). But of course there are many possible ways of painting the 'globalization from above' picture. The most common way is a top–down perspective, and the top is understood as peak multinational corporations and multi- or supranational political organizations. This common view of globalization from the top is often developed by those at the top or by those who adopt their standpoint; particularly economists, as Stiglitz (2002) indicates. Further, this view is widely proselytized by right-wing think tanks, many national governments and much of the popular media. It is from this perspective that we hear of the so-called new and consensual economic world order. As Waters (1995: 116) explains, this is an ideological conception that seeks to obscure very real differences of interest and military power. The master narrative is neo-liberal economics with its associated calls for structural adjustment in national economies and state promoted 'free' trade. The underlying logic is deterministic: economic globalization that accords with the neo-liberal agenda, portrayed as unstoppable. The logic is often also advocatory – globalize (according to neo-liberal prescriptions) or perish. This 'neo-liberal globalism' Beck (2000: 9) associates with 'the ideology of rule by the world market' which, he argues, 'proceeds mono causally and economistically . . . reducing the multi-dimensionality of globalization to a single, economic dimension, that is itself conceived in a linear fashion'. Neo-liberal globalism 'liquidates' the distinctions between politics and economics. Further, as Massey (2005: 82) observes, under this rubric 'spatial differences are convened under the sign of temporal sequence' and hence ultimately this is an 'aspatial view of globalisation' which occludes the 'nature of the relations at play' (2005: 83).

A second broad set of ideas associated with the notion of 'globalization from above' is less deterministic and advocatory, and seeks to be more analytical and scholarly. It attempts to identify two main things; the key historical shifts and the major material and cultural patterns associated with globalization. There is a particular interest in, and debate about, what can be understood as new, and what is rather a continuation of the recent or distant past.[2] A main set of debates in sociology and anthropology revolves around whether globalization is an acceleration of modernity (high/late/reflexive), capitalism and colonialism or whether it is a recent and distinctive phenomenon associated with such 'post' processes as post-industrialization, post-modernization, post-colonialism. Whatever the case, the focus is often on processes of detraditionalization, particularly the movement away from traditional institutional formations and anchors of identity. Some see this as a good thing, some do not and some try to describe rather than evaluate it.[3]

In very general terms, there are three ways of theorizing these shifts and patterns. One set of accounts is structuralist. The driving force of globalization is the all-powerful relationship between global capital, markets and digital technology, and their associated colonizing imperatives. In this view, cultural transfer is seen in terms of global corporate/cultural homogenization, Americanization or Westernization. As Waters (1995: 3) explains, 'this does not mean that every corner of the planet must become Westernized and capitalist but rather that every set of social arrangements must establish its position in relationship to the capitalist West . . . it must relativise itself.' Another set of accounts adopts either a more dialectical view or a view drawing from structuration theory: the relationships between global/local, integration/fragmentation and structure/agency are key concerns here. The codes are now widely acknowledged via the notion that 'the global now helps to shape our everyday worlds and by our everyday acts we help to shape the global' (Giddens 1999). Of course, there is considerable debate about how this global/local dialectic is manifest and increasingly grounded studies identify a range of local interactions and inflections that are not so easily thought of in such binary terms. We will turn to them later. A third set of ideas draws on the notion of 'complex connectivity'. Because this is the general view we take in this book, we will enlarge on it before elaborating further on the relevant concepts and foci of those who focus on globalization from above.

'Globalization refers to the rapidly developing and ever-densening network of interconnections and interdependences that characterize modern social life', argues Tomlinson (1999: 2). He calls this 'complex connectivity' and identifies the different modalities of 'interconnection and interdependence' involved. He argues that the task of globalization theory is to 'understand the sources of this condition' and to 'interpret its implications across the various spheres of social existence' (Tomlinson 1999: 2). When Tomlinson explores the multidimensionality of globalization, he insists that it needs to be understood in terms of 'simultaneous complexly related processes in the realms of the economy, politics, culture, technology, and so forth' and 'involves all sorts of contradictions, resistances, and counterveiling forces' (1999: 17). Similarly, Held, McGrew, Goldblatt and Perraton (1999, in Benyon and Dunkerley 2000: 11) claim that contemporary globalization 'is not reducible to a single causal process, but involves a complex configuration of causal logics'. Giddens (1999) contends that globalization is 'a multi-causal; multi-stranded process full of contingency and uncertainty'. Waters (1995: 3) defines globalization as a 'social process in which the constraints of geography on social and cultural arrangements recede and in which people become increasingly aware that they are receding'. Scholte (2000: 3) agrees, but also argues that deterritorialization (supraterritoriality and the emergence of transworld spaces) is a key feature of globalization that gives it a 'new and distinctive meaning' and that represents an important contemporary historical development.

The notion of complex connectivity is well illustrated in Appadurai's theorization of the global cultural economy and the 'fundamental disjunctures between economy, culture and politics' (2000: 95). He identifies five dimensions of global cultural flows; financescapes, technoscapes, ethnoscapes, mediascapes and ideoscapes, and argues that 'one way of exploring such disjunctures is to look at the relationship among' them. These scapes are, he says, fluid, irregular and multiply constituted and perspectivally registered (Appadurai 2000: 95). It is the latter three that are most pertinent to this book. Appadurai calls the 'landscape of persons that constitute the shifting world' an 'ethnoscape' (1996: 33). Mediascapes and ideoscapes are 'closely related landscapes of images'. The former are produced by electronically distributed news-papers, magazines, TV stations and film production studios. The latter are more 'directly political and frequently have to do with the ideolo-gies of states and the counter-ideologies of movements explicitly ori-ented to capturing state power' (1996: 36). They include 'a diaspora of key words, political ideas and values'.

The key concepts and concerns of 'globalization from above' scholars include time/space reconfiguration and compression (Giddens 1999; Harvey 2000), transnational interconnectedness, networks, flow, speed, virtuality, fluidity, flexibility and the reshaping of power. There is a fas-cination with disembedding, with the 'fluid firm', with 'flexible' man-agement and labour and with the governmental and other technologies that permit/encourage them to exist. Much associated attention is thus paid to deterritoriality, the porousness of borders and boundaries, and to the mobility or flow across national borders to different places all over the globe of information, ideas, images, trade, investment, labour, commodities and people.

Global media forms, such as film, television and the Internet, are instrumental in the global circulation of culture, information, images and imaginaries; 'mediated globalization' Rantanen (2005) calls it. Hence, there is an intense curiosity amongst these globalization schol-ars about the fresh configurations of time and space that they permit and produce; about the spacelessness and placelessness of images, screens, virtual worlds and simulated, hyper-real and 'imagined spaces' (Soja 1996) and 'imagined worlds' (Appaduri 1996, 2000). Equally, there is an interest in 'non-places', particularly those that have arisen along-side intensified travel and tourism, and the emergence of a hyper-mobile global cosmopolitan elite.

In general terms this literature concentrates on such things as advanced corporate and 'cultural economies' (Appaduri 1996), interna-tional organizations and multi- or supranational political institutions, their modes of operation and their effects. In other words, the focus is on what can be understood as the control centres and controllers of the global economy and culture, the means by which they spread their power and influence, and the nature of this influence; hence the par-ticular interest in global cities as well as global elites. As Waters (1995: 51) explains, 'transnational corporations set up global linkages and systems of exchange so that the globe is increasingly constituted as a single market for commodities, labour and capital'.

Alongside this line of inquiry and analysis is the acknowledged paradox that there are now serious limits to such power and influence. These are related to the risks associated with ever-present threats of ecological disasters, global economic collapse and the spread of war and of international health epidemics. Beck (1992) calls these 'high consequence risks' and argues that they universalize and equalize regardless of location and class position. But he also considers the manner in which risks are distributed, claiming that class disadvantage can lead to risk disadvantage; that poverty and risk attract each other. Giddens (1994: 20) says that humanity is driven by its collective fear of the threats it has created and it is thus that survival values unite us all.

Just as high-consequence risk is seen as a feature of globalization, so too is reflexivity. Indeed, reflexive modernity is seen as an intimate companion to globalization. It is Giddens's (1994) view that reflexivity is a structural aspect of contemporary life. Expert systems are repositories of technical knowledge that can be deployed over a wide range of contexts. They are thus, as he explains, highly mobile and well suited to deterritorializing times. He argues that today's reflexively ordered societies are regularly and rapidly shaped and reshaped by cycles involving the production and application of new knowledge. Indeed, the intensification of this process has led to 'burgeoning institutional reflexivity'. Risk and radical doubt feature because of the many available sources of knowledge, multiple experts and the lack of traditional or 'final' sources of authority. Giddens claims that, globally, we are involved in frequent attempts to 'colonize the future' through the reflexive organization of knowledge. For instance, risk of all sorts and reflexivity are companions, and 'risk management' has become a major preoccupation of government and institutional policy makers. It involves 'discovering, administering, acknowledging, avoiding or concealing such hazards with respect to specifically defined horizons of relevance' (Beck 1992: 19–20). As the risks increase, so too do empty promises of security. Giddens (1994) points to the re-regulation that is occurring within and beyond nation-states as they respond to the 'high-consequence risks' of globalization.

Throughout this book, we are alert to many of the major trends and patterns associated with globalization that we have outlined thus far, particularly complex connectivity and global disjunctive flows. But our focus is on if, how, and the extent to which they are manifest in out of the way places in 'developed' Western places; we do not want to fall into the trap of universalizing phenomena. We were prompted, in part, to look 'underneath' the big patterns of globalization by criticisms of the literature that consider globalization from above. Several are pertinent here. The first is that some such studies, particularly those that focus on information technology and its relationship to capital, are informed by a determinist and thus problematic logic. A second is that some (not all) such studies of globalization suffer from an ethical emptiness. Harvey (2000) explains how on some occasions they talk of globalization when they might more aptly talk of imperialism or colonialism. The third is that many studies operate at high levels of generalization and abstraction and are, as Scholte (2000: 1) observes, 'empirically thin'. As several, particularly feminist, critics point out, much of the 'globalization from above' literature is highly selective in the scales, spaces, flows, networks and subjects of globalization that it chooses to analyse (Nagar, Lawson, McDowell and Hanson 2001). This selectivity means that it offers readers a rather skewed version of globalization (Kofman 2000), often from the standpoint of the overdeveloped West. Indeed, some argue that the broad scale of much of this analysis draws attention away from the implications of globalization for other equally pertinent sites, flows, networks and actors in 'peripheral' spaces and places. Often obscured from view are the implications of globalization for the daily/nightly practices of households, diverse local workplaces and organizations, face-to-face communities, and non-elite embodied and socially embedded actors. Thus how different places and people are drawn into the relations of globalization in different ways and with different and unequal consequences is muted in analysis. Such foci also, it is said, draw attention away from the manner in which the spaces and scales of globalization are multiple and intersecting.

Globalization from below

The sorts of criticisms outlined above have provoked an assortment of literature that seeks to extend and deepen understandings of globalization by focusing on what is variously called mundane, vernacular or indigenized globalization or 'globalization from below'. We will use the latter term as a convenient shorthand for those terms that precede it, with due apologies to Falk (1999). This work attends to intersecting geographic scales and to the uneven and particular aspects of globalization. As Waters (1995) notes, deterritorialization has proceeded most rapidly in the West and how it is experienced differs from place to place. The globalization from below literature is, then, especially sensitive to globalization's unevenness. It also identifies in detail globalization's paradoxical integrating and fragmenting tendencies, power geometries and their implications for global, regional, national and local stability and justice. Held and McGrew (2002a and b) observe that cultural divisiveness and nationalist fragmentation are being reinforced and are growing as a result of global inequalities.

Predictably, studies of 'globalization from below' have a 'bottom–up' standpoint in terms of their theoretical, methodological and moral concerns. A strong theoretical orientation here is culturalist but this is also accompanied by the theoretical orientations noted above; namely structuration theory, the dialectical and that which also stresses 'complex connectivity' and global disjunctive flows. While, again, much of this literature is descriptive and analytical, it also often has a strong moral imperative, concerned as it is with the power inequities associated with the current 'geographies of centrality and marginality' (Sassen 1998), with representing the particular in ways which do not diminish it, and with speaking back to the power elites of the global economy on behalf of the local and non-elites (Escobar 2001). Such studies also try to distinguish that which is part of globalization and that which remains apart from or opposed to it. Indeed, more so than studies of 'globalization from above', studies of 'globalization from below' tend to heed the advice of the eminent cultural theorist Williams (1982: 204–5), who insists that one remain alert to the historical interplay of competing tendencies. He calls these dominant, residual, oppositional and emergent tendencies and urges commentators not to focus too exclusively on analysis of dominating tendencies and the new. We heed Williams's advice.

One focus in this literature is on the extent to and manner in which globalizing processes are mediated in embedded and embodied ways including 'inside the head' (Robertson 1992). Attention is paid to diverse people's and places' complex and contradictory experiences of, reactions to, and engagements with, various aspects of globalization as they intersect with their lives and identities over time (Luke and Ó Tuathail 1998; Urry 1995). Of related concern are the particular lives and spaces that are made poorer and 'marginalized' by the trade and investment patterns of economic globalization, particularly in the so-called Third World or the South (Afshar and Barrientos 1999; Freeman 2000). Asymmetrical dependency, the rich/poor divide and the causes and consequences of Third World debt are very much a part of this agenda (Potter 2000). A further interest is in those social movements that have mobilized in opposition to 'globalization from above', especially various aspects of corporate globalization like that associated with Wal-Mart (Yuen, Rose and Katsiaficas 2001).

Those with an interest in 'globalization from below' are of course also interested in deterritorialization, flow, networks, the reorganization of time and space, virtuality, the fluid, the flexible and the new. Equally, they are interested in global trade, investment, de- and re-regulation, and issues of cultural transfer. However, their interest is in localized inflections of these, in how and the extent to which such globalizing processes modulate material and territorial place, space, cultures, identities and relationships, and how these modulate more global trends. The embedded, embodied and 'in the head' mediation of such matters is a key focus here.

Placing and displacing identities

The focus of this book requires us to specifically consider the ways in which 'place' and identity figure in discussions of globalization. Place, in the context of globalizing processes, is a key concern of many for, as Scholte (2000: 3) observes, 'the rise of supraterritoriality has by no means brought an end to territorial geography; global and territorial spaces coexist and interrelate in complex fashions'. Clearly, as a consequence of such globalizing processes, dispersed places have become more interconnected and dynamic. Theorists thus adopt a view of place that recognizes this. Hence Sassen (1998: xix) observes that '[p]lace is central to many of the circuits through which economic globalization is constituted'. Held and colleagues (1999, in Benyon and Dunkerley 2000: 10) argue that 'even though most people remain rooted in a local or national culture or a local place, it is becoming increasingly impossible for them to live in that place disconnected culturally from the world in which it is situated'. Giddens (1990: 19) explains that 'place becomes increasingly phantasmagoric' as it is more 'thoroughly infiltrated by and shaped in terms of social influences quite distant' from it; 'stretched out'. While pointing to the obvious enduring physical distance between people and places in the world, Tomlinson (1999) argues that, as a function of global media images, there exists an increasing sense of worldwide 'proximity' and that this sense is accompanied by the very real connections that arise through economic, environmental and communicative links and through long-distance travel, tourism and migration. Such imaginary and real 'proximities', he observes, alter the nature of localities and affect what he calls 'dis-placement' (1999: 9). Distant events and powers infiltrate local experience. Equally, he observes local events; practices and lifestyles are increasingly considered in terms of their global implications and consequences. This set of connections has led Giddens to claim that many people now take 'action at a distance' and that, thus, many of their experiences are 'disembedded'. Indeed, for him, time–space distanciation, disembedding and reflexivity mean that complex relationships develop between local activities and interaction across distances. And, finally Beck (2000: 46–7) talks of cultural de- and re-location and says that 'local cultures can no longer be justified, shaped and renewed in seclusion from the rest of the world . . . there is a compulsion to relocate detraditionalized traditions within a global context of exchange, dialogue and conflict'.

Such views of place prompt a consideration of the relationships between Appadurai's scapes and place; that is, the ideas, people and cultural forms that flow though place, the ways in which people mediate these scapes in place, and the implications for local cultures. And this takes us back to discussions about global/local relationships. There is considerable interest among cultural anthropologists and ethnographers in observing the ways in which global cultural forms interact with local cultures. This literature examines *in situ* the 'traffic in culture'; cultural interaction and exchange – the movement of meaning systems and symbolic forms, and the extent to which, how and why these are assimilated, hybridized or resisted locally (Hannerz 1991). As we explain further in Chapter 2, the methodological imperative here is to follow Held and colleagues' (1999, in Benyon and Dunkerley 2000: 11) call for inquiry to register the nature of the encounter and to attend particularly to interplay, interaction and cultural creativity. In other words, the drive is to show how reception is localized – to show if, how and what local meanings are attached to what is globally imported, and if and how the global is interpreted differently in different cultures and locations (Miller 1995).

Despite this interest in various forms of mobility, those who theorize place in globalizing circumstances nonetheless agree that place, more traditionally defined, still matters, and certainly matters in some locations and for some people more than others. The more traditional definitions of place see it as relatively tied to space and time, and as involving a sense of contiguity, homogeneity, and physical and social borders. In such places, kinship, friendship, work and leisure relationships and networks are relatively stable. Indeed, Sassen (1999) notes that we need an approach to place-based analysis that counters the overemphasis in the globalization literature on speed, hyper-mobility and so on – one which acknowledges 'material conditions, production sites and "place-bounded-ness"' (Sassen 1999: xxiii). Tomlinson is at pains to point out that 'local life occupies the majority of time and space'

(1999: 9) as most people stay in one place most of their time. Not all of place is displaced in people's lives, he says, but it is increasingly hybridized, for, as Appadurai (1996: 33–4) argues, the 'warp of stability is everywhere shot through with the woof of human motion as more persons and groups deal with the realities of having to move or the fantasies of wanting to move.'

Such considerations of 'the warp of stability' have provoked renewed interest in the role of tradition, heritage and roots, in notions of home and memory, and in the manner in which these and traditions intersect with the present. There is a revived interest in the established, the settled, those who choose to or are locked in place and, overall, the politics of stability and its relationship to the politics of mobility.

Some suggest that globalization may well have revived local solidarities and particularisms. For instance, Scholte (2000: 137) says: 'When faced with the vastness and seeming intangibility of globality, many people have turned away from the state to their local "home" in order to nurture their possibilities of community and self-determination.' Indeed, in the face of homogenizing economic and cultural globalization, there has been a proliferation of cultural particularisms and pluralisms. These have included a push for territorial means of identification involving surges in local, regional and national sensibilities (Robertson 1992). The forces for homogeneity, it is argued, in fact accentuate heterogeneity and fragmentation. Indeed, some who take a longitudinal perspective show how, over time, in the shadow of the 'global other', localities and even nations have reacted with attempts to revive local and national alternatives. Moreover, the rise of local nationalisms and identities and the post-colonial insistences on diversity have, in turn, contributed to further global fragmentation. This has involved many attempts to reconstruct tradition and to revive or reinvent the particular: Giddens (1994: 84) argues that our 'runaway world of dislocation and uncertainty' – our world of 'manufactured uncertainty' – often results in calls for a return to particular traditions. Here he makes specific mention of fundamentalism that he says is 'a defense of tradition based on the tradition it defends' (1994: 83). Fundamentalism tends to sentimentalize, romanticize, oversimplify and misrepresent the past. Gender fundamentalism and family fundamentalism are obvious examples. Further, in various instances, the technical and symbolic resources of globalization have been used to revive and stimulate the local. In such circumstances local cultural entrepreneurs may be those who help to translate the global locally or, equally, those who seek to promote the local locally or indeed globally.

As indicated earlier, another feature of studies of globalization from below is their concern for the ways that globalization reconfigures certain geometries and geographies of power and reinscribes others. Such studies focus on the webs of power that constitute 'scattered hegemonies' (Grewal and Kaplan 1994) in hierarchical interconnections of space (Grosz-Ngate and Kokole 1997). As this indicates, such power relations are often considered 'through the prism of space' (Urry 1995: 14). Matters of interest here are wide ranging and include the power relationships between spatial units as all-inclusive as the 'West and the rest', between nation-states and regional alliances and between other spatial entities such as different cities, localities and neighbourhoods. Some are geographies of hope (Harvey 2000), trust and security, and others are geographies of high risk, uncertainty and future panic. Their relationships with each other are also emotionally coded; for instance, as places of fear and danger or places of desire. In other words, globalization has an emotional geography.

The views outlined above are usefully complemented by the conceptual work of cultural geography that offers a more nuanced view of place than that provided by globalization scholars. In developing a critique of universalizing theories of globalization that are informed primarily by the notion of time-space compression, Massey (2005, 1993) draws attention to the 'politics of mobility'. She states that such theories ignore the relationship between social differentiation and time–space compression. In other words time and space are compressed in different ways for different people, and in some cases not much at all. Poverty, age, place of birth and disability need to be factored into the analysis. She adds that many, if not most, people are still located in a routine or home base, a locality to which they return regularly and in which they spend a significant proportion of their social life. Like Sassen, she argues that the local remains important and should not be lost in a certain social theory's obsession with speed and the new. Massey accepts that any understanding of locality or place must not be constrained by the notion of boundaries and must recognize a complex range of external links and layers in space, not all to do with globalization (Massey 1994: 120). She terms this the 'simultaneous multiplicity of spaces' and argues that spaces are cross-cutting and intersecting, existing in relations of paradox and antagonism. To Massey (1994: 3), place remains an important focus for social inquiry in globalizing times if it is understood in this manner and if it is also recognized that places do not have single unique identities but are full of internal differences and conflict. Indeed, in her most recent book she talks of place as an 'event', a 'constellation of processes' and stresses its 'thrown togetherness' involving sets of negotiations between history and geography, humans and nonhumans including changing landscapes and climates' (Massey 2005: 140–1). And, as Lippard (1997: 7) evocatively illustrates in *The Lure of the Local*, 'place is latitudinal and longitudinal within the map of a person's life. It is temporal and spatial, personal and political'. In a multicentred world, there are many senses of place.

Globalizing identity

There is now considerable speculation and debate over what globalization means for people's sense of who they are. This debate, which is central to this study, is layered over and builds on the long-standing debates about identity and identification, subjectivity and subjectification and the self, and how best to understand them (Hall 1996).

Some who explore the issue of globalization and identity proclaim the emergence of new identities that reflect and affect current global circumstances. These lines of argument tend to arise in association with two bodies of scholarship which, by and large, have very little to do with each other and which we will bring together throughout the book. The first focuses on globalization, reflexive (high/late) modernity and what this means for selfhood. The second focuses on global culture, the global–local cultural nexus, global mobility, and their implications for identity. These perspectives do not map easily on to the above–below distinction. We will briefly outline the main contours of each line of thought.

The suggestion by some key sociologists is that reflexivity is not only a structural aspect of current times as noted earlier (in 'reflexive modernization' theory) but also a feature of current individualized biographical projects of the self. As the power of older modalities of identity formation is reduced, individuals are propelled to consciously design their own specific identities and futures (Bauman 2000; Beck 1992; Giddens 1991, 1994). According to Giddens (1991: 187–201), contemporary times have provided 'new mechanisms for self-identity'. In Giddens's view, we have moved to a 'post-traditional order' which is a result of the many current challenges to traditional ways of doing things, organizing our lives and interacting with nature. These challenges include the declining influence of traditional agencies of socialization (church, family and school), the rise of other major influences (the media, popular culture), developments in scientific and technical knowledge and their applications to nature and our bodies, new social movements, the clash of values brought about by the rise of global differences, and the spread of different cultures around the globe. Such

changes and challenges, Giddens (1994: 83) argues, have forced traditions into the open, they have been 'called to account', and are obliged
to justify themselves.

These structural conditions call into play reflexive identities; 'we are,
not what we are, but what we make of ourselves', says Giddens (1991:
75). As many traditional anchors of identity are stripped away, a con-
fusing array of choices emerges. People have to decide about many of
the things that once were taken for granted or regarded as natural.
While freedom from old constraints offers more apparent choice and
autonomy, it also generates new uncertainties and fragmentations
around gender, family, work, knowledge and authority. Central to the
contemporary reflexive project of identity formation, or self-making,
then, are issues of risk, trust and ontological security.

A second broad way of considering matters of globalization and identity is associated with debates about global culture and the global/local
nexus. One focus here is on the emergence of what some describe as a
globalized culture. Waters, for instance, argues that 'A globalized culture
admits a continuous flow of ideas, information, commitment, values
and tastes, mediated though mobile individuals, symbolic tokens, and
electronic simulations' (Waters 1995: 126). While there is much debate
about the extent to which this can be defined as a culture, there is a
broad agreement that this 'culture' is disembedded, deterritorialized and
highly differentiated and segmented. According to Waters again (1995:
126), a globalized culture is chaotic rather than orderly, its meanings
are not unitary or centralized but are, as noted earlier, 'relativized' in
relation to the West and the United States.

With regard to identity, then, the claim is that as a result of this rise
in interconnectedness and interdependence, more and more people
around the globe are coming to comprehend the world as one, albeit
diffuse, place. Such altered experiences of proximity, or what some call
'new geographies', have produced certain sensibilities, identities, communities and solidarities that are not necessarily grounded in geography or the nation-state. These trans-border identifications are along
various lines that include such things as religion, work, politics and
various forms of consumption. Such increased interconnectedness and
interdependence have, however, also intensified the collision of cultures
and histories that has long characterized the human condition. This has
also contributed to the simultaneous processes of homonegenization
and fragmentation, disintegration and reintegration that we have
already discussed. Appadurai (1996, 2000) observes that global cultural
processes are:

products of the infinitely varied mutual contest of sameness and difference on a stage characterized by radical disjunctures between different sorts of global flows and the uncertain landscapes created in and through these disjunctures.

(Appadurai 2000: 100)

More people must resolve, somehow, the implications for the self as they negotiate multiple affiliations and overlapping communities (territorial and non-territorial). They must, as Appadurai argues, 'navigate the perspectival set of landscapes' associated with the global cultural economy (2000: 95). In sum, then, the emphasis in this quite extensive body of literature is on globalized sensibilities and hybridized identities and identifications.

Of course, such broad patterns contain an even more complex story. This is possibly best told by globalization-from-below scholars who tend to emphasize the particular contexts of reception, that is, the rereading, creative appropriation, resistance and subversion of global tendencies and cultures by local peoples. They point to imitative and plagiaristic negotiations, trading and raiding in circumstances of unequal power and with diverse effects for locality and identity. The logic follows what Mercer (1994: 63) calls a 'syncretic dynamic which critically appropriates elements from the master-codes of the dominant culture and creolizes them, disarticulating signs and rearticulating their symbolic meaning otherwise'. This raises questions about what people bring to the dynamic and it is at this point that matters associated with histories, habits, memories, customs, rituals and conventions come to the fore. As Cvetkovich and Kellner (2000: 134) argue:

Today, under the pressure of the dialectics of the global and the local, identity has global, national, regional and local components as well as specificities of gender, race, class and sexuality. . . . This situation is highly contradictory with reassertions of traditional modes of identity in response to globalization and a contradictory mélange of hybrid identities.

They point to the continued importance of tradition in contemporary constructions of identity while at the same time arguing that the global/local nexus is producing new matrices for identity, thus 'expanding the realm of self-definition' (Cvetkovich and Kellner 2000: 134) and providing new options for selfhood.

A global sense of masculinity

The relationship between globalization and masculinity was of little interest to masculinity scholars until quite recently. Until this point, sociocultural studies of masculinity were largely preoccupied with the micro-politics of different masculinities in specific social sites, or in relation to particular cultural forms, or with the macro-politics of national politics of masculinity. For example, Whitehead and Barrett's (2001) edited anthology of sociological studies of masculinity includes depictions of Chicano/Latino (Mirande 2001), African-Caribbean (Sampath 2001) and South African (Wood and Jewkes 2001) masculinities. Whitehead and Barrett (2001) also include accounts of masculinity and national institutions, such as Barrett's (2001) discussion of the US navy and Segal's (2001) analysis of schooling in Sweden. Such situated modes of inquiry resonate with the theorizing of masculine identities embedded in place that we undertake as the study progresses. However, their views of places and institutions are not overtly linked to globalization theory and neither do they involve Massey's notion of a 'simultaneous multiplicity of space'. As such, studies of masculinity and globalization need to be clearly distinguished from such sociocultural analyses of masculinities in terms of the intellectual trajectory they build upon and the divergent forums of academic application they speak to.

The imperative for masculinity studies to adopt a global sensibility was established by Hooper (2000a) and Connell (2000a, 2001). The foundational work of these theorists was then drawn together in the work of Haywood and Mac an Ghaill (2003). These studies have put globalization on the agenda of masculinity studies but, as we will argue, there remains considerable scope for conceptual and empirical refinement.

Writing from a feminist perspective on global restructuring, Hooper's[4] (2000a) work on 'Masculinities in Transition' offers a critical cultural examination of 'integrated global elites of (largely) White male professionals and businessmen' (2000a: 59). In sympathy with Massey, Hooper argues against dominant ideas about space and time often associated with globalization, such as the ways in which discourses of globalization theorize 'the world as a single social space, shrinking time and space' (Giddens 1990, in Hooper 2000a: 59). In contrast, Hooper makes the case that the locations in which 'the global' actually constitutes a single space along which different states of masculinity 'flow' smoothly are highly select and privileged. Further, she contends that there is a range of ways in which traditional hegemonic masculinities, which she terms 'frontier masculinities', have been reinscribed or recontextualized in relation to globalization. For instance, the kind of masculine behaviour that was integral to the processes of English imperialism and American frontiers (Hooper 2000a: 63) has been updated and become fundamental to global corporate zones of influence, such as the international stock market. Such global masculinities exemplify many of the ways in which 'the shiny new discourse of globalization draws strength from old formulas of racism, masculinism and imperialism' (Hooper 2000a: 69). Further, they deploy 'imagery which integrates science, technology, business, and images of globalization into a kind of entrepreneurial frontier masculinity' (2000a: 67). Hooper explicates the ways in which the economic fabric of the developed Western world has become a terrain in which contemporary hegemonic masculinities are able to control Third World resources. There are few changes in power dynamics here; rather, there is an intensification of the scale upon which certain male elites are able to exert their power.

Connell's (2000a) *The Men and The Boys* takes a similar trajectory to Hooper's critique of corporate global masculinity. He also considers what globalization might mean for masculinity studies. This entails situating masculinity in relation to a 'world gender order' (2000a: 40–3). Here gender is produced through relational processes between men and women, nations and citizens and across first and developing world contexts. The notion of 'transnational business masculinity' (2000a, 2001: 370) is a core concept of Connell's. Particularly, he (2000a: 53–4) contends that:

> the hegemonic form of masculinity in the current world gender order is the masculinity associated with those who control its dominant institutions: the business executives who operate in global markets, and the political executives who interact (and in many contexts merge) with them. I will call this pattern 'transnational business masculinity'

He names a range of ways in which hegemonic masculinity is being re-invented and redeployed across First and Third World globalizing contexts.

There are some positive ways in which contemporary processes of globalization might open out masculine possibilities and also the ways in which people read masculinities, Connell argues, saying:

> the global gender order contains, necessarily, greater plurality of gender forms than any local gender order. This must reinforce the

consciousness that masculinity is not one fixed form. The plurality of masculinities at least symbolically prefigures the unconstrained creativity of a democratic gender order.

(Connell 2001: 372)

A bi-focal definition of globalization is adopted by Haywood and Mac an Ghaill. They state that

At a general level, globalization may be understood as referring to the processes, procedures and technologies – political, economic and cultural – underpinning the current 'time–space' compression which produces a sense of immediacy and simultaneity about the world (Brah et al. 1999). However, this emphasis on transnational phenomena often eclipses the significance of local voices, issues and histories (Taylor et al. 1996). It also tends to neglect the power of imagined national communities that reconfigure and localize global processes.

(Haywood and Mac an Ghaill 2003: 84)

This dual perspective is analogous to the perspectives of 'globalization from above' and 'from below' that we outlined earlier and it leads their work to develop along these two somewhat different trajectories.

First, Haywood and Mac an Ghaill undertake some comparative, but not global studies of masculinities in different national contexts. In undertaking cross-cultural examinations of masculinity, among other things they are concerned with 'how masculinities are mediated through (and constructed within) different cultural contexts and how specific social and cultural interrelationships reshape the meanings of manhood' (2003: 86). The material that forms the core of such discussions explores the lived, everyday or vernacular expressions of global processes. The second way in which Haywood and Mac an Ghaill develop their work on globalization and masculinity is by adopting a transnational perspective (pp. 92–9). They read international politics, global capitalism and globalized desires as gendered and also as tied into economies of sexual desirability (pp. 96–100). Here global politics is seen to involve various forms of global gendered performativity 'from above' (pp. 85–100). In so doing they continue a line of analysis adopted by Hooper and Connell and deploy a notion of global hegemonic masculinity.

For our purposes, there are several points to be made about this set of literature on globalization and masculinity. The first is that it involves important theoretical moves for the field as it points to a research agenda that is long overdue for development. Indeed, given the avalanche of literature on globalization it is surprising that the masculinity and globalization literature is so sparse in comparison. The second point relates to the ways in which globalization is understood. While, Connell and Hooper are clearly critical of the views of globalization promoted from the top by those at the top, they nonetheless focus on the control centres and controllers of the global economy and culture and the nature of their power and influence. As Connell says, '[t]o the extent particular institutions become dominant in world society, the patterns of masculinity embedded in them may become global standards' (2000a: 45). Even though they discuss the global hegemony of related forms of masculinity, explaining how such hegemony is secured 'inside the head' in places beyond the worlds of the business elite is not a feature of their work. In a similar vein, yet deploying slightly broader theoretical brush-strokes, Haywood and Mac an Ghaill (2003) condense contemporary standpoints on globalization from above and below, but do not reconceptualize them.

Overall, there is little indication that this small body of work seeks to advance theories of globalization or to engage in theoretical dialogue between studies of globalization and studies of masculinity. Our thinking differs from this in the sense that we synthesize perspectives on globalization from above and below through the notions of place that we outlined earlier, and in particular through Massey's (1994) notion of a 'progressive' sense of place. Rather than perceiving the local as acted upon by global processes, we work with the idea of a globally progressive sense of place. The ways in which places engage with processes of globalization are contingent upon their located specificities.

The third point to be made about this literature is that business persona and investments in immaterial labour are understood to constitute decisive aspects of the globalized/globalizing masculinities. Hooper's entrepreneurial global frontier masculinity and Connell's transnational business masculinity arise in relation to global deterritorialized contexts. But what constitutes the global frontier? Where is it? And, if we are unsure where it is, what is the masculinity that it inscribes? The same questions apply to the notion of the transnational. A global sense of place problematizes such notions. It asks about the different ways in which masculinity is becoming globalized, and if and how Connell's 'world gender order', orders, reorders or disorders place and identity. Are some masculinities globalizing (the CEOs of Wal-Mart in Ashland for instance) while others are globalized (the local young men who purchase their global merchandise)? These questions are similar to those posed by Sassen (1998) with regard to who constitutes a global worker in the global city.

Inspired by such questions, we seek to contribute to a theoretical dialogue between studies of globalization and studies of masculinity. More specifically, we aim to open up the field of masculinity studies to an analysis of globalization as it is lived in place and space, with place, space and masculine identities conceived in symbiotic relation. To assist us in this project, we turn, again, to the work of cultural geographers with a particular interest in gender and place. With their focus on gender, they help to refine for us the notions of globalization, place and identity that we outlined in the previous section.

In the early 1990s Jackson put out a call to 'map masculinities' (1991). She was one of the first geographers to 'explore the various instabilities and contradictions that inhere with the notion of masculinity and [to] make a concerted effort to uncover the spatial structures that support and maintain dominant forms' (1991: 210). Since Jackson's call there has been something of a surge of studies of masculinities, space and place (e.g., Berg and Longhurst 2003; Little and Panelli 2003; Nespor 2000b; Shire 1994) and an emerging interest in gender, geography and globalization (e.g., Nagar, Lawson, McDowell and Hanson 2001). This literature explores the changing gendered discourses, identities and relations of specific places and spaces and points to place/space-based variations in the construction and reconstruction of gender. It asks why, for instance, '[w]hat it means to be masculine in the Fens is not the same as what it means in Lancashire' (Massey 1994: 178).

Such studies address four broad themes, not all of which speak directly to questions related to globalization. First, they look at how changing economies and policies impact differently on different places and different genders, and how such changes may (or may not) reconfigure gender relations in local institutions and in the overall gender order of the locality (Walby 1997). The gender implications for particular male workers and workplaces are of concern here. Examples include the computer industry in Cambridge (Massey 1995), merchant banking in London (McDowell 1997). Thinking more globally, uneven economic growth and development, changing economies on various scales are also of interest for, as Sunder Rajan (1993: 6) observes, 'uneven development both shapes and draws on gender relations'. A second focus is on gendered symbolic meanings and use of space/place/landscape and the implications of this for constructions of masculinity. Examples here include Woodward's (1998) study of male soldiers and the rural landscape and Dowler's (2001) research on Irish nationalism and masculinity. A third focus is on the connections between space and social difference and/or discrimination, especially that associated with gay men and men of colour. See, for example, the work of Majors (2001) on black masculinities and sport and Mirande (2001) on Chicano/Latino masculinities.

Finally, a fourth focus in these studies is on the relationship between place, space and time (Berg and Longhurst 2003; Knopp 2004; Little 2002). While acknowledging globalizing changes, those who work within this theoretical trajectory are not necessarily convinced that traditional anchors of identity, such as gender, have dissolved in the manner described by certain globalization 'from above' theorists. They are not, to borrow Appadurai's (1996: 33–4) metaphorical references to weaving, convinced that with regard to gender relations and identities, 'the woof of human motion' takes precedence over the 'warp of stability'. Indeed, along with their considerations of 'new geographies', they remind us of the gendered implications of such things as history and habit, ritual and reminiscence.

A conceptually inventive example of work arising from gender and cultural geography is Nespor's (2000b) 'Topologies of Masculinity', where she argues that different kinds of spaces produce divergent intraspatial modes of masculinity. To develop her arguments she draws heavily on Latour's (1987) identification of three kinds of intraspatial relation. These are bounded clusters of similar objects (local clusters), distributed networks (which operate across distances), and fractured or permeable social spaces in which relations leak between zones and bounded areas mutate. Nespor relates these to masculinities, arguing that bounded clusters are most likely to be associated with hegemonic masculinities, leaky spaces with 'ambiguous' masculinities, and distributed networks with imagined masculinities that pass between locations, from Hollywood to the playground, for example. Here Nespor draws on Appadurai (1996) in considering the role of mediascapes in the construction of young men's sense of masculine possibilities. Nespor (2000b: 40) considers such a role in terms of her interest in a three-dimensional, spatial, temporal and sensory engagement. Through three-dimensional engagement with mediascapes and other affective kinds of connection, masculinity becomes configured as a network rather than a form of embodiment. Nespor contends: '[i]n one sense, bodies . . . organized across such mediascapes . . . are no longer the bodies-as-bounded-region that are self-contained.'

She also argues that 'along with complex gender topographies there are multiple "gender topologies"' (2000b: 32). She deploys Mol and

Law's (1994: 643) notion of 'a mathematics of spatial form that "doesn't localize objects in terms of a given set of co-ordinates. Instead, it articulates *different rules for localizing* in a *variety of coordinate systems*"' (emphasis in original). With regard to the implications for masculinity, she explains:

> Instead of arguing that masculinities assume a particular topology, I want to suggest that multiple masculinities are constructed, on differing scales, sometimes in reinforcing layers and other times in tension, within all three topologies. Body-reflexive practices take different forms in the context of different topologies.'
>
> (Nespor 2000b: 33)

Nespor's notion of three-dimensional spaces of masculinity enhances Massey's notion of a 'progressive' sense of place, which implies a set of nested contexts, but it complements her notion of 'the simultaneous multiplicity of spaces'. Equally, Nespor's use of the concept 'topology' speaks to Massey's (1993) notion of 'power geometry'. In these terms, her work is certainly useful for us. However, we adopt the view that, while some spaces are more bounded than others and while some boundaries are more firmly patrolled that others, all spaces are potentially leaky and particularly so as a result of what Appadurai calls global disjunctive flows. The notion of networked spaces thus becomes redundant. Further, it also implies chains of relay and reaction which Appadurai's ideas also problematize. Appadurai is less concerned with relays of specific images and ideas than with the ways global mediascapes may inspire imagined and mobile lives. Such scapes point to notions of space and place that are highly porous.

Overall, as can be inferred from these standpoints, scholarship on geography, gender and identities has much in common with that on the global/local/identity nexus discussed above. It recognizes that identities are formed through complex geographies and geometries of multiple differences. These include 'uneven and fractured' (Bakker 1996: 19) globalizing processes that are economic, cultural, social and political. Such an interest in multiple axes of identity within irregular globalizing processes points to the necessity of considering both the 'fixity' and the porousness of place and the implications for identity formation.

Within such a conceptual framework, masculine identity is viewed as historically and spatially situated. Masculinity as a social, cultural and spatial construct involves a global nexus of 'dominant, residual, oppositional and emergent' (Williams 1982: 204–5) patterns of meaning, power and affect. But how is it embedded in, and formed through, territory itself and through territorialized institutions and communities? How is it formed through mobility, deterritorialization and associated real and imagined worlds? If it involves 'mobile locatedness' (Massey 1993), and the invocation of globally differentiated speeds in place and space, what are the links between pace, place and masculinity?

* * *

Throughout this book, we explore the ways in which globalization, place, masculinities and change intersect. In so doing we draw together and mutually enrich divergent trajectories of scholarship – sociological, cultural and geographical. The literature discussed in this chapter provides a rich set of theoretical resources with which to begin our explorations. In the chapters to follow we will work with it in several ways. In some instances we will elaborate upon it. We will, however, put some key concepts under empirical pressure to see how well they hold up. Those that have particular resonance for our inquiries will be deployed and also provided with some empirical thickness. Where apt, we will bring additional existing concepts into the picture. However, we will also show that such things as reconfigured masculinities, emergent spaces, reordered economies and the globalization of affect require some new conceptual resources and we will develop these. In conceptual terms, our ambition is to theorize afresh masculinity, place and globalization.

2
Place-Based Global Ethnography

Numerous Internet sites and web-based newspapers tell stories of economic and industrial change in the US town of Philomath in Oregon. These electronically mediated accounts illustrate the ways in which timber corporations virtually annihilated the forests surrounding the North American country town and neighbouring smaller logging towns. This corporately engineered environmental devastation was precipitated by the rise of mechanization in the timber industry. As logging technologies became increasingly advanced, logging labour became progressively more redundant. Many of those who were left unemployed by the timber industry needed new jobs and new vocational identities. One account, of Philomath man George Shroyer, emerges from a number of cyber stories. George's tale speaks of difficult and often almost fatal risks encountered in the Philomath forests by the town's loggers. George began working in a Philomath sawmill as a teenage boy. He was employed in various facets of the timber industry for his entire working history. His identity became embedded in his work and in the Philomath logging industry. At the age of 91, George was still behind the wheel of his truck (Hall with Wood 1998).

However, not all Philomath workers have remained so intrinsically connected to the now troubled Philomath logging industry. The shifts in the local economy have meant that people of Philomath had children who were not raised to 'work at the mill'. Rather, new industries that sprang from the reskilling and redeployment of timber industry labourers also fuelled a new generation of workers and Philomath citizens.

35

Tourism and hospitality are being emphasized as strengths in the Philomath economy. Much of the publicity that presents Philomath as a tourist destination notes that the township is located close to the mountainous terrain known as the 'Coast Range'. For example, the primary Internet site promoting the town's assets markets Philomath as 'The Gateway to the Oregon Coast' (Philomath Chamber 2004). The same site highlights the fact that the distinctive shape of Mary Peak, one of the Coast Ranges' notable mountains, frames the highway into Philomath. It seems that as they become increasingly aware and proud of the natural beauty that the logging industries once harvested, people's approaches to the district are changing.

There are many other representations of the social changes precipitated by the demise of the logging industry in Philomath. Most come from community media and Internet sites, produced by those with diverse political investments in the past or present cultural fabric of Philomath. For example, there have been extended media debates surrounding education scholarships in Philomath. These tales tell of Rex and Ethel Clemens, people who did well from the logging industry. In an attempt to put back into Philomath some of the wealth the countryside had offered them, in 1959 the Clemens established an educational trust fund worth in excess of 30 million dollars (Clemens Foundation 2004). The trust is now administered by 'The Clemens Foundation', which suggests their monies are available to fund any student in Oregon County (Clemens Foundation 2004); any student, as long as they are not gay or lesbian, not committed to environmental politics, or are unwilling to support the Philomath logging industry as their career progresses. Only logging-friendly students need apply. A story in the online Philomath journal *Education Reporter* (2003) which details this case is but one of many media accounts of Philomath which have populated the American press over the past few years. The *Education Reporter* articulates the community tensions which are embodied in this case, tensions brought about by the loss of traditional work, the rise of new industries and the influx of new ideas as a small town works to reinvent itself and cope with the backlash produced by change. The journal reconstructs the history of this politically hostile situation by suggesting that:

anti-logging sentiments and other manifestations of radical environmentalism and political correctness have invaded the [Philomath] school, causing [the Clemens] foundation board chief Steve Lowther to drastically alter the scholarship programme. If Lowther and the board stick to their decision, Philomath High School students will no longer be eligible for the scholarships, and other students will be able to apply . . . Lowther asserted that some teachers and administrators use their positions to promote radical politics in the classroom. He and other board members also object to the immodest dress and body piercing now popular among many students, and to the school's gay/lesbian club. [Lowther argues that] 'We are not going to use timber dollars to send the professors' kids, the physicians' kids, the teachers' kids to school, because they are the ones helping to shut down the timber industry with donations to Greenpeace.'

Lowther's class-based argument ('the professors' kids, the physicians' kids, the teachers' kids'), couched in a blue-collar versus white-collar ideology, ignores the deeper causes of the decline in the logging industry. Clearly, Philomath teachers, physicians or professors are not responsible and the responsibility rests with key decision makers within the logging industry itself and the wider market and environmental economies within which it operates. An irony here is that it's the broader logging industry, which Lowther defends so stoically, that has effected such rapid economic and ecological change in his hometown.

These mediascapes point to local/global configurations of continuity and change, power and politics and old and new identities and identifications. It is for these reasons that Philomath is the sort of place that has much appeal for ethnographers of the various hues that we will discuss in this chapter; namely critical ethnography and what has come to be called global ethnography. For instance, the various media stories suggest different angles of analysis along the lines suggested by Massey's simultaneous multiplicity of spaces and her progressive sense of (global) place. In terms of masculinity, they point to the potential of deploying Nespor's gender topographies and topolologies. Such stories also exemplify the politics of representation, and in so doing suggest the politics of knowledge production associated with ethnography itself.

We indicated at the outset that this is a place-based global ethnography and add here that it links ideas associated with critical and global ethnography. Our first purpose in this chapter is to elaborate on the ideas associated with these methodological approaches and to offer a sense of the developments and debates that have arisen with regard to them. Our second purpose is to consider the relationship between studies of masculinity and ethnography with a view to explaining the key features of a global ethnography of masculinity. Our third purpose is to introduce our approach.

Changing times, changing ethnographies

Ethnography is finely attuned to the horizons and rhythms of everyday lives. It involves the extended engagement with, and careful observation and interpretation of, everyday life *in situ*, and observes, probes, describes and seeks to understand the means, motivations and minutiae of human behaviour. Conventionally, it focuses on the particular, the local and the contingent. In fields as diverse as cultural studies, anthropology, sociology and education, ethnography has played an important role in the development of understanding about masculinities and gender relations. Indeed, an argument can be sustained that the literature on youthful masculinities that has had the most impact and resulted in the most significant theoretical developments has arisen from ethnographic research. For example Willis (1977) and Mac an Ghaill (1994) both conduct innovative ethnographic studies which identify key social and cultural factors influencing white working-class boys' schooling in industrial (Willis 1977) and post-industrial (Mac an Ghaill 1994) England. Further, as the role of consumption has assumed greater importance in identity formation, ethnographic studies of masculinity have increasingly focused on young males' creative everyday appropriations of media and consumer culture (Dimitriadis 2001, 2003). Much such work is conducted within the terms of what has come to be called critical ethnography (Thomas 1993), which draws on various versions and in various ways from critical and post-critical theory (see, respectively, Carspeckon 2001; Foley 2002; Simon and Dippo 1986).

Critical ethnographies

Critical ethnographers use a range of ethnographic techniques to generate data about 'real life', bringing this into creative tension with conceptual frameworks that are pertinent to their central research questions and, as Willis says, 'seek to deliver analytic and illuminating points not wholly derivable from the field but vital to conceptualising its relationships' (2000: xi). Amongst much, critical ethnographers seek to engage in and address pressing social issues and debates, to uncover and expose the complex and often unequal power dynamics and relationships in specific social and cultural settings and to show how they link to wider power geographies. Critical ethnographies look to connect history, daily life and biography, local everyday realities and large-scale structures. They understand these as operating in a reciprocal, if uneven, relationship. Willis explains it this way:

> Of fundamental importance to the ethnographic imagination is comprehending creativities of the everyday as indissolubly connected to, dialectically and intrinsically, wider social structures, structural relations, and structurally provided conditions of existence.
>
> (Willis 2000: 34)

Within this genre, ethnography and ethnographers are understood as operating within the politics of knowledge and the wider power dynamics associated with institutionalized knowledge industries and broader society.

Critical ethnography arose as one of many responses to the problematization of ethnography. In turn, this arose as a result of the epistemological tumult that has occurred in the social sciences and humanities since the 1980s. This has involved challenges to:

> the founding assumptions of most of the disciplines that constitute the human sciences. The politics of knowledge of this era has been one of its defining features. Under the labels postmodernism and then cultural studies, a bracing critical self-examination was initiated by many practising scholars in the social sciences and humanities. This examination of their own habits of thought and work involved reconsiderations of the nature of representation, description, subjectivity, and objectivity, reconsiderations even of the notions of 'society' and 'culture' themselves, as well as of how they have materialized objects of study and data about those objects to constitute the 'real' to which their work had been addressed.
>
> (Marcus 1999: 6)

It is apt that we mention at least a little of this recent history in order that we may methodologically situate our study. We will then discuss in more detail global ethnographies and our particular approach to them.

Early ethnographic traditions largely subscribed to the Platonic notion that signs/language are mirrors of reality (Stoller 1999). This positivist and objectivist account of reality was accompanied by three other notions: that of the objective observer; the view that valid data could only be produced through testable and standardized methods; and the notion that reality could be accurately represented in text (Hammersley and Atkinson 1995). It followed from such notions that ethnographers identified the facts of social and cultural life and that their representations of their findings provided truths about the human condition. Such views constitute what is seen as ethnography's 'traditional' and 'modernist' epistemological base (Denzin and Lincoln 1994). However, they have endured an extended period of criticism.

Many doubts have been voiced about the ability and appropriateness of ethnographers' claims to provide a 'realist' account of social and cultural life. Indeed, there has been much debate about the practice, truth claims and future directions of ethnographic methods, thus effecting something of a 'crisis of representation' for ethnography (Lincoln 1995). Much of this has come from cultural, feminist, subaltern, colonial and post-colonial studies. Theoretical developments in literary and language studies have also provided some of the impetus for such debate and for new ethnographic writing practices. So, for example, in this context, ethnographic writing came to be seen as 'fiction' on an equal par with other fictions (Bochner and Ellis 2002; Daly 1997; Pillow and St Pierre 2000). Such critique also came from within the disciplinary home of ethnography, anthropology itself. Indeed *Writing Culture: The Poetics and Politics of Ethnography* by Clifford and Marcus (1986) is a landmark study that, as the title suggests, also problematizes the poetics, epistemology and politics of ethnography. Denzin and Lincoln term the 1980s and beyond, a 'post-modern moment' and describe it as 'a messy moment, [with] multiple voices, experimental texts, ruptures, crises of legitimation and representation, self-critique, new moral discourses, and technologies' (Denzin and Lincoln 1994: 581).

This 'representation crisis' made hazardous not only the processes and products of ethnographers' work but also the moral and intellectual authority of ethnographers themselves, thus also leading to a legitimacy crisis. Geertz (1983) argues, for instance, that if ethnographers produce interpretations of interpretations, then the researcher can have no privileged voice. Further, this line of thought made problematic the translation of ethnographic fieldwork into the written account. As Gubrium and Holstein (1997: 101) observe, ethnographers are located in the highly ambiguous border between the fictions of reality and the realities of representation. Such observations and critiques cleared the way for 'a spate of highly narrativised ethnographies in which the presence of the ethnographer was acknowledged, truth was partial and the . . . epistemological assumptions of the Enlightenment were questioned' (Stoller 1999: 700).

Ultimately, the critical and post-critical turns in the social sciences and humanities have meant that ethnographers are now much more sensitive to matters of truth and representation, power and authority (Davies 1999). However, the manner in which such sensitivity is manifest in ethnographic practice varies widely, as does opinion about the merits or otherwise of the various intellectual stands and strands that make up the 'post-modern moment'. Indeed, Marcus points to 'a pervasive nervousness about the legacy of this self-critical ferment, a lack of confidence in the relevance of all the theory, a sense that maybe the so-called crisis of representation has been only an intellectual crisis, offering little possibility of effective theoretical or analytic engagement outside academia' (Marcus 1999: 6).

Critical ethnography in its various manifestations is but one outcome of this ferment. It, too, has come in for its fair share of criticism and has engaged in its own self-criticism. This is not a debate we wish to get into here. Rather, let us mention where we stand within it. We subscribe to the view that ethnographies are historically, culturally and spatially located. Further, we believe that it behoves ethnographers to make clear their theoretical and political sympathies and to acknowledge that they produce partial, situated and interested knowledge. Our views are informed, in part by Haraway (1991), who argues that situated knowledge claims do not assert their transcendence or universality. Because situated knowledges are locatable they can be called to account, unlike views 'from above, from nowhere, from simplicity' (1991: 195), unlike certain relativist post-modern accounts. As she says, 'the alternative to relativism is partial, locatable, critical knowledges sustaining the possibility of webs of connection called solidarity in politics and shared conversations in epistemology' (p. 191). It is in this sense, then, that we subscribe to a very specific notion of critical realism.

Let us spell out aspects of this view of critical realism. We do not claim a privileged connection to truth *per se*. On the other hand, we do seek to produce knowledge that is recognized as a credible depiction of the situation by those well placed to know. In this sense, our approach can be called to account on inter-subjective grounds. Willis calls this the 'Ah-ha effect' (2000: 117). Further, our position is neither empiricist nor idealist. One crucial epistemological conversation takes place as the ethnographer seeks to interpret the relationship between theory, the fieldwork and the empirical record, and to record the final ethnographic account in text. We believe central features of such a conversation are instinct, inventive tension and interruption. Emulating the approach to ethnography advanced by Willis (pp. 112–21), we contend that the ethnographer must be willing to try various theoretical possibilities, to let go of those that do not deepen appreciation and to move with and/or generate those that do. Equally, data and language must be deployed in the final text so as to illuminate, not necessarily to fully represent or validate. The broader responsibility of the ethnographer is to participate in contingent and reflexive conversations that seek to enhance comprehension of some aspect of the human condition. As Willis argues (p. 121), this is especially necessary in times of rapid social change, when on-the-ground experience may have outstripped the capacity of the concepts available to comprehend it. A more specific responsibility is to participate forcefully in the politics of meaning making around issues central to bettering the human condition with regard to questions of justice. One requirement of such powerful participation is that the ethnography does its job properly – it makes meaning 'at the highest level of achievable quality, methodological, theoretical and textual' (p. 119). It can thus be defended as trustworthy on both *epistemological* and *ethical* grounds. Finally, if the ethnographic account provides a sufficient basis for others to build upon in subsequent research or political action, then it can be defended on *pragmatic* grounds.

Ethnographies and globalization

For some critical ethnographers the crises of representation and legitimation noted above are of somewhat less significance and concern than two other issues. These are, first, trying to comprehend the processes and repercussions of globalization and, second, considering the implications of globalization for ethnographic methodologies. The imperative here is to ensure that ethnographies have global reach and relevance. Let us take each of these points in turn, noting the work of theorists who have sought to grapple with such issues.

The Editors of the scholarly journal *Ethnography* (Willis and Trondman 2000) argue that:

> There is now an urgent need for the detailed and grounded empirical study of the myriad changes that are remaking the face of 'late modern' societies as a result of the sweeping restructuring of economy, society, culture, and politics across the globe

Many agree with this claim and contend that the scholarship on globalization needs to move past its abstraction and its focus on disembodiment. Some meta-narratives of globalization are so steeped in abstraction and enmeshed in the politics of academic discourse that they erase the complexities of the ways in which it is lived in different parts of the globe for different peoples. For instance, Gille and Ó Riain (2002: 275) make the case that many theorizations of global mobilities fail to properly attend to questions of power, human agency, sense making and embodiment. Such critiques are usually followed by the claim that critical ethnographic inquiry, constructed in order to engage with the global, is a vital means by which comprehensive understandings of globalization can be further developed. Synthetic statements about global change can be built from individual and comparative ethnographies and thus theories of globalization can be refined. For instance Ong (1999b: 31) argues that ethnography offers a valuable methodology through which to understand globalization and also to refigure social theories in relation to its lived effects.

Many ethnographies and other qualitative studies about such changes are emerging and a comprehensive overview of these is offered in Gille and Ó Riain (2002). These sorts of studies are variously called 'global ethnography' (Burawoy et al. 2000), 'ethnographies of globalization' (Kraidy 1999), Tsing's (2000) anthropology of '[t]he global situation', and 'cosmopolitan ethnography' (Appadurai 1996). Research that pursues similar objectives to 'global ethnography', yet under different names, includes Comaroff and Comaroff's (2003) work on 'postcolonial anthropology and the violence of abstraction' and Gille and Ó Riain's (2001) review essay 'Ethnography after Locality', where they discuss 'place-making projects'. Taken together these studies indicate that 'global ethnography' is an emerging, interdisciplinary and multimethod genre. This is in the process of realizing its potential to enhance understanding of globalization and to develop new conceptual resources that might assist such understandings.

For instance, the diverse ethnographies of 'grounded globalization' in the Burawoy and colleagues (2000) collection, demonstrate the fruitfulness of this approach, offering a nuanced view of global dynamics marked by unevenness and counter-tendencies, and showing that globalization involves the creation of many new and varied connections between local and global spaces. Ong's *Flexible Citizenship: The Cultural Logics of Transnationality* (1999a) also signals a comprehensive advance on theories of globalization by showing how 'places in the non-West differently plan and envision the particular combinations of culture, capital, and the nation-state' (Ong 1999a: 31).

All that said, globalization has prompted considerable debate about the capacity of ethnography to adequately comprehend the complexity of globalization. For instance, Ong (1999a: 31) argues that established ethnographic research methods 'are no longer adequate to capture the range of political formations and self-positioning in different parts of the world'. In Stacey's (1999) view, globalization poses theoretical and logistical challenges to ethnography, and the methodological and analytical repertoire of ethnography must expand to address them. Such claims are part of a broader debate about the 'metatheoretical, epistemological and political implications' for the social sciences of the sociohistorical changes associated with globalization (Gille and Ó Riain 2002). This in turn has led to discussion about how ethnographic methods might need to alter if ethnography is to be up to the task. We will turn to this matter shortly, but, first, we consider why it is that globalization has made ethnography so apparently problematic.

There are three primary reasons why globalization and ethnography appear to be mismatched. The first is because of the ways that place has traditionally been defined within anthropology and sociology, and the implications of this for ethnographic methods. The second reason concerns the capacity of ethnography to deal with matters associated with transnational scale, and the third involves the difficulty ethnography has in attending to the mobilities associated with globalization. Let us take each in turn.

Ethnographies are often conceived around the notion of the ethnographer's naturalistic immersion in local, bounded sites that contain unique cultures. And, as we indicated in Chapter 1, many globalization theorists have problematized the notion of place or locality inherent in such views. They have posited the demise of the local, as economic, cultural and political relationships are increasingly caught up in transnational conditions. Deterritorialization, such theorists argue, means that social life is *de*creasingly organized around territorial centres and *in*creasingly dis-embedded from the particularities of locality or place. As a result, social relations are 'stretched out' across ever-widening expanses of space (Giddens 1999). A further common observation is that 'the world is on the move' (Appadurai 1996) and that the flow of people, money, goods, services, ideas and images characterizes globalizing times.

An associated notion is that local cultures are washed away in the tide of such global movements. It is such constructions of contemporary locality as well as ethnography that lead Burawoy (in Burawoy et al. 2000: 1) to ask, somewhat rhetorically: '[h]ow can ethnography be global? How can ethnography be anything but micro- and ahistorical?' Appadurai's (1996: 52) answer is that '[t]he task of ethnography now becomes the unravelling of a conundrum: what is the nature of locality as lived experience in a globalized deterritorialized world?' Gille and Ó Riain (2001: 301) label this general phenomenon 'Appadurai's dilemma', because going to the local no longer provides straightforward access to the social or the cultural (2002: 273). They explain that such notions of globalization put under pressure traditional notions of the ethnographic site and ask 'Where is the "there" . . . where global ethnographers should be?' (Gille and Ó Riain 2002: 272).

Sassen (2001: 260) argues:

> The multiple processes that constitute economic globalization inhabit and shape specific structurations of the economic, the political, the cultural and the subjective. Among the most vital of their effects is the production of new spatialities and temporalities.

A key feature of theories of globalization is that various aspects of the social and the cultural have been, to some extent, detached from place. As a consequence, new scales of social action and social power have emerged. These take ethnographers within sociology and anthropology beyond their spatial comfort zones – the local and the nation-state for instance. The transnational has thus come to be understood as a social space involving and invoking transnational social and cultural activities and formations. Further, place also comes to be seen as embedded within the complex power geometries of the 'politics of scale' (Brennar 1999, cited in Gille and Ó Riain 2002: 278). This involves a 'destabilization of existing hierarchies of spatial scales' and new arenas for social action beyond the local and the national (Gille and Ó Riain 2002: 278). It requires ethnography to rethink its relationship to space.

Movements are a preoccupation of many theorists of globalization. As we indicated earlier, they have been conceived of variously as flows, mobilities, scapes and networks. These potentially alter the relationships between space, time and power and the local and the global. Indeed, they destabilize existing sociological and anthropological categories (e.g., locality, community) and also many of the binary concepts associated with some forms of globalization theory, the local/global binary for instance. But more significantly for us here, ethnography is not technically or conceptually well equipped to deal with global movements.

So what are the implications of globalization for ethnographic methodologies? Burawoy (2001), a foremost theorist of global ethnography, argues that narrow and static views of place, ethnography, the field and fieldwork must be surpassed if ethnography is to properly engage with the transnational flows associated with globalization. Ethnographers must not be completely bound by local place and time. Rather, they must reconceive of place, and reflexively pay attention to both embodied and local habits and cultures and also to global flows; they must attend to 'fluidities and mobilities' as well as 'stoppages and fixities', as Gille and Ó Riain (2002: 275) put it, or to 'dwelling as well as travelling', 'routes and roots' as Clifford (1997: 20–2, 24–5) suggests. For Marcus (1998), ethnographers working in global times need to engage with questions of movement, scale and multiple sites. He urges researchers to 'follow the people . . . follow the thing . . . follow the metaphor . . . follow the plot, story or allegory, . . . follow the life or biography, [and/or] follow the conflict' and conduct 'multi-sited ethnography' (pp. 90–5). Such a globally aware kind of ethnography defines its

> objects of study through several different modes or techniques. These techniques might be understood as practices of construction through (preplanned or opportunistic) movement and of the tracing within different settings of a complex cultural phenomenon given an initial, baseline conceptual identity that turns out to be contingent and malleable as one traces it.
>
> (Marcus 1998, 90)

Such an approach would seem well suited to mapping global flows, but as Gille (2001) observes, it is easier said than done. Interestingly, she abandoned it in favour of applying Massey's progressive sense of place to global research contexts.

According to Gille and Ó Riain (2002: 278): 'Places matter because it is in places that we find the ongoing creation, institutionalization and contestation of global networks, connections and borders.' These sorts of argument mean that the ethnographic notion of a field site must no longer be thought of in isolation or as bounded, and that ethnography has the potential to involve a 'diversity of empirical sites and scales' (Collier and Ong 2003: 1). Indeed, this may mean that the conventional notion of 'the field' must be extended, even rethought, and that new understandings of field site are possible; global flows, networks or scapes can, for instance, be understood as sites for ethnographic investigation. They might also, for example, be conceived of, Burawoy and colleagues (2000: 5) argue, in terms of the multiple global forces, connections and imaginations that are associated with and cut across that site.

Burawoy and colleagues' three axes of globalization have come to feature strongly in understandings of the objects of inquiry for global ethnography. *Global forces* are understood as those pressures on place that emerge from such overarching, often intersecting structures as capitalism, modernity, colonialism and imperialism. Ethnographic studies of global forces explore the means by which these operate on the ground and in the flesh, and their impact on local lives and livelihoods. The term *global connections* is used to refer to the translocal and transnational links between such people or groups as migrants, tourists and social movements. A *global imagination* refers to the mobilization and deployment of meanings about globalization itself and the power and politics of such meaning making. These combine to produce what Gille and Ó Riain (2002: 279) refer to as 'complex multi-scalar place-making projects'.

These and other elaborations of the possible foci of contemporary ethnography have led Marcus (1998) to argue that ethnographies of globalization must be 'multi-sited'. Drawing on Marcus, Gille and Ó Riain (2002: 286) explain:

> Multi-sited research is designed around chains, paths, threads, conjunctions, or juxtapositions of locations in which the ethnographer establishes some form of literal physical presence, with an explicit, posited logic of association or connection among sites that in fact defines the argument of the ethnography.

They go on to observe that 'multi-sited' ethnographies do not only attend to new possible sites but also to 'multiple places and spatial scales' and to the ways that places and mobilities (flows, networks) 'constitute one another' (Gille and Ó Riain 2002: 272–5). In practical terms investigating these means developing a 'logic of associations' arising from the field itself and from theory, and then pursuing its trails and traces. This invokes the pursuit of many possibilities, including people, objects, narratives and images. Marcus (1998: 50) discusses such a method of research, and suggests that: 'An ethnography of complex connections, itself, becomes the means of producing a narrative that is both macro and micro.'

In addition though, Gille and Ó Riain (2002) warn against an overemphasis on fluidity and movement and indicate that the construction of spatial borders and boundaries is also legitimately part of contemporary ethnographic inquiry. Attention may be paid to the ways in which some borders might, under some circumstances, be fluid, but also to how and why some may be held in place and with what social and cultural consequences. In drawing attention to the borders of places, they make the point that the 'production of differences between places' extends to the 'political contestation of place' via a consideration of the 'politics of scale' noted earlier. This they call place-making projects, 'new kinds of places with new definitions of social relations and their boundaries' (pp. 272–8).

Global ethnographies understood largely in Burawoy and colleagues' (2000) terms, then, are a means of tracing the diffusion of global forces, connections and imaginations locally, and of tracing the manner in which these spiral outwards from the local to other scales. Albrow's (1997) notions of 'socio-sphere' and 'socio-scapes' are useful here for he, like Massey and others, insists that the associated networks are uneven in their scale, intensity and territoriality and that in understanding them, more attention needs to be paid to the local and the individual actor. His notion of 'socio-sphere' refers to a specific territory or cluster of interest (pp. 51–2), whereas the term 'socio-scape' is used to refer specifically to people's 'fluid imaginings of spatial belongings . . . that reach beyond the locality' (Gille and Ó Riain 2002: 278). A socio-scape is the vantage point from which intersecting socio-spheres can be observed.

It is our view that Appadurai extends Burawoy's notion of global imaginations and Albrow's notion of 'socio-scape'. In discussing deterritorialization and its implications for ethnography, Appadurai focuses on 'the role of the imagination in social life' (1996: 52), arguing that:

> In the last two decades the deterritorialization of persons, images and ideas has taken on a new force . . . More people throughout the world see their lives through the prisms of the possible lives offered by the mass media in all their forms. That is, fantasy is now a social practice, it enters, in a host of ways, into the fabrication of social lives . . . The biographies of ordinary people are constructions (or fabrications) in which the imagination plays an important role . . .
>
> (Appadurai 1996: 54)

'Possible lives' is a key concept and he makes a case that these 'complex, partly imagined lives' must form the bedrock of ethnography. Indeed, he says if ethnographers are to remain relevant in deterritorialized times, they must be alert to 'the fact that ordinary lives today are more often powered not by the givenness of things but by the possibilities that the media suggest are available' (p. 52). 'Thick' description takes

on a new meaning as it seeks to portray the impact of the deterritorialized imagination on local experiences and individual life roots and
routes. 'Thickness with a difference', he calls it. The 'reality' that ethnography seeks to portray has many new meanings. A qualification is
required though, for Appadurai points out that 'Not all deterritorialization is global in its scope and not all imagined lives span vast international panoramas. The world on the move effects even small geographic
and cultural spaces' (p. 61). Which images and ideas flow through space,
how they travel and what people do with them in and out of place
become central issues in his conception of global ethnography.

We mentioned in Chapter 1 that some globalization scholars argue
that globalization and reflexive modernization are closely related
(Bauman 1991; Beck 1992; Giddens 1990, 1991; Lash 1993). Briefly, the
argument is that individuals and institutions are involved in a reflexive
self-monitoring process that is now so pervasive in society it has become
structural. It is thus possible to see the post-modern ferment in the
social sciences and humanities that we noted earlier as part of reflexive
modernity and thus of globalization. Indeed, this view is implied,
although not stated in *Critical Anthropology Now*, a collection of ten
ethnographies edited by Marcus (1999).

The broad purpose of the Marcus collection is two-fold; to examine
whether post-modern critique is a feature of power/knowledge appara-
tuses outside of the academy and so to enter 'unconventional field sites',
and develop whatever methods are appropriate to study them. As
Marcus argues:

> the impact of the so-called post-modernist critiques of anthropology
> lies not in further discussions of post-modernism, but in the enact-
> ments of new kinds of research projects in anthropology, differently
> problematized and innovatively conducted.
>
> (Marcus 1999: 7)

The Marcus collection focuses on the professions, corporations, publishing, the military, finance, politics and policy, science and technology. In other words, much of it focuses on groups, institutions and
practices that participate in the processes of globalization in quite influ-
ential ways. They are, as Marcus says, 'devoted to the pragmatic, ratio-
nal control of social problems' (1999: 11). The collection examines the
extent to which and how reflexivity is a feature of these different groups
and settings. It points to the 'the contemporary anxieties, "cracks,"
and acknowledged indeterminacies in otherwise confident expert and

common-sense discourses' (p. 9). The sites investigated range from the boardrooms of multinational corporations to the chat rooms of the Internet, and a strong argument of the book is that 'new and more complicated research locations are giving rise to shifts in the character of both fieldwork and fieldworker' (p. 2). Further, one of the reasons for conducting ethnographies of the sort in the Marcus collection is to advance understanding of the knowledge politics of contemporary times. Interestingly, it would seem that the post-modern ferment equipped us well to look beyond the academy to examine such politics.

Overall, then, sophisticated global sensibilities and sensitive globalizing methodologies are called for (Stoller 1999). Three very general imperatives for global ethnographies arise. First, they must be sufficiently fertile to take into consideration transformations of space, place, time and identity. This includes factoring into analysis some, or all of the following: large-scale economic and cultural shifts and influences, their social and cultural manifestations in place and space, and their implications for identity and the imagination. Second, such ethnographies must include theories and techniques that help to make sense of complex, uneven and diverse globalizing trajectories and local–global relations, and provide the opportunity for the comparison of their different manifestations. Third, they must expand notions of the field to include deterritorialized sites not usually thought of as sites *per se* and adopt foci not necessarily within the comfort zones of ethnographers. The aim, then, is to achieve layered and liquid methodologies that are sensitive to the intricacy and mobility both within and across localities broadly defined. Clearly, all of this involves a certain disciplinary and theoretical promiscuity, as Stacey argues (1999), and a supple ethnographic imagination.

In many ways critical ethnography, as we have defined it and as it is employed in cultural studies particularly, is well placed to undertake such inquiries. Unlike more traditional ethnographies from anthropology, it has a view of place that is, as noted, dynamic and contextual. With its expressed interest in the links between specific locales and wider sociocultural patterns, it already has at its disposal the appropriate dispositions to study the dynamic relationship between the local and global. Further, it has a wide view of what might be considered a 'field' site. With its long concern with cultural appropriations of media and commodity forms it has experience in examining the role of the imagination in social life.

In addition to these qualities, critical ethnography is well disposed towards surprise in the field. This means it is also open to what is new

– open to that which exceeds the conceptual resources currently available. It might thus be inferred from this and from earlier critical ethnographic studies that methodological approaches that have previously proved effective for critical ethnographic studies can be taken into global contexts unchanged.[1] However, this is not totally the case, for thinking about globalization has clearly created space for critical ethnographies to pursue to a much greater extent questions of scale, transnational complexity and global flows.

Ethnography and masculinity studies

In his sociological review of masculinity studies as a field of inquiry, Connell (2000a: 8–9) suggests that ethnography is one of two 'core' research methods employed in studies of the social construction of masculinity. The first of these is ethnography and the second is 'life-history methods' (p. 8). He considers the period from the 1980s to 2000 as 'the "ethnographic moment" in masculinity research, in which the specific and the local . . . [are] in focus' (p. 9). Connell expands this argument by noting, 'this is not to suggest that the work lacks awareness of broader issues – Moodie's (1994) research on South African mining, for instance, is a classic study of the interplay of race, class and gender structures' (p. 9).

In his view, ethnography has offered scholars a way of engaging with and understanding masculinities which is more complex and culturally aware than other forms of social research. Indeed, Connell (2000a: p. 9) suggests that '[t]he ethnographic moment brought a much-needed gust of realism to debates on men and masculinity, a corrective to the abstractions of role theory'. We have already shown that ethnography is a highly specific research method, and that there is a range of particular approaches to ethnography within the broader rubric of the method. To collapse two decades of masculinity scholarship into an 'ethnographic moment' is rather sweeping. But this apparent lack of interest in extended methodological discussion seems to be symptomatic of the field.

Despite the prevalence of qualitative sociological methods in studies of masculinity (Connell 2000a and b; Haywood and Mac An Ghaill 2003; Mac an Ghaill 1996; Whitehead and Barrett 2001), there are surprizingly few substantial discussions of ethnography, or indeed of qualitative research methods more generally. Take, as an example, Whitehead and Barrett's (2001) extensive edited collection. Most chapters therein undertake qualitative research on men from specific demographics, but few explicate the research methods deployed in generating data, or the methodology from which such methods were derived. The papers in the edited anthology *Dislocating Masculinity: Comparative Ethnographies* (Cornwall and Lindisfarne 1994) are a little more expansive, but not much.

This rich collection contains a range of different discussions that include reflections on the authors' employment of ethnography as method. This said, the reflections are brief and to a great extent terms such as 'ethnography' and 'anthropology' are taken for granted. Cornwall and Lindisfarne (1994) problematize the scholarly history of anthropology as a method for understanding gender relations (pp. 27–9). They note that early ethnographies in anthropology tended to be carried out by men researching women's social roles in ways that re-enforced patriarchal power structures. They observe that in the 1970s, and subsequently, feminist critiques of such studies and feminist ethnographies counteracted this situation. The critical reconsideration of ethnography as a tool through which to better understand shifting dynamics of gendered power was, they explain, then furthered within studies of men and masculinity. While there are a number of theoretical moves in the collection that are very insightful, the discussion of the ethnographic method itself falls short of explicating specific approaches and does not involve any reflexive discussion of research method. So, although the editors, and the analytic strength of the studies in this collection, indicate that ethnography is indeed an apposite method with which to study masculinities and gender relations, the method itself is neither refined nor debated. We acknowledge that in the strict economy of publication there is not always space to discuss method, and that theory is often seen as a more weighty matter. However, lack of explicit attention to method in masculinity studies is odd and not particularly healthy, especially in comparison with the frequent and explicit attention paid to such matters in feminist studies (e.g., Pillow and St Pierre 2000; Wolf 1996).

Six years after the publication of the Cornwall and Lindisfarne (1994) collection, Connell suggests that the 'ethnographic moment' (2000a: 9) in studies of masculinity has lost its interpretive power. In line with certain ethnography scholars mentioned earlier, Connell argues that ethnography is no longer dexterous enough to sufficiently engage in global issues:

> the 'ethnographic moment' in masculinity research . . . needs to be supplemented by work on a larger scale . . . Ultimately, the large his-

torical context, the big picture, is essential for understanding the small picture, the ethnographic details. This logic must now be taken a step further . . . to understand local masculinities, then, we must think in global terms. But how?

(Connell 2000a: 14, 39–40)

Taking this line of inquiry further, Connell devises the global theories of masculinities and theories of globalizing men which we noted in Chapter 1. However, he does not explore ways of developing ethnography so it may better attend to matters of scale, or what global ethnographies of masculinity might involve, or indeed what the methodological debates about global ethnography might have to say to masculinity studies. Moreover, it can almost be inferred from what he says that he does not see how 'small pictures' can illustrate the workings of 'big pictures'; even though, as noted, he says that some ethnographies have in fact captured broader issues. Further, his notion of the 'big' and the 'small' overlooks 'complex multi-scalar place-making projects' (Gille and Ó Riain 2002: 279) and the mutual constitution of place and mobility already mentioned here. To focus only on questions of scale is to overlook the debates about how ethnography might redefine its notion of site and deal with contemporary global spatialities, temporalities, mobilities and imaginations; how it might become multi-sited as Marcus (1998) suggests.

While we agree with Connell that individual ethnographies of masculinity may not be able to adequately capture contemporary global conditions, it is still the case that together comparative ethnographies in such collections as Cornwall and Lindisfarne's (1994) do illustrate the diverse and uneven ways that masculinity is taken up around the globe and can, to some extent, also speak to matters associated with spatial borders and the production of, and contestation over, place-based differences. In this sense, collectively they can be the basis for synthetic, even if mainly comparative, statements. However, it is also clear that such accounts do not either explicitly or, in most cases, implicitly deal with the 'myriad changes' (Willis 2000) associated with globalization. Neither, therefore, do they necessarily help to reconfigure theory about masculinity and its relationship to globalization. So what of those global ethnographies that focus on men?

Global ethnographies of men

Methodologically aware examples of global ethnography that feature men, can be found in Burawoy and colleagues (2000).[2] A striking feature of these is that while they are self-consciously fashioned as global ethno-graphies, they do not usually draw on theories or indeed other ethno-graphic studies of masculinities. We have already outlined the ways in which this collection streams 'global ethnography' into studies of *global forces*, *global connections* and *global imaginations*.

The *global forces* section considers the implications for lives, livelihood and institutions of an 'evermore integrated global economy' and 'the shifts in relations between capital and labor' (2000: 93). And under this theme Gowan (2000: 74–105) studies globalization as loss, based on several episodes of ethnographic research with 25 homeless male recy-clers in San Francisco. Her study illustrates global ethnography as a research method, giving a clear example of how global economic trends were the primary factors leading to the unemployment and disposses-sion of these men. Drawing together Castell's discussion of global spaces – spaces of flows and [binding] spaces of places – with a detailed con-sideration of the global economic climate engulfing these men's biogra-phies, Gowan shows how globalization changes some men's lives, and unpacks what these men and their dispossession can tell us about *global forces*. The men's nostalgia unearths an 'under-side' to neo-liberal eco-nomic discourses of worker mobility, casualization of the labour force, multi-skilling and flexible employment. Gowan explains:

> the instrument I use to hook into the big picture is nostalgia, the nostalgia of the dispossessed for the lives they have lost. In each case, individual regrets and losses connect to the large-scale shifts set off by what we call globalization . . . their nostalgia for the past helps us explore globalization as loss.
>
> (Gowan 2000: 75–6)

Global forces, and certainly 'economic global forces', are critical agents acting upon bodies as sites of the production of contemporary mas-culinities. However, the production of masculinity itself remains outside the scope of Gowan's analysis. While she theorizes loss as a complex cultural, economic, psychological and physiological matrix, she does not specifically consider the ways in which masculinity is part of this complex. In other words, she does not consider the ways that the emo-tional geography of globalization links with that of masculinity. Her reading of homeless men remains focused on their recycling of public waste and theorizing the significance of their alternative economy in the light of mainstream neo-liberal economic discourses. The discussion of methods here is more notable than in other analyses of ethnographic studies of men (e.g., Cornwall and Lindisfarne 1994), yet is still far from comprehensive. The nature of Gowan's analysis offers the reader insight into her time in the field, which she extends to include engagements with some global popular cultural texts – Hollywood films (2000: 98) and American print media (pp. 76–7). However, the explicit discussion of methods remains scant, and a direct engagement with theories of masculinity is outside her analytic focus.

Still within the conceptual lens of *global forces*, in another exploration of the economic and lived fallout for men of global deindustrialization in America, Blum (2000: 106–36) theorizes the changing working lives of men in the San Francisco shipyards. His insightful pseudo-biographical analysis is a 'global ethnography' in the sense that he consistently considers the global contexts giving momentum to forces of deindustrialization and its lived effects. His discussion of method does not explicitly identify aspects of his research process that are 'global ethnography', as opposed to ethnography. His concern with global ethnography is only evident through his consideration of global issues and the chapter's contextual position within the collection. Blum's discussion also excludes any consideration of the kinds of masculinities produced by steelwork in shipyards, and how processes of globalization are changing ways of being men as much as they are changing what men do.

A final example in Burawoy and colleagues (2000) is within the *global connections* section which is concerned with 'the transnational social' (p. 139) and analyses 'the way emerging global connections create new regimes or sets of social relations in which the "material" and "discursive" moments are inextricably linked', and in relation to which new social possibilities emerge (p. 140). George's (2000: 144–74) chapter within this strand illustrates the capacity of global ethnography to self-consciously engage with gender relations and dynamics; although she too uses few direct studies of masculinity. Her study is of gendered relations between Indian men and women living in the United States and focuses on the lives of Indian nurses and their husbands. George is concerned with global markets for services as much as with cultures of immigration and conflicting cultural belief systems. Pursuing these multiple interests, she notes that: 'the incorporation of Kerala Christian nurses into the Indian labor force created a reservoir of migrant workers for a global market' (p. 153). It is the associated migrations that bring about shifts in masculinities, femininities and gender dynamics, and alter the balance of domestic labour and men's role in the church. George remains consistently reflexive about her research method, which consists of two years of multi-sited fieldwork, one year of which she spent in Central City in the United States and one in Kerala in India. Still, George does not explicate what she takes 'global ethnography' to mean. Even so, George's chapter illustrates some ways in which global ethnography as method can be deployed to study masculinities.

While, clearly, Burawoy and colleagues' (2000) collection as a whole models global ethnography as method, each of the studies included could be more exacting about how the methods they employ are 'global ethnographic' methods rather than simply ethnography with a global focus. But more to the point here, the chapters we have discussed not only missed the opportunity to engage the rich field of inquiry that constitutes masculinity studies, they also missed the chance to contribute overtly to the development of global ethnographies of masculinity.

So what might count as a global ethnography of masculinity? Do the other studies of masculinity and globalization that we mentioned in Chapter 1 help to flesh out this notion? These questions clearly echo the debates we have canvassed so far in this chapter. Is Hooper's discussion of transnational business masculinity (2000a), an example? She theorizes transnational 'frontier' business masculinities in global developed Western world cultures. Yet we would not consider her work to be global ethnography, because it is a textual analysis of *The Economist* magazine format newspaper. It does not involve extensive, direct immersion in lived culture. In order to construct a comprehensive ethnographic understanding of globalized and globalizing masculinities, one must at the very least undertake direct immersion in a range of fields (or sites) of lived cultures and consider global economic forces together with transnational connections and cultural imaginaries as they relate to the complex power geometries associated with masculinity. This approach to global ethnography is more in line with Nespor's (2000b) theorization of 'Topologies of Masculinity'. Nespor examines located and mobile gendered connections between pre-adolescent boys; connections made evident through fieldwork observation and interviews as well as through broader social and cultural considerations. Nespor's is a useful early example of a global ethnography of masculinity.

Our approach

This study explores the complexity of what goes on in out of the way, but nonetheless globalizing places in developed Western countries. We do so in order to ascertain how globalization is experienced and constituted in the everyday lives of the local people, but particularly young males.

Our focus, in the first instance, is on four diverse places in Australia, each quite different, as we indicated in the Introduction. In many ways our actual data-gathering techniques are typical of ethnographic methods. For a three-year duration we spent extended periods in our four fieldwork sites observing people going through their daily routines in their own settings. In each place, in-depth semi-structured interviews were carried out with 36 young people. On a weekly basis, for a six-week period, the 24 males who were involved in the study were interviewed individually and the 12 females were interviewed fortnightly. They ranged from 13 to 16 years of age. Loosely structured focus and affinity group discussions were held with senior boys and senior girls in the school (16–18 years of age) mothers, fathers, community members, teachers, and youth and welfare service providers. Informal conversations were held with a wide range of local people. We spent time at a variety of community and youth-specific locales (e.g., the school, beach and main street) and events (e.g., sporting matches, discos, local carnivals). In addition to this fieldwork, we considered relevant government statistical data banks, and local documentary materials such as histories, visual archival material and town records. Our final sources, and this is where we depart from convention, were popular media and marketing representations of out of the way places including references to masculinity, gender dynamics and change. We developed an archive of relevant TV programmes, films, documentaries, advertisements and promotional materials, websites and newspaper articles. We also included in this archive web-based self-representations by similar globalizing locales in other countries.

In some respects our view of the field is quite conventional – four different sites, four different fields. Equally, we address matters that are the conventional stuff of ethnography: local habits and cultures of dwelling; the dynamics of face-to-face interaction; localized forms of social organization; and internal differences and conflicts. But given that we do not have a bounded view of these places, this is only part of the story of each place and of masculinities in place, and thus of our approach to ethnography.

Because we conceptualize place via Massey's (1994: 3) notion of the 'lived world of a simultaneous multiplicity of spaces' this means we investigate the links between our lived cultural research sites and other related spaces, places and media representations outside, yet connected to, such locations. We link the global, the state, the city and other out of the way places with the lived cultural sites of our fieldwork. Extending Burawoy and colleagues' (2000) notion of global ethnographic studies to include Massey's (1994) concepts of spaces and places, we consider these links in terms of multiple forces, connections and imaginations. Drawing on Appadurai (1996) we refine these rather broad concepts through discussions of his (1996) disjunctive scapes, particularly ethnoscapes, mediascapes and ideoscapes. Each of Burawoy's three axes of globalization is linked to the flow of ideas, people and images into and out of place. In turn these are concerned with people's lived and 'possible' lives, both of which are continually being remade and rethought by young men and others in peripheral places, and by the global media that represent them and their sorts of places.

The global trajectories of masculinity we consider were, in the first instance, suggested by the theories of globalization, place and of masculinity outlined in Chapter 1. These provided us with some sensitizing concepts for investigation. Their particular manifestations emerged as we engaged with each place, explored if and how they were expressed 'on the ground', and traced and compared their social, cultural and subjective affects and effects. Most such trajectories are not treated as sites for investigation *per se*, as proposed by some proponents of global ethnography. Rather, they are understood as woven into the fabric of each 'place-making project' and each such project is understood as enmeshed in wider scapes. It is in this restricted sense that this might be considered a multi-sited study along the lines proposed by Marcus (1998).

In summary, the *forces* that concern us are the contemporary global economy and its ideoscape companions, including economic reflexivity and risk management as these are mediated by the state and as they hit the ground and ricochet out. The *connections* of concern are, first, those associated with the ideoscapes of global corporate cultures as they flow into and rearrange the spaces and signs of the local. The second set of connections of interest are those associated with ethnoscapes; with the flows of people in and out of place; and the politics of the imaginative worlds that accompany them. In considering *imaginations* we depart from Burawoy to focus on global mediascapes and the imaginative worlds that they conjure up. These take two forms, first, the youth cultural images that circulate globally and become a source of young men's 'imagined lives'; and second, the mediascapes that represent out of the way places and people, including those that represent the changes they are experiencing. These all help to construct imaginings of life and masculinity beyond the metropolis. They also provide the contexts for cultures of place-based masculinity in the globalizing local.

*   *   *

As implied throughout, we seek to contribute to discussions about critical and global ethnography by reinstating place, but in ways that speak to contemporary manifestations of place in mobile, uneven and unfair globalizing circumstances. We also develop an approach to ethnography that takes seriously questions about the role of the imagination in social life, particularly the role of the media in imagining place and imagining global connections between comparable places that are grappling with similar global issues. Further, we bring about a meeting of ethnographies of masculinity and global ethnography with a view to considering how each might enhance the other and critically extend the methodologies of both. The book as a whole offers an example of one way to undertake a contemporary place-based global ethnography of masculinity in which the global is read primarily through the embodied and disembodied specificities of place, time and space.

3
Reordering Work

High country cattlemen on their horses rallied in the city of Melbourne in June 2005 and left a lot of horseshit in their wake. Their protest was over the Victorian government's proposed ban on cattle grazing in the Alpine national park. Many of the signs of the Australian bushman were on display – Drizabone coats, Akubra hats and R. M. Williams boots. The ban was constructed as an attack on Australia's tradition, heritage and identity – on the *'Man from Snowy River'*.[1] Was this scene of farmers protesting in the city a particularly Australian phenomenon? Far from it. At the turn of the twenty-first century, similar scenes were being played out across Europe and the Western world. In Poland in 1999, angry farmers 'protesting against the destruction of their livelihoods' and 'demanding a halt to foreign food imports and higher prices for their own products' set up roadblocks (Tyler 1999a):

> [H]undreds of Polish highways and several major border crossings were paralysed for days. Farmers parked their tractors and other heavy machinery across the carriageway, blocking some 200 major highways. . . . The German daily *Frankfurter Rundschau* commented, 'What occurred on some streets was almost like a scene from a civil war: The farmers set fire to tyres and threw Molotov cocktails at the police. The most effective weapon has proved to be the liquid manure spray – in most places the biting stench forced the state powers to withdraw without a fight.'
>
> (Tyler 1999a)

In Brussels in 2001:

> Belgian riot police, some on horseback and others wielding water cannons, were unable to hold back thousands of angry farmers converging on the European Council Building . . . Farmers blocked surrounding streets with some 1000 farm tractors, putting the building under a virtual state of siege.
>
> (London 2001)

In France, farmer-turned-activist Jose Bove achieved international notoriety for his attack on a McDonalds restaurant in the French city of Millau. Bove claimed the attack was intended as a protest against globalization, genetically modified crops and other alleged evils of the 'modern age' (Common Dreams 2001). Significantly, as Bove was tried for the attack in 2000; he received support from farmers worldwide, including the president of America's National Family Farm Coalition, Bill Christison, a self-described 'family farmer' from Missouri who characterized Bove's action as a 'quest for economic and social justice' (Christison 2000). On 22 September 2002, in what organizers claimed was 'the largest demonstration ever seen in the UK' (Countryside Alliance 2002), protesters in the Liberty and Livelihood march poured into the centre of London to 'highlight the problems of the farming community.'

> (Suroor 2004)

These news stories would seem to suggest that around the world the countryside is in trouble. But is such trouble manifest in different ways in different places and does it provoke and invoke different masculine modalities? Indeed, can we assume that all non-metropolitan areas and males are experiencing problems? Could it be that some such places experience globalization in less problematic ways and that alongside various forms of protest masculinity, including the 'lash back' bucolic masculinities noted above, are other formations of masculinity? This chapter considers what happens to masculinity beyond the metropolis when local men's worlds of work change. We explore how such changes alter local places and cultures, the ways in which males survive, give up, reskill or move on, and how their adjustments loop back into the working cultures of place and the working identities of young men.

Changing work, changing workers[2]

Structural shifts in the economy in developed Western countries have involved a move away from primary and secondary to tertiary industries, particularly to the service sector, and to sign-saturated economies (Bauman 1998a and b; Kearns and Philo 1993; Lawrence 1987; MacCannell 1999; McDowell 2003; Ray and Sayer 1999). This has been variously described as a shift from Fordist to post- or neo-Fordist and from industrial to post- or deindustrial production (Amin 1994; Bauman 2000; Harvey 2000). These shifts have often included the closure, restructuring, downsizing, and 'off-shoring' of 'heavy' manufacturing industries and of primary industries. Further, the centre of economic gravity has altered and become more global and less national and local. Survival needs and the drive for competitiveness have led small businesses to either close or to join bigger ones and led larger businesses to become international or global. Many public enterprises have become private and then followed this pattern (Beresford 2000). Local business sensibilities have either been replaced by national or by non-territorial sensibilities. Global corporations have an increasing presence everywhere. Workplace restructuring has usually included the reduction of the workforce, intensification (longer working hours, increased productivity and less pay), casualization and technological enhancement. New approaches to management include the elevation of the entrepreneurial as well as, ironically, increased concern about risk.

Despite the neo-liberal rhetoric about leaving economic growth to market forces – and despite various practices of deregulation – governments have acted as mediators between global, regional, national and local economic trends. They have sought to sustain national and state economies by steering them in particular directions away from certain industries and business practices and towards others. Such imperatives take the form of policy advice, various deregulating and regulating practices, sundry incentives and disincentives, state 'compensation and readjustment' packages and subsidies and strong intervention in the ideological climate, particularly around notions of free trade. Indeed, in this context the state absorbs many of the financial and social costs of economic globalization (Waters 1995: 24).

But how are these broad patterns manifest in particular places outside of the cities? As Massey (1995: 189) explains, production has a geography and this involves 'spatial divisions of labour' and, we argue, an emotional geography. Different patterns of economic activity in different locations alongside uneven economic growth and decline mean that the broad patterns associated with economic globalization and the associated changes in the world of work are manifest differently in different places. Deindustrialization, for instance, is not evenly spread and there is an increasing tendency to relocate production from developed Western to 'Third World' countries or to distribute it across multiple sites (Harvey 2000). Further, as economic production in developed Western countries is increasingly dematerialized, and veers towards the production of services and symbolic goods, as described by Lash and Urry (1994), those places involved in primary and secondary material production, usually places beyond the metropolis, are economically disrupted. For instance, as McMichael and Lawrence (2001) indicate in their discussion of 'globalizing agriculture', many places involved in agriculture have been destabilized by the reduction in world prices for agricultural products, technological change and the so-called liberalization of the agricultural sector, with harmful consequences for farm income and employment. The economic base of such places is also altered by ecological globalization. In the interests of environmental sustainability, governments now undertake risk management in local economies and this involves industry restructuring. For such reasons these places are particularly subject to the flight of capital, the associated restructuring, downsizing or closure of local private and then public industries and services. Local economies are, then, challenged to change, to search for alternatives to conventional practices in a range of industries. Such challenges include the imperative to reflexively apply new scientific and technical knowledges to nature, genetically modified crops being the most obvious example. Traditional industries are constantly re-evaluated and increasingly detraditionalized (Giddens 1994). Local entrepreneurs are those who seek to reinvent the local in the interests of economic recovery. In this chapter we will show how places that extract and process natural resources, through mining, power generation, logging, fishing, horticulture and viticulture experience this situation.

Contemporary workers: flexible, reflexive and feminine?

In present-day circumstances workers' conditions are consistently reconfigured and their identities challenged. The developed Western 'global' work order consists of a small labour elite (the highly skilled, highly privileged professions) and an increasing number of people in casual, poorly paid and insecure work (May 2002). In general, the key features of desirable workers for the contemporary developed Western work order include mobility (they must not be rooted in place), flexibility (they must be prepared to work in any mode, at any time, for any pay), increased expertise (they must have more technical rather than manual knowledge and skill), and increased cultural (style) and social (networks) capital. Loyalty to tradition, enduring respect for geographical location and class-based cultural norms are usually understood by business and industry as impediments to growth. Individualized workers are called upon to be more autonomous, self-monitoring, reflexive and enterprising in order to make themselves employable. Overall, such imperatives frame the present-day worker and work place. But, again, how are such imperatives differently inflected in diverse industries in different places and what do they mean for young males in terms of their gender identities?

It is often argued that the contemporary work order is feminized. The notion of the feminization of work commonly refers to the trend for an increasing number of workplaces to emulate the work and working conditions that have historically pertained to the 'female' retail and service sectors. This involves the gendered *convergence* of labour market and work experiences to the extent that males' experiences in the world of work are becoming more like those of females. A more specific line of argument is that the feminization of work has occurred, particularly in 'the post-industrial service sectors of the economy in metropolitan centres' (Adkins 2002b: 56) where the cultural economy reigns. It should be emphasized that the focus in such analyses is on cultural economies rather than political economies, as Adkins explains, and the question thus arises as to what extent this focus restricts the purchase of the analysis. Nonetheless, the claim is that the associated aestheticization of the economy calls into play amongst workers 'feminine' attributes associated with image, style and affective dexterity. In turn, this is seen to feminize and detraditionalize masculinity. There is no doubt that the claims about the 'feminization of work' carry a heavy conceptual burden and that they need to be more thoroughly spatialized with regard to place and workplace and to be put under more empirical pressure. We undertake to do such work throughout this chapter with the assistance of Bakker's (1996: 7) complexification of the feminization thesis via what she calls the 'gender paradox of restructuring'. This involves, she argues, the 'contradictory effects of the dual process of gender erosion and intensification'. We will unpack both these processes with regard to masculinity and certain worlds of work outside the cities. We will also deploy Adkins (2002a and b), who closely examines the feminization thesis through notions of gender reflexivity, mobility, and de- and retraditionalization.

The existing research on young, mostly urban males points to the ways that some are inventing themselves as 'new workers' and to the fact that some others, particularly those who subscribe to 'macho masculinities', are not (e.g., O'Donnell and Sharpe 2000). However, such research offers insufficient sense of place and of the gendered ways in which males address the identity issues that arise in relation to the diverse and uneven 'new' work order that includes, but certainly goes beyond, so-called feminized work and labour markets. The issues that arise as gender is refashioned across the generations have also attracted insufficient attention. We address matters of place, generation and gender here.

Melancholic masculinities and intergenerational angst

The men of Flint in the United States bore the brunt of General Motors' relocation. The factory they had given their lives to left them for dead. As depicted in Michael Moore's 1989 documentary *Roger and Me*, the town of Flint was decimated. General Motors had closed down multiple factories – factories that had employed the majority of men working in the town and had fed its economy. General Motors (GM) found cheaper labour in Mexico and moved production across the national border. Flint fell apart. In this traumatized town 20,000 people queued for free food. The federal government tried to reinvent Flint as a tourist location. The Hyatt even built a brand new world-class hotel. Nothing could repair the massive economic, cultural and psychological haemorrhage that occurred when GM pulled out of Flint and left the men of the town without work and dignity. The symbolic and cynical gesture of Ronald Regan taking 12 unemployed citizens out for a pizza rubbed salt into their wounds.

Michael Moore's polemical and poignant story of economic change in Flint and the contested accounts of change in Philomath that we discussed at the start of Chapter 2 point to the community effects and affects of certain forms of economic globalization and suggest some ways in which labour, community and identity are being reconfigured. One of many core issues at the heart of both stories is emotional intensity grounded in loss and the associated gender erosion and intensification. Together, these can produce the sorts of 'protest masculinities' (McDowell 2003: 200–19, Poynting, Noble and Tabar 2003: 132–55) illustrated in the news stories at the start of this chapter and they can also produce a form of masculine melancholia.

Brought into the ideoscapes of contemporary Western thought by the work of Freud[3] (1917, republished 1995: 584) in psychoanalytic terms:

The melancholic displays something else besides which is lacking in mourning – an extraordinary diminution in his self-regard, an impoverishment of his ego on a grand scale. The patient represents his ego to us as worthless, incapable of any achievement and morally despicable; he reproaches himself, vilifies himself and expects to be cast out and punished.

Such a psychological condition has economic and sociocultural dimensions, a point well demonstrated by Nicholls (2004) in his study of *Scorsese's Men*. In the context of Scorsese's films, such as *The Age of Innocence* (1993), *Raging Bull* (1980), *Taxi Driver* (1979), *GoodFellas* (1990) and *Cape Fear* (1991), Nicholls articulates the ways that melancholia, nostalgia and loss become entwined and come to define certain masculinities. The irony he identifies is that the melancholic male, incapacitated by his wounds, may be cherished for his melancholic state and even 'enjoy' it. Melancholic masculinity becomes almost honorific. The situations in Morwell and Eden illustrate this state of affairs and also point to some of the emotional costs of economic globalization.

For many years the main economic base of the country city of Morwell has been power generation and that of the coastal town of Eden has been fishing and timber. The history of work in each location is closely tied up with what has conventionally been thought of as men's work and with particular manifestations of masculinity. Males earn respect and reputation by performing a job well and diligently, and by working hard to earn a decent wage. Logging and fishing occur out in the elements and involve battling with nature and extracting its bounty. They entail physical danger and call into play the camaraderie that arises from shared risk. In contrast, the industrial work associated with the power industry in Morwell involves the mastery of machinery and males develop close affinities on the shop floor. The masculinities invoked in both instances equate with what Vashti Kenway (2001: 7–8) drawing on Connell (1995) calls 'hegemonic industrial working-class masculinity'. As she points out, this includes 'a "hard bodies", "hard emotions" response to the world [and] a mode of embodiment that signifies strength, mobility, autonomy, solidarity and a capacity to dominate space'. Morwell and Eden have historically developed their self-concept around a particularly place-based version of 'hegemonic industrial working-class masculinity' that is central to the manner in which identities, work and all relationships are valued. Emotional and intellectual work play little part in the dominant masculine identities of each place. Indeed, such labour is either ignored or belittled for its softness and lack of physicality. The broad economic changes outlined above have, however, challenged the gendered identities and relationships of local people in both places. These people are workers who have, in the words of Bauman (1998a: 18) 'watched helplessly, the sole locality they inhabit moving away from under their feet'. As we will now explain, the various reactions of many white working-class males to such industry changes are defensive, reactionary, uncertain and confused. Yet there are also different patterns of effects and affects in both places.

'Men were put on the scrap heap'

Located near rich deposits of brown coal that are excavated for the production of electricity, Morwell was once an economically thriving town that made its money from power generation.[4] But the neo-liberal privatization and deregulation reform policies pursued, since the late 1980s by successive Victoria state governments undermined Morwell's economic base. Morwell's main industry is now directed by international conglomerates based in the United States, England, Ireland and Canada. Many decisions about Morwell are now made beyond Australia. The privatization and restructuring of the State Electricity Commission (SEC) has involved major job losses (Kazakevitch, Foster and Stone 1997). This has had a significant social and psychological impact on the locale, or 'distributional impacts' as they say in the jargon of those who seek to orchestrate globalization from above.

Before this restructuring, jobs for local men were plentiful, secure and well paid and there was intergenerational employment for males. Ingrid Meltzer, a youth service worker, explains: 'You could always get work at the SEC. It was slow, easy and comfortable. You didn't need an education, you started at the bottom and just worked your way up.' Boys whose fathers worked at a power station were almost guaranteed an apprenticeship. However, local people's conversations, now, are suffused by a melancholy discourse of loss and defeat that flows into pessimistic views about the present and future of Morwell. Sometimes this discourse is also taken up by the young, who portray Morwell as a 'ghost town'; a 'lonely city'.

The industrial foundations of many workers' identities have been lost and much of the town, it seems, is unable to resolve the grief this precipitated. With the dramatic downsizing of the power industry came worker redundancy and the search for new employment. Some men have used their redundancy payouts to start small local businesses. Some survived, many failed. Others have searched for work locally, but, unable to find it, have reluctantly 'gone on the dole' (government benefit). Others feel they have no tolerable choice but to leave their families and join the many 'mobile' and 'flexible' new workers displaced and on the move due to economic globalization. Some have found work elsewhere and fled with their families thus contributing to what has become known as the rural drain. Others have stayed behind because their children are settled and they own a house. Yet, as some boys tell us, even fathers who have found local employment are not necessarily a strong presence at home. As Ted Prevost (age 14) notes, without bitterness and with some pride, they are 'too busy to be worried about us kids'.

The families who have stayed in Morwell are the 'locally bound'; left behind as capital and influence have flown. They have to do what Bauman (1998a: 8) calls the 'wound licking, damage repair and waste disposal'. The gendered dynamic to being 'locally bound' in Morwell is a clear example of 'gender intensification' (Bakker 1996) for females, who are required to stay and care for children. The absence of fathers means that increased family work falls on mothers whether they are in paid employment or not. This work includes dealing with the psychological fallout of neo-liberal economic globalization, the emotional upheaval that often accompanies the forced loss of men's jobs, status and identity and the subsequent stresses of change, a matter we return to in Chapter 5. Despite the implications for women, children, families and the town itself, this changing economic context is largely framed as a 'crisis' for men and boys. Elizabeth Marot, a long-time local, observes: 'Men were put on the scrap heap. There was a feeling that they were useless.'

When fathers lost their jobs and could not get work, this impacted on sons in melancholic ways. The fact that significant numbers of hard-working, able-bodied men were not wanted by their employer or even by many subsequent potential employers, cast serious doubt on their worth and on their particular ways of being male. They seemed socially surplus and disposable or what McDowell (2003) calls 'redundant.' However, such deeply entrenched ways of being male are not at all easily disposed of by the males themselves. Notions of worthwhile work and the admirable worker remain from the past and are carried across the generations. Local ideologies of hegemonic working-class masculinity have not been weakened, even though there is less of an economic base to support them. Indeed, in some ways, they have been magnified and mythologized and become even more honorific than they once were, a form of melancholic excess. This is evident in the hopes of quite a sizable proportion of young adolescent males and in their views of education.

Local middle-class entrepreneurs consider education an important part of an economic renewal strategy for Morwell, hence the moves to establish an Education Precinct on the regional campus of Monash University. This is based on the notion of borderless and 'life-long education', a notion informing the Australian government's attempts to build a globally competitive 'knowledge economy'. Upper-secondary schooling, vocational education and training and university courses are to be provided on one campus, allowing students to move relatively easily between them. However, certain boys in Morwell don't readily accept such ideas, expecting rather to leave school as soon as possible and get an apprenticeship in the trades. 'Having a trade is like having a job for life', says Ted Prevost (age 14). Terence Hillebrandt (age 15) is typical:

> I am not really interested in . . . being a lawyer or accountant . . . I want something that is hands-on. I hate sitting there and doing nothing . . . If there is paperwork and stuff involved I will do it, but I would rather be out in the machine shop doing something.

As Collinson and Hearn (1997) observe, from the point of view of male manual workers, paper work is not 'real work' and, indeed, although Terence does not say so, it is also seen as effeminate.

Boys like Terence (and their parents) think that boys who are 'good with their hands but not their heads' should just do 'hands-on' at school and go into a trade. Yet, as teachers and youth workers tell us, many contractors cannot afford to take on apprentices and the restructuring of the power industry has reduced the apprenticeships offered. Further, those few that are available locally are highly competitive, involving 'lots of aptitude, medical and psyche tests'. 'Non-academic' students compete against high academic achievers and usually miss out. In turn, this can cause family conflict, especially between fathers and sons. Particularly, some fathers cannot admit that a trade is no longer 'a job for life', even though this notion has been so patently undermined by the Morwell experience.

Despite the restructuring of the Morwell economy and the changed nature of local employment, many fathers cannot *unlearn* the attitudes associated with regular skilled manual employment and local hegemonic working-class masculinity. This involves more than the sorts of loss that Gowan (2000: 74–105) discusses, they have become *melancholic* figures, unreflexively living in the past and sidelined in the present.

They have become resolutely attached to feelings of failure, hopelessness and anger. As such, melancholic masculinity has become a local cultural norm sustained by unresolved feelings of loss and characterized by an inability to move on, psychologically or politically. An intergenerational repetition of this process is that some young men refuse to rewound their already wounded and humiliated fathers by adopting a more reflexive and mobile form of masculinity. Intergenerational angst and young men's loyalty to their fathers inhibits their ability to engage with the imperatives of the new work order. Indeed, their badge of honour, worn for their fathers, is their immobile masculinity. But also, feeling forlorn and fearing that the psychological labour involved is pointless, they are ill prepared to negotiate changing labour markets – be they local or elsewhere.

The story of globalization in Eden has some things in common with the Morwell story but also involves some significant differences associated with what Giddens (1994: 20) calls 'high-consequence risk'. The key themes in Eden are associated with the government's regulation and 'risk management' of the timber and fishing industries in the interest of environmental conservation. In addition, the flight of global capital has meant the closure of a large processing plant. Overall, there have been significant job losses (Eden Business Challenge 2000).

Eden has suffered social dislocation similar to Morwell, or, in the language of neo-liberalism, it has experienced: 'the transition and adjustment pressures of structural reform'. A middle-aged male timber worker puts it bluntly; 'Eden is a working-man's town but it has no jobs.' A study of the social impact of the changes to the Eden timber industry identified higher levels of stress and insomnia, increased use of prescription drugs, feeling of powerlessness, heightened fear of family break up, of not being able to meet financial commitments, and higher levels of physical and verbal violence (Bochner and Parkes 1998: 18–20). This despondency is not restricted to adults. Many young people feel that they have no future due to the lack of jobs, and their subsequent feelings of worthlessness are exacerbated by the strong local work ethic. Prior to the closure of the cannery/processing plant there was a sense of hope and, indeed, quite strong resistance to the globalizing forces associated with environmental regulation. This was evident in a truck blockade of Parliament House in Canberra and in similar protests in Sydney against the New South Wales government. These nationally visible, high-profile protests occurred in the early 1990s. Protest masculinity invoked a form of melancholic agency – it politicized loss.

The government and 'the greenies', 'ignorant' city dwellers, 'outsiders with no understanding of local issues', and government departments for sustainability and the environment were all seen as the root of the problem. The town is now split. According to Grant Tamerlane (age 15): 'The loggers don't like the greenies, the fishos don't like anyone, the greenies don't like the fishos or the loggers.' And then there are the 'druggos', the 'alternative lifestylers' and the 'hippies', all of whom want to 'close down the chip mill' and 'get rid of jobs' many boys tell us. Generally, environmental regulation and the Save the Forest Campaign conducted by environmental activists were seen as an attack on the values associated with local lifestyle and on the timber cutters themselves. As Bochner and Parkes (1998) show, the timber workers felt confused about their negative public image and suffered an overall loss of self-dignity that left them feeling resentful of outside interference. This spilled over into serious conflict with environmental activists. Many stories have been shared with us about the 'provocative' behaviour of 'greenies' and equally the hostile and sometimes violent behaviour of those protesting men who opposed them.

Before the restructuring of the timber and fishing industries, boys in Eden found it easy to follow their fathers into work. But now there are not enough jobs for the current workforce. Some fathers have difficulty understanding why their sons are finding it so hard to get a job, when they 'just walked' into their jobs when they were of legal working age. There is quite a commonly held view that 'If you're prepared to put in the hard yards [the hard work], you'll always get a job.' Thus some fathers blame young men for their lack of work.

Young men without work are often an embarrassment and annoyance to their fathers. Such sentiments are illustrated by this father's comments about his son: 'I get out of bed about 7 or 8 a.m., but he doesn't get out of bed until 10 a.m., and he will just sit around the house all day in his boxers and watch TV.' The context of globalized restructuring of traditional industries, the new work order and rising unemployment are unaccounted for in such fathers' constructions of young males. Such denial prevents them from acknowledging the importance of flexible and mobile masculinities for their sons – the importance to them of the loss of a sense of loss in order that they might move on.

However, such established narratives of masculinity have begun to wane. In instances where fathers are not melancholically bound to dated notions of what 'men' and 'men's work' should be, they are heeding the 'greenies' and the government's lessons about the future. The following statement illustrates this point:

> I come from a long line of timber cutters. I followed my father into the industry. But I am not going to let my sons follow me . . . Its just not acceptable these days – because of the greenies and because it is a dying industry.
>
> (Fathers' Focus Group)

Environmentalism is also putting some young men off primary industries. James Banks, age 16, typifies this view:

> The chip mill, all the major industries like fishing . . . they can't go on forever the way they are doing it . . . and that is why I don't want to be a fisherman. These industries are going to be gone eventually . . . So it is just a waste of time getting a job in logging.

Clearly the young males of Eden are negotiating some powerful, conflicting local, state and global forces associated with the world of work and with global ecology. To be valued as males in the local culture, they are expected to have work but there is not enough work for all of them, and the available local work is either insecure casual work in the traditional local industries or in the fledgeling tourist industry. Further, they have grown up in an atmosphere hostile to outsiders and the outside world, and this implicitly discourages them from migrating elsewhere for work. Yet to stay locally is to be subject to a depressed and depressing economy and culture. If they seek to reinvent themselves in tune with the tourist industry, this is seen as subscribing to 'ritzy' values that are alien to this 'working-man's town' or, worse still, to the feminine values associated with women's work. Young men who do so, put others' perceptions of their masculinity at risk. Note the remarks of a long-time male resident (age 65):

> This town is made up of the Ockers, you know like the timber industry, the bush fellas and the fishermen. They are hard-working types . . . They work with their hands and they can't be turned into office boys. They'd be out of place if this became a big tourist industry. There is an outdoor working culture. Their jobs have diminished. There are tourism jobs for girls, but that doesn't help a hard-working person.

So what do boys do when they leave school? Some, but not many, leave town for further study or work, some get casual work when it is available, some go on the dole and some get into trouble. Those who stay in town, but remain outside the full-time workforce, have time on their hands. Many of these young men go surfing – a topic we return to in Chapter 7. Despite all its masculine virtues, fathers do not regard surfing as a valuable way for their under- or unemployed sons to spend their time. Also, some senior teachers associate surfing with what they scornfully call 'beach culture', which is seen to distract local boys from the serious work of schooling.

Ironically, this scorned beach culture is also the basis for the multi-purpose wharf that local entrepreneurs hope to build in order to rescue Eden's economy. Some local entrepreneurs also see tourism as the answer to their town's plight, although others vigorously oppose it unless it is the sort of tourism that involves 'those who'd want to come here and get their hands dirty' (elderly local male). Local educational entrepreneurs have developed a marine studies programme at the high school. This includes units of study such as diving, safe boating and Coxin's certificates, and provides students with a qualification to undertake work in any marine area from deckhanding on a fishing boat to running tourist charter boats. It incorporates young males into the expanding tourist industry in ways that draw on the masculinities most valued in Eden.

Many young men who see the old natural industries as dying and obsolete are turning to hospitality. These boys are also adopting a reflexive stance with regard to work and gender and are redefining work that has traditionally been defined as feminine as now being masculine. This gender reversal challenges the traditional local masculine/feminine binary and signals a local refashioning of gender. For example, Garth Kochan (age 14) thinks that retail work is for women, but that 'In the hospitality trade, it's better to be a man, like in the kitchen or something like that.' Despite their fathers' views about threats to their masculine identity, some Eden schoolboys have embraced tourism and are taking up courses and work experience that will lead them to a career in hospitality. Sadly, fathers who have invested in the forms of masculinity associated with hard physical outdoor labour find it difficult to respect sons who undertake such 'feminized' work; as one says sceptically: 'What future is there for boys with aprons?' Wearing an apron signifies the feminization of masculinity and is not an acceptable form of masculine mobility.

Making and marketing frontier masculinities

Notions of the frontier and of pioneering men on the frontier occupy a central place in historical and spatial imaginings. They are the stuff of many films, novels and the place mythologies of the tourist and advertising industries. The North American 'Wild West' is the best known traditional frontier in the global imagination. The difficult lives of tough men labouring for survival characterize such traditional frontier places and place myths. These men have physically rugged and psychologically steely masculinities. Desert topography and typologies of men lured to such landscapes by the promises they hold have long been features of such frontier fascination. This involves the sense that people can rediscover their true selves in the desert as the film *Paris Texas* (1984) suggests. For example, the Virgin Valley Black Fire Opal mined in Nevada is marketed as 'best opal, bar none, to come from North America' (Arizona Rock Shop 2004). Black Fire Opal is thought to capture the seductive promise, exhilaration and elusiveness of desert places. People still flock to Nevada, some to seek the Black Fire Opal, others to gain a novel frontier experience. Indeed, Nevada, now famous for its tourism, is an example of the ways in which the tourist industry contributes to global frontier imaginings by hyping up the hopes associated with desert-like spaces and by further commodifying traditional frontier masculinity.

'Global frontier masculinities' intrigue Hooper (2000a) as we explained in Chapter 1. But her conceptualization of the global frontier is confined to corporate, transnational contexts. The disembedded, privileged and powerful 'frontier masculinities' she describes are indeed produced by and in relation to the time–space compression associated with the global mobilities of elite males. Connell defines these in terms of transnational business masculinity. But, as our example of Nevada suggests, this is a limited reading of what a 'global frontier' is, where global frontiers are 'located' and what global frontier masculinities might be. In turning our focus to working masculinities in Coober Pedy, we take up and extend Hooper's notion of global frontier masculinity.

Frontier frictions

Coober Pedy's history is thoroughly entwined with the opal. 'Frontier men' and 'pioneers' are terms that were once used to describe the opal miners of Coober Pedy. The white history of the town is dominated by stories of the shocking living conditions and the heroic feats of survival undertaken by those men who first mined for opal. The 'opal-rush' in the years following the First World War enticed the most hardy and hopeful of men to travel vast distances and live in the harsh climate and tough terrain to seek their fortune. The early miners and some intrepid others arrived on camels, horses and by foot. The legendary 'Iron Man', Jim Shaw, arrived in Coober Pedy in 1921 having pushed a wheelbarrow for some 225 kilometers (*Coober Pedy Times*, April 1995: 19). The mining was done by pick, shovel and a few sticks of dynamite. The working culture that developed was unequivocally masculine; there were very few women and families. The only regulation in this 'wild zone' was self-regulation. A 'Progress Society' established in 1919 looked after the settlement's affairs and if the few 'laws of the frontier' were broken, the offender was banished to the desert.

Memories and discourses from the early frontier are evident in certain articulations of masculinity in Coober Pedy today. Men and boys are still expected to be hardy and heroic, or at least self-sufficient and without pretensions, men still gamble on striking it rich and their families, at least those who stay with them, live in hope too. The fact that Coober Pedy is enveloped by empty space and separated from other settlements by vast distances continues to confer a sense of freedom and individuality on the Coober Pedy working man. Such sentiments also invoke contempt for those who live the soft, secure and polite life of the city. Some Coober Pedy men still prefer a 'do-it-yourself' approach to justice – with the odd mining dispute still solved with a stick of dynamite.[5]

Such notions of 'unregulated' frontier masculinity characterize some young men's views of working masculinity. For example, Charlie Belew, 14, helps patrol the 'dog fence'. This fence is 5300 kilometres long and runs from eastern Queensland to the far west coast of South Australia. It is designed to keep roaming dingoes from the north attacking sheep and cattle stations to the south and passes just north of Coober Pedy. Hunters are employed to check the fence and shoot any dingoes on the wrong side. For Charlie this form of employment is perfect. He attests:

> I love to go shooting along the dog fence. You get to use your gun and stuff . . . It's great being out there on the back of the Ute,[6] checking the fence.

But, in the longer term, most local young men want to make enough money to allow them to escape Coober Pedy.

There is an enduring community belief in Coober Pedy that its location has somehow lifted people out of reach of the rules and regulations that apply elsewhere. 'People used to come . . . because it was a totally free place and it was far enough away from government so that you could pretty much do what you wanted', an older local resident remembers. She explains the restrictions and resentment that arose when various forms of government moved in. The arrival of government services, such as the school, hospital, social welfare and the creation of a local shire council, were accompanied by increased bureaucratic control and surveillance. The establishment of such services has also resulted in public servants living in the town, including a larger percentage of women and children. New modes of manhood are now evident; they involve head work not hand work, rationality not physicality (du Gay 1994). Connell argues that 'professional' work, such as that undertaken by bureaucrats and managers, 'has been structured historically as a form of masculinity'. This is:

> Emotionally flat, centred on a specialized skill, insistent on professional esteem and technically-based dominance over other workers.
> (Connell, in Whitehead 2002: 135)

'Cold calculations' (Spicer and Jones 2003) now guide the governing of Coober Pedy. The influx of such 'city masculinity' gets short shrift from the miners. Rather than seeing it as a different performance of masculinity, it is equated with feminization – with making the people 'soft'.

These changes to the working culture of the town have had a significant impact on the discursive constructions of miners as workers. Miners work when they like, for as long as they like, and as Charlie Belew indicates, their culture endorses those who are 'willing to work but not overwork'. However, the arrival of bureaucracy with its regulatory regimes, systems of classification and its collection of statistics has resulted in some significant discursive shifts. This, accompanied by the alternative work ethic of the white-collar workers, has helped to redefine the miner as shiftless and feckless; as trusting too much to luck and as taking too little responsibility. New and 'respectable' townsfolk often think of miners as wasters and 'bludgers' – terms without a history in this once like-minded community. Miners' sons are similarly constructed as unmotivated and unreliable.

Tourism has opened up Coober Pedy to global ethnoscapes. Its physical remoteness lessened in 1987 with the completion of the Sturt Highway, which allowed air-conditioned tourist buses to make the journey north to Alice Springs and to stop over on the way. Thus time and space have been reconfigured for this remote locale. International tourists now come in considerable numbers, many as part of prearranged package deals organized often through global tourist operators. The resultant tourist boom has transformed the economic base of Coober Pedy and has had a significant impact on community identity more generally. 'It was more of a single man's town – more of a mining town', a local resident points out, 'but now I see it more as a tourist town'. Indeed, in line with Lash and Urry's notions of the increasing link between aesthetic reflexivity and economic accumulation, Coober Pedy's economy is becoming 'more culturally inflected and [its] culture is more economically inflected' (1994: 64). This has entailed a further shift in power and status that has left the miners feeling even more marginalized:

> Tourism and mining go hand in hand. The tourists come here because of the opal. But the council does tend to forget about mining sometimes and focus too much of its attention on tourism.
> (Geoffrey Johns, mining manager)

Tourists come to Coober Pedy for the opal, but they also come to see the rugged, hard-working 'Aussie men' and photograph them as mementos of the outback. Indeed, Coober Pedy is now part of the global image economy and the state government is eager to market it further. A South Australian Tourism Commission study indicates how Coober Pedy has been re-imagined:

> The transport linkages, opal and unusual landscape features such as the Breakaways provide a market unique to Coober Pedy in the region. There is great potential to attract Asian visitors to Coober Pedy who would not otherwise visit the Outback. The opal town, with its underground living could become the region's desert icon.
> (Gutteridge, Haskins and Davey 1997: 10)

Tourists come for an 'authentic' outback experience; to consume frontier culture. And Coober Pedy and the desert lifestyle are being reconfigured to satisfy tourists' desires in what might be seen as an increasingly 'staged authenticity' (MacCannell 1999). Indeed, entrepreneurial masculinities are being called upon to market frontier masculinities. The Mail Run Tour is one of many examples. The mail is delivered once a week to the outback stations surrounding Coober Pedy. This delivery route has been commodified and tickets are now sold. The brochure describes the Tour thus: 'All dirt roads – a genuine outback safari.' The central street is dotted with cafes, opal shops and backpacker accommodation. An underground hotel, The Desert Cave, provides 'luxury in the frontier'. Certain locals feel that the town's identity and culture are thus being erased. Indeed, the reconfiguration of time and space is seen overall as a challenge to the traditional masculine identity of the place.

The place myths of Coober Pedy and the 'Outback' are now being heavily marketed and local culture and frontier masculinity are part of the package. While, ironically, frontier masculinity is on the decline, it has been elevated symbolically. Indeed, various caricatures of it are made available to tourists. A common sport among some of the young men is to drive down the main street, ogle the good-looking women tourists, hang their heads out of the window and pant or wolf-whistle. These young men perform for the tourists what they imagine is the tourists' view of them. Take a further example. 'Crocodile Harry' is promoted as a local character. The tour buses all go to Crocodile Harry's dugout home, inside of which there is a coarse collage of local art work and photos of heroic masculine frontier acts. A touch of parody here is that Harry's walls are festooned with pictures of him fighting crocodiles – hardly an authentic desert experience.

Earlier we noted Hooper's (2000a) contention that certain aspects of the traditional masculine behaviour that were integral to the colonization of frontier lands have also became fundamental to the promotion of transnational corporate zones. Paradoxically, the physical and aesthetic embodiment of such traditional masculinities in places beyond the metropolis is also a marketable, global commodity. In a global marketplace, images of such traditional 'frontier masculinities' help to sell products and services. Here the Coober Pedy man is also a global frontier man. He may well be aestheticized, and indeed stylized, but beyond this he is not feminized. Traditional frontier masculinity is front-staged, intensified and also erased. In the process of the bureaucratization and commodification of the town, the Coober Pedy man has lost much of his centrality and credibility.

Fruit, wine and masculine ambivalence

Ontario Job Futures, a Canadian employment agency providing training and information for work seekers, paints a bleak picture of life on the farm. Its vocational information website says:

> Employment for this occupation is expected to decline . . . The overwhelming majority of job openings will occur from replacement needs as older farmers retire. The long-term trend toward a smaller number of larger farms results in fewer employment opportunities for this occupational group.
>
> (*Ontario Job Futures* 2004)

This industry profile of farming in Ontario is eerily disenchanting. The profile almost conjures up images of ghost-farms run by machines where, for example, cattle are herded via remote-controlled implanted computer chips, where fruit is harvested by New Age designer machines, and where 'farmers' are Computerized Central Processing Units in metal boxes, running off power generated from the farm.

The notion of reflexive accumulation points to the widely acknowledged recognition that knowledge, information and technological enhancement are central to contemporary economies. Work in this context has a heightened reflexive element. But as Lash and Urry (1994: 61) argue, current economies do not just involve 'information intensity as a way of coping with a complex and uncertain environment'. Reflexive accumulation also means that the 'norms, rules and resources of the production process are constantly put into question'. As we noted in Chapter 1, this has led to 'burgeoning institutional reflexivity' and 'radical doubt'. In the face of increasingly globalizing processes this is certainly the case in the fruit and wine industries. But what are the implications of burgeoning reflexivity in these industries for males? Do they too experience 'radical doubt'?

Renmark's economy, like that of the other Riverland communities, relies heavily on its horticulture and viticulture industries.[7] Its produce includes grapes, citrus, stone fruit – including apricots, peaches and plums – and almonds. One of the major contributors to the area's recent economic growth has been the wine industry. Escalating grape prices have seen a lot of growers either changing over to grape production or increasing the percentage of grapes on their blocks. The area produces two-thirds of the state's wine grapes, equating to one-third by volume of Australia's total wine grape production (Ratsch 1995). 'Australia used to ride on the sheep's back, maybe now it's riding on the back of a grape harvester', says the Australian Bureau of Statistics (2000b: 1).

Traditionally, the 'fruit block' has been as much a way of life as a source of income. It has involved the family working the land together, even if the 'domestic/productive divide' has been naturalized along gender lines in ways akin to those discussed in Davidson (2001: 204–13) with regard to the dairy industry. The following remark from an old-timer typifies older generations' views of this way of life:

It's the attitude towards working the land and relationship with the land . . . I think it's a positive thing for kids to see all the manual work that goes along with making a living. In the city, children don't get the chance to see that side of life. Life's not just offices and concrete and glass. It's dirt and getting dirty and working hard . . . and contributing to the family survival.

Such views draw on the view that farming is an 'inherently noble and virtuous pursuit, symbolically opposed to the moral corruption and individualism of city life and the bureaucratic inadequacies of and unnecessary interference of government' (Lockie and Bourke 2001: 8). Boys are expected to adopt such a view and to work, year round, on the block. But such traditions are under pressure, even though Renmark is currently experiencing a boom.

Its horticulture industry and that of the wider Riverland region have long experienced cycles of 'booms and busts'. Although grapes are currently doing well, in the past vines have had to be pulled out due to the low prices. A local historian tells us that federal and state governments had Vine Pull Schemes and growers were paid to pull out their red grapes, including Cabernet Shiraz, subsequently in high demand. She also informs us that 'This cycle of boom and bust has gone on forever up here, and not just with wine grapes, also with stone fruits and citrus.' This repetition is familiar and normalized for young and old. Mick Dean (age 16), spells out the situation:

> When we bought our fruit block . . . everyone was pulling out their vines and planting apricots and oranges and mandarins, thinking that the vines were going to go hopelessly. Nowadays, everyone is pulling out their citrus and apricots and putting in vines. They think there's more money in it, but who's going to drink all this wine?

Others tell the same story with similar levels of scepticism while also acknowledging that this reflexive cycle of planting, pulling and replanting is almost a Renmark tradition. Indeed, reflexive accumulation is central to the world of work in Renmark. As it becomes increasingly enmeshed in global trends, reflexive cycles of reinvention and market-based redefinition have intensified.

Renmark is dealing increasingly with the deregulation of domestic markets as well as increased competition in international markets. For example, in the 1970s regulations that supported the dried fruit industry were lifted, which caused domestic markets to be flooded by cheaper Turkish apricots. At the same time traditional export markets in the United Kingdom that were based on Commonwealth agreements were significantly reduced, which meant that growers had to find markets elsewhere. The consequences of such things include the collapse of the

local Farmers' Cooperative and the rise of large-scale processing companies. As the big companies are growers themselves, there is very little
market share left over for others and so the former cooperative ethic
has given way to intense competitiveness in a context that is characterized by escalating mergers and aquisitions. This scenario is reminis-
cent of much wider struggles in the global wine industry, as illustrated
in the documentary film *Mondovino* (2004) made by Jonathon Nossiter.
As Nossiter says, 'There is an essential notion in the world of wine which
is the idea of *terroir*, the idea of a sense of place' (in interview with Jillie
Copeland, ABC National Radio 04/09/2005). He associates this with territorial and cultural identity and distinctiveness and with transgenera-
tional wine families that stay in place. However, as the film powerfully
illustrates, this sense of place has been challenged by the globalization
of the wine industry, the increasing homogenization of production and
marketing formulas, and the huge rise in significance of such figures
as the global wine entrpreneur – the consultant and the critic. Indeed,
in the broader scheme of things, 'capitalism and the countryside'
(Lawrence 1987) are more and more associated with economies of scale
involving non-local and large-scale production (Bourke 2001).

This situation makes it much harder for family-run small properties.
Indeed, another impact of globalization is their limited profitability and
an associated trend towards increasing farm size. Samson Hughes, a
training officer in the horticultural industry, explains that properties are
getting bigger and more commercial and that small family blocks are
disappearing. He says: 'It used to be much more casual and people were
more worried about the lifestyle than the money situation.' Dino
Kyriakakis observes: 'Blocks now require owners to have business management skills; they need such skills to survive.' Survival in international markets also now depends on quality. 'Quality has become a big
issue', declares Samson Hughes, 'The fruit has to look perfect or else
they can't sell it – or it gets sold for juicing and they get a lot less money.'
Fruit companies buy only the best fruit and have rigid schemes by which
they judge it; any blemishes vastly reduce the price paid. Quality assurance is now the name of the game. Here, we are reminded of Lash and
Urry's (1994) observations about the heightened role of aesthetic reflexivity in present-day production and consumption.

A further change associated with global processes is the increased use
of technology, and especially mechanization, within the fruit industry.
The grape industry, for instance, has recently seen the development of
a mechanical harvester. Technology has allowed growers to farm larger
tracks of land with less labour costs and this has dramatically changed

fruit-growing practices. 'Now with mechanization, they just whack the whole lot out, plant it all with grapes and there's a grape harvest in: within one night and she's finished' (Fathers' Focus Group).

Together these changes are indeed reorganizing space, time and identity in Renmark. They are altering the character of blocks and block work and requiring new worker identities. Big, highly mechanized blocks are having a particular impact on low-skilled workers, the young and on the family lifestyle associated with block work. More expertise is necessary to run the business, manage the risks, 'assure quality', and achieve soil, water and landscape literacy about environmental impacts. There is increased pressure for educational qualifications. Further, mechanization means that the hard manual labour of the past is no longer so necessary. In turn this has reduced labour costs for block owners. Kristov Szekelyi, a local grower, says: 'This is bad for employment but good for the farmers.' Mechanization has reduced the available low-skilled work associated with picking, drying and packing. And when handling is necessary, quality assurance requires more skilled workers, those who can work at speed without blemishing the fruit. But profit margins remain low and so the payment for the unskilled labour that is required is also low.

Overall then, despite the recent boom in the locality, there is also an air of vulnerability. This is partly attributable to the regular boom/bust cycles but it can also be attributed to the pressures and vagaries of global competition and the new demands, uncertainties and identities it brings. The fluctuations in global markets leave people feeling out of control. This air of uncertainty is also attributable to the 'bigger is better' sensibility that accompanies globalization and to the predatory behaviour of various businesses, in the viticulture industries in particular. While some businesses are doing well, others still struggle. While some block families have escaped back-breaking work with bigger blocks and more mechanization, others have not. These disparities are increasingly evident.

All of this is of consequence in intergenerational and gender terms. Fruit blocks have traditionally been passed on from father to son and in the interim sons have worked for an income on the family farm. As in many regions of Australia, sons have been given inheritance preference over daughters even if the daughters show more interest and aptitude (Bryant 2001). But this inheritance process is changing, not in favour of daughters, however, in the case of Renmark. Barbara Lee makes clear why: 'Because there is not enough profit off one farm to support two adult males.'

The hard grind is losing its masculine cache. As Sophie Buchanan, a Technical and Further Education (TAFE) college manager, observes, 'People are leaving the horticulture industry because it is seen as bloody hard work.' Further, block work is often now seen as a dead-end job. Like in Morwell and Eden, young males are trying to come to grips with the implications of a particular combination of local/global changes. The 'dirt and getting dirty and working hard' which our old-timer values so greatly has much less appeal to the young men. Gem Johnston, (age 14) expresses this view in no uncertain terms: 'I'm sick of doing block work . . . It's hard . . . All it is, is just packing oranges, or . . . just picking grapes. It's just no good.'

The hard work, the uncertainty, the stigma and the family pressure now mean that quite a number of young men want to get off the family fruit block. Oscar Hayes is one example. Oscar is 14 and lives on a family fruit block that has been in the family for several generations. Oscar would like to go to the city, but his father is putting a lot of pressure on him to stay and be a 'blockie.' Like many boys in Renmark, Oscar imagines his future elsewhere, away from the daily grind of block work.

Yet as we noted, block work is changing. It is becoming less physically demanding and more intellectually demanding. Reflexive production is aimed at the reflexive global consumer. Much more knowledge of produce, markets and contracts is required. This is particularly the case in viticulture, which local entrepreneurs see as offering very good career prospects and travelling opportunities. 'They can start from picking and end up as a wine maker', says Sophie Buchanan from TAFE. Despite these opportunities, many young men in the locality are not especially attracted to the viticulture industry. This is such a concern for the local horticultural industries that they have pooled their resources to establish their own training programme. Through this they seek to increase the numbers of skilled workers in the area and to promote the industry to potential employees. New local narratives of workplace success for males in Renmark are now available. Old masculine scripts of self-reliance have given way to 'self-improvement' scripts, associated with what Connell sees as professional masculinity and also with what we describe below as entrepreneurial masculinity.

It is something of an irony that the boys in this boom-town don't particularly want either the old work or the new. There are many possible reasons why. Perhaps they do not trust the promises of the local entrepreneurs because they have memories of the serious ebb and flow of good fortune. Perhaps they are aware of the risks associated with the global economy and the dangers for them of the greed and growth behaviour of big business in the industry. Perhaps they have so absorbed the notion that manual work is masculine work that they find professional masculinity feminizing. Maybe the sophisticated new knowledges associated with production, management and marketing that are being deployed to manage change in the industry are understood as more feminine than masculine and thus as less desirable. Perhaps boys want to escape the obligations of the family work/lifestyle and be more individual and independent. Whatever the case, it seems that burgeoning reflexivity in the industry has led to the gendering of radical doubt with regard to masculinity, and to gender ambivalence.

Grape escape: the flight to McDonalds

McDonalds employees in Renmark feel fortunate to have a job that is not fruit block work and doubly fortunate to have one at McDonalds. Seamus Doyle has been working at McDonalds for three years. He used to do 'block work' but much prefers working at McDonalds, as it is a really social place with lots of his friends working and hanging out there. He found it easy to get a job at McDonalds. However, others have not. Many talk about the unspoken specifications required. You need to be a cool kid. Gem Johnston (age 14) complains: 'If you're not popular, you won't get a job. It's a simple as that.' Robyn Gilligan (age 13) agrees with Gem, adding: 'The good-looking girls get work first because they attract customers.'

We mentioned at the outset the attacks against McDonalds by French activist farmer Jose Bove (Christison 2000) and the worldwide support he received from country lobby groups. Clearly McDonalds signifies loss and affront to such country folk. But for many young people in out of the way places, McDonalds signifies progress, a point we explain further in Chapter 4. Also the young understand it as a place of social opportunity. Such notions have clearly spilled over into the idea of working at McDonalds. It is THE place to work and the work itself is understood as social. Further, its association with 'popular' kids and good looks means that to work at McDonalds is a status significr.

In some ways gender is being unsettled in relation to McDonalds. Traditionally, in Renmark, young school-age males are expected to undertake outdoor, 'hard yakka' work on fruit blocks. Many still do, but increasingly, as we have shown, they resent the expectation and some, like Seamus in McDonalds, are re-imagining themselves as workers. This not only implies a devaluing of the ways of being male associated with block work, it has also meant that the hospitality industry has been re-imagined in terms of masculine and feminine identities and gender relations.

McDonalds might be seen as an example of the feminization of work. But gender has become rather muddled in this situation and involves what Adkins (2002b: 75) sees as 'more complex logics than those of hybridity or reversal.' At first glance, it certainly appears to have reversed a traditional gender division of labour. Young males work 'out the back' (they don't say 'in the kitchen') and they cook. And, like the hospitality boys in Eden, some construct 'the back' as a male space that is superior to the feminine and deficient 'out the front', where girls have to go because they 'can't cook' and where their good looks and affective dexterity can be put to use commercially. But boys who are attractive and sociable also work 'out the front.' As is the case with the girls, they can trade on their looks and their sociability. In both senses masculinity has become feminized and detraditonalized and gender has been hybridized. Even so, other boys still try to create a gender hierarchy of value with regard to the front and the back. Yet far from being a deficient space, 'the front' offers the chance to develop portable skills and to becoming a manager. In the McDonalds narrative, girls too are detraditionalized: they are out of the kitchen and have other employment pathways available to them. At one level the boys do actually know that the visual and emotional components of labour are now seen as very desirable. Even so, girls' work 'out the front' is not understood by the boys (and indeed some girls) as a matter of recognized skill, but more as a matter of their natural cultural and social capital. So too is the work of the out-the-front boys. In this sense girls' femininity is retraditionalized and certain sorts of feminine masculinity are diminished. As Adkins so powerfully argues, aesthetic and emotional reflexivity do not de- or retraditionalize gender unambiguously.

Entrepreneurial masculinities

Local entrepreneurs are the people, often but not always male, who help to craft local renewal strategies and we suggest that these are related to a form of entrepreneurial masculinity. In Eden, such people are promoting the multi-purpose Navy wharf, a growing aquaculture industry and holiday/tourism. In Renmark they are developing a highly professionalised wine industry and a sustainable holiday industry based around a growing houseboat market. In Morwell education is promoted, and in Coober Pedy it is mainly tourism. Bourke (2001: 328) makes the point that many places in Australia 'located on the coast, in wine-growing regions and near natural features such as bushland, beaches and wetlands' have experienced a surge in tourism and these places are no exception. In fact the tourism, holiday and leisure culture industries have become increasingly important across the board. Even Morwell has established a Power Industry tour and display centre called *Power Works*. Economic and ecological globalization has led each locality to examine how it might survive and secure its future, and local entrepreneurs have devised strategies whereby they might manage and benefit from such global change. The local entrepreneur thrives on the 'challenges' posed by competitive global markets and aims to deliver local progress and prosperity. With the aid of state compensation packages and subsidies, local councils have taken on the job not only of developing regional economic plans but also of promoting the region to prospective industries, employers and residents. They seek to entice capital flows into their locality. Other local organizations have been established for the same or similar purposes. Place managers and marketers have formed a mutually beneficial alliance, seeking new combinations of the local factors of production. This is common in the selling of places, as Kearns and Philo (1993) demonstrate.

There is 'increasing competition between places to present themselves as attractive to potential investors, employers, tourists and so on, to promote themselves, to sell themselves as service and skill rich places' (Urry 1995: 23). Local entrepreneurs are now in the business of lobbying for and marketing place: giving it an image, a personality, attaching it to certain feelings. As a consequence, they have had to become increasingly attentive to economies of signs as well as spaces. Aestheticizing and lifestylizing the local have become integral to their work. They combine their hard-edged knowledge of management and marketing with an openness to risk and a passion for place. This masculinity is not associated with a denial of emotionality as is that of the professional and the working man. Emotionality has become a resource to be harnessed: affective reflexivity, particularly the ability to link emotion to geography, a skill to be celebrated. They present as local heroes, as community saviours and visionaries, which in some senses they are, as Cheers and Luloff (2001) show with regard to a range of other rural communities. But ultimately local entrepreneurial masculinities re-imagine places, spaces and people as objects and commodities; in this sense they feminize them. However, as we have shown with regard to Coober Pedy, such feminization may also summon and reconfigure traditional masculine symbols.

Regional entrepreneurs are selling particular places, but it is important to note that they are also pushing the metropolis to reconceptualize out of the way places and people – to understand their difficulties, complexity and importance. A role of the local entrepreneur is thus to bring such matters into wider cultural consciousness; to participate in the politics of the representation of out of the way places. For example, English news headlines about the crisis in the countryside often focus on the emotive issue of fox hunting, which galvanizes public opinion and sparks strong, divided reactions. It also serves to distract attention from other more prosaic concerns, such as the rising cost of housing in the country, the closure of schools and worsening unemployment (*The Guardian* 2004). The masculinities that engineer protests such as the Liberty and Livelihood march seek to craft the cultural landscapes of images and ideas about place and change. They employ sophisticated media strategies to protect and promote the countryside.

In 2002, hundreds of thousands of people took part in the 'Liberty and Livelihood' march in London, an event billed by its organizers as 'the day when the country came to town' (Suroor 2004). Organizers – including a group called The Countryside Alliance – claimed the march was intended to express 'growing frustration at Westminster-based politicians' refusal to recognize the many and various rural issues that need to be addressed urgently' (Suroor 2004). The Alliance was infuriated when a government Minister attempted to reduce their concerns to the issue of fox hunting alone:

> The Alliance has criticised as 'untrue and unfair' several comments reportedly made by Minister Alun Michael about Sunday's massive Liberty and Livelihood march . . . Mr Michael who appeared to have embarked on a concerted media offensive in the lead-up to the march, was widely reported to have claimed variously that the Alliance's march had been 'highjacked by the pro-hunting lobby', that the Alliance had originally claimed the event's purpose was only 'about hunting' but had subsequently changed this, and that the demonstration had a 'confused message' . . . Alliance Chairman John Jackson today hit back: 'To accuse us of highjacking our own march is laughable. Moreover Mr Michael, and the rest of the Government, knew full well from the start exactly what this march was about. We published an explicit credo on its aims and purpose, which made clear that this march was about much more than hunting.'
>
> (The Countryside Alliance 2002)

The Countryside Alliance spokesperson, Mr Jackson, emphasizes the complexities of issues in places beyond the metropolis and uses them to link the march to the unjust ways in which media representations can erase the complexities of peripheral places. The Countryside Alliance piece continues:

> 'hunting formed the centre piece because the way in which the hunting issue is resolved has become the countryside's touchstone for the Government's attitude to rural policy more generally.' Mr Jackson added, '... this massive demonstration's key message was that the countryside cannot be treated as a single-issue place. Nor is the Alliance a single-issue organization. And nor are our supporters single-issue people. The countryside is a complex place.'
>
> (The Countryside Alliance 2002)

In response to this pointed marketing of the issues, the government minister, Mr Michael, and the press covering the incident, largely retained a one-dimensional focus on the symbol of the fox and hound and the contested sport of hunting. Their insistence on the erasure of complexity continued.

Another example of the work of such local entrepreneurs can be found in the Centre for Rural Strategies in the United States, an organization that, in its own words, 'seeks to improve rural life by increasing public understanding about the importance and value of rural communities' (Rouvalis 2003, in The Centre for Rural Strategies 2003). The Centre's mission statement attests to its sophisticated grasp of the politics of representation. It describes its attempts to 'use media strategically to reframe the broad public discourse that defines rural communities', and 'to design and implement information campaigns that educate the public about the problems and opportunities that exist in contemporary rural communities'.

The Centre's entrepreneurial media strategies were evident in a controversy in the United States that centred on the depiction of rural people. Seeking to 'cash in on' the global success of the wave of reality television programmes, CBS television explored the prospect of producing a show called 'The Real Beverly Hillbillies.' The plan involved finding a real family from the American countryside and transplanting them to a Los Angeles mansion where they would be filmed. No doubt it was hoped that their inept attempts to deal with city life would prove a rich source of mirth. Heading out to peripheral places in order to find an appropriate family – a selection process that one commentator described as a 'hick hunt' (Rouvalis 2003), CBS found precisely the opposite of what was anticipated. Rather than a plethora of men chewing hay and women in gingham frocks nursing babies, the CBS crew was presented with a carefully managed, well-planned intervention into their process, by the Centre for Rural Strategies (2004). The Centre lobbied against the production of the television show, on the grounds that it was perpetrating negative images of people in places beyond the metropolis. As a result, plans for the show have been shelved. Clearly, local entrepreneurs are actively intervening in the ways that mediascapes and ideoscapes represent and acknowledge places beyond the metropolis.

The symbolic politics of entrepreneurial masculinities can be seen as qualitatively related to Hooper's (2000a) global frontier masculinity. Mr Jackson of the Liberty and Livelihood march is a particular inflection of this kind of masculinity. He is an action man pioneering a new global frontier: remapping the mediascapes and ideoscapes of non-city life and livelihood. Mr Jackson is fighting against the reduction of country complexity into simplistic symbols and is seeking to change the ways that the materialities of the countryside are imagined. Around the world such local symbolic entrepreneurs know how to market memory and custom and manipulate the symbols, myths and fictions of rural masculinity. They even know how to manufacture melancholia. For instance, behind the Australia high-country cattlemen who rallied in Melbourne in June 2005 is the organization Country Voice whose slogan is 'Enough is enough'. This organization self-consciously deployed the gender codes of country men as a way of drawing attention to their concerns.

* * *

So, has the globalization of work and workers generated processes of detraditionalization in which males beyond the metropolis are set free from the structural conventions of work? Have they taken up more reflexive and flexible identities in the workplace? Has gender been eroded? We have argued that answers to these questions are differently inflected in diverse industries in different places. Certainly workplaces beyond the metropolis no longer provide the clear support for young males' working identities that they once did. Our research supports the arguments that many current workplaces require the take up of a more reflexive and flexible stance with regard to gender. By and large, boys beyond the metropolis are not in the position to, nor do many want to, reproduce their fathers' working cultures. But this does not mean that tradition has become irrelevant. The detraditionalization of work in out of the way places involves collisions and collusions between traditional and contemporary masculinities, and thus between the generations. And, as we have shown, when memory and custom are brought forward into the present, intergenerational relationships between males may be haunted by sentiments of melancholia and loss. In turn this can invoke attempts by boys to repeat the past through a form of gender intensification and inflexibility that prevents them developing alternative forms of expertise. Masculine melancholia thus becomes a form of social constraint but it has also been mobilized politically and symbolically. Further, this is only one aspect of the refashioning of gender in globalizing workplaces outside of developed Western world cities. Bureaucratization, professionalization, burgeoning reflexivity, casualization, aestheticization and commodification are also part of the story. These cannot simply be described as involving feminization or indeed gender convergence or intensification, reversal or hybridization. They are best seen as complex manoeuvres that involve intergenerational and spatial power struggles over the meanings of manhood and the purposes of work.

4
In and Out of Place

Males in the city and in the country can appear further apart than any measurable distance suggests. *The Adventures of Priscilla: Queen of the Desert* (1994) is a film about feminine masculinities and the social, affective powers of landscape. It maps emotional, ideological, financial and cultural differences between males in metropolitan spaces and those in desert terrains. Set in the harsh surrounds of the Australian desert, the film tells a fictional tale of four men's journey through the country's centre in a pink bus called 'Priscilla'. Despite the title, the film is more about masculinities and space than it is about the bus – albeit an alluring vehicle, complete with a giant glittery silver shoe adorning its roof. The landscape that these men travel through inspires them, challenges them and brings them closer together. The local men these metropolitan tourists meet are as foreign as the landscapes around them. As their chosen means of transportation suggests, the men travelling across the outback are decidedly camp. Indeed, the silver stiletto adorning their bus is a remnant of Sydney's Gay and Lesbian Mardi Gras: a popular Gay Pride parade.

The different cultural frameworks upon which the bus-travelling men and local country men build their identities come into a violent juxtaposition when one traveller, high on ecstasy and looking for sex, decides to chat up the local outback men while in drag. His mission is very successful until hand-to-hand with another man, their physical similarity becomes apparent. The men of the outback turn on him like hyenas faced with an appetizing meal. Yet what these angry men tear apart is not just the physical presence of this cross-dresser, it's also the

threat that such fluid identities pose to the masculine fundamentalism of the outback. Local masculine solidarities are intensified by the despised other, the outsider within.

Mixing different trajectories of masculinity can be a volatile business.
As the tale of the drag queen in the outback illustrates, the maps of masculinity in non-metropolitan places can be very restrictive. Taking up
such cartographies as a call to examine the politics of space, place and
masculinity, this chapter asks: What are the trajectories and boundaries
of masculinities in out of the way places? How are they configured and
reconfigured, what solidifies or changes them?

We commence by establishing the affective powers of place for young
men beyond the metropolis. We do so through the notion of 'live and
dead zones'. In developing this idea of places being either lively or dull,
we also examine the roles consumer culture plays in establishing different powers of place for young people. We theorize some different
ways in which the relationships between place and identity are configured by the young. In so doing, we take into account the gendering
nature of spaces and consider how the divergent qualities of space and
place are implicated in the logics of masculinities beyond the metropolis. We then widen our analytic lens to consider how places, like males,
can be reconfigured by corporate bodies and how such processes of
reconfiguration shift the possible coordinates of young men's identities
in place.

Throughout, we identify various constructions of out of the way
places, showing what identities some places are ascribed by young
people and the basis for their imaginative ascriptions. We also illustrate
how globalization both informs and changes these places' identities via
media images and corporate flows. In undertaking such lines of inquiry,
we develop some conceptual tools that assist us to think through such
embedded and disembedded complexities of the spatial politics of place.

Globalizing places

In Chapter 1, we introduced place as an important focus for social
inquiry in globalizing times. More than this, we argued that place needs
to be conceptualized in an increasingly nuanced manner if contemporary scholarship in this area is to be productively deployed. We introduced Massey's (1994) version of place, which we expand and build
upon here. Such an understanding of place recognizes a complex and

mobile range of links to other places. Embedded within this notion are links to other types of spaces, including virtual spaces created by the mediascapes and ideoscapes associated with corporate globalization.

Massey (2005: 140) sees place as an 'event', arguing that 'what is special about place is precisely that thrown togetherness, the unavoidable challenge of negotiating a "here and now" (itself drawing on a history and a geography of thens and theres); and a negotiation which must take place within and between both human and nonhuman.' Massey (1994) has developed the notion of a 'progressive' sense of place as a concept that is both spatial and temporal. She argues that places can be understood as 'particular moments' in the 'articulation of social relations which necessarily have a spatial form' (1994: 120). She says, '[s]ome of these relations will be, as it were, contained within the place; others will stretch beyond it, tying any particular locality into wider relations and processes in which other places are implicated' (p. 120). Place is conceived as an intertextual, or compiled, spatial form, constructed through its social relations with other places and objects. This 'progressive sense of place' is in line with McDowell's (1999) conceptualization of place as a set of 'fluid, socio-spatial relations'. Both McDowell and Massey argue that places are constructed through time and the ongoing intersection of the past and the present, and the 'in here and the out there' as Giddens says. Building upon McDowell (1999) and Massey's (1994) conceptualizations of place as multifaceted, lived connections of time, biography and sensory surroundings, we develop the complementary notions of spatio-temporal and spatio-sensual assemblages.

Spatio-temporal assemblages articulate the ways in which diverse spaces – cyberspace, open outback space, shopping centres and so on – operate within distinct temporal zones. Young men are connected to the temporal trajectories of the places they inhabit. Thus they are part of specific spatio-temporal assemblages. Boys' being in place is also linked to their senses and the established and shifting senses that material places evoke. Places involve spatio-sensual assemblages. These notions offer embodied micro-political extensions, and practical applications of Massey's (1994) spatial and temporal 'progressive sense of place' and Knopp's (2004) 'ontologies of place'. We also build on Nespor's (2000b: 33) notion of the body in place as 'a location, a set of densities', the production of which 'is always tenuous, the result of ongoing struggle'. The terms upon which such struggles occur and the contexts in which points are assembled into bodies are two key lines of our inquiry. We begin by establishing the affective nature of place through the notions of live and dead zones.

Live and dead zones

Young people in out of the way places usually don't choose to live in their place. It is allocated to them and provides a context in which they develop a sense of self and other, being and becoming, longing and belonging – their identities and identifications. When talking about 'their place', the young men we studied regularly deployed metaphors associated with life and death. In localized and complex ways, notions of live and dead zones relate to such things as landscape, opportunities for mobility (of both bodies and signs), relationships and available activities. We argue that live and dead zones are space–time foldings that bind young people to a certain 'ontology of place' (Knopp 2004). Different zones require different ways of living.

When young people call an out of the way place 'dead', they mean it's a place that asphyxiates; it is a dead weight. Dead zones relate to the view that there is nowhere accessible to go beyond the locality itself. The isolated and bleak landscape of Coober Pedy, for example, and the costs of moving beyond it tie young people to place. Time and space are not compressed for most of these youth; at least for most of their time. Time goes slowly. Further, in some ways, the 'progressive sense of place' that Massey talks about is denied to people living in the desert. Despite the abundance of space, there is nowhere to roam; certainly there are no nearby towns to connect to or to define oneself against. The young people of Coober Pedy have little choice but to stay put, imprisoned in place, as many imply, but surrounded by space. The vastness of the landscape appears to offer boundless freedom; however, the harsh climate limits this. Young men experience a spatial paradox, for although there is an apparent freedom of space there is little freedom of movement.

A critical element of a dead zone is the locality's lack of the signs and symbols commonly associated with youthful consumer pleasures. Many young people in Coober Pedy and elsewhere feel the pull of global consumer culture. Their constructions of dead zones are formed in relation to an assemblage of globalized desires – dead zones are breaks in a global chain of connection between consumer icons and youth cultures. A dead zone is a place bereft of the commodity forms that young men have come to identify with and long for. Indeed, dead zones are associated with a longing to be elsewhere, with objects and actions seen from a distance, not 'action at a distance'.

The qualitative natures of such places evoke specific temporalities. In turn, these time zones provoke different ways of being and feeling in place – temporality and temperament are symbiotic. The enmeshment of place and pace is brought together in evocative ways in May and Thrift's (2001) edited collection. But here we focus on Knopp's (2004) discussion of the 'ontology of place' and the 'ontological weight' (p. 131) of being and becoming in place. He contends that a cartographic imagination should have the capacity to focus upon:

> the messy and most ephemeral aspects of the experiences and prac-tices we call 'place' (including those involving non-human forces). Rather than objects that need to be specified theoretically or even fully understood, places . . . are 'disclosive', in the sense that they evoke, enable, and denude simultaneously. They are conjunctions of (frequently empowering) time and space-specific material practices and events at the same time that they are generative (and reflective) of meaning.
>
> (Knopp 2004: 129)

There are parallels here between Knopp's imagining of place, in which he draws on a 'topological imagination [which] focuses on connections, flows, simultaneity, situatedness, contingency, and "becoming" (p. 126) and Nespor's theory of multiple "gender topologies" – multiple mascu-line and feminine spaces' (2000b: 32). Both angles of vision account for the complexity of place: it is multi-dimensional and thus somewhat fluid in its capacity for motion, yet it is also situated and powerful in its material fixity. We take up Knopp's (2004: 129) suggestion that place is an assemblage of 'conjunctions of . . . time and space-specific mater-ial practices'. We consider specific temporal zones alongside the spatial coordinates that are required to imagine and understand place. It is our contention that various spatio-temporal assemblages happen by virtue of being in space and they affect young men's identifications and disidentifications with particular places. Dead zones are a specific kind of spatio-temporal folding. They are slow, binding, heavy and largely bounded.

What do dead zones look and feel like? Charlie Belew's story offers an example. Charlie, age 14, has only recently moved to Coober Pedy from rural Victoria. He has been having difficulty adjusting to life in the desert. For him, Coober Pedy is the definitive dead zone, largely due to his reading of the landscape: 'There is nothing here; it is just dirt.' Other young people in the town echo Charlie's reading of the place as a barren locale. Pailin Rieflin says: 'Coober Pedy is a hole.' Samantha Cohen calls it 'a crusty town, a dust bowl', and Luke Rosen proclaims

it 'a wasteland in the middle of nowhere'. The burnt-red desert landscape of Coober Pedy and its surrounds, framed by flat broad blue horizons, offers a forceful testimony to their claims. But there is more to the
construction of a dead zone than just a desolate landscape. Charlie
elucidates:

> Coober Pedy is probably the worst place I have ever been in. Coober
> Pedy has nothing. The other places I have been to, you walk up the
> street and there are trees around, and pavements, seats. You can go
> and see your friends and have fun up-town, buy roller blades or
> something . . . Here, all you see is people sitting around, doing
> nothing.

This narrative highlights the key aspects of dead zones, most of which
also apply in various ways to some young people's views of our other
research locations and other out of the way places in the developed
Western world. For example, Bone, Cheers and Hil (1990) illustrate the
perspective of one 17-year-old girl in the Whitsundays, who feels that
life in regional coastal towns can also be pretty dead when you're not
a tourist: '[There's] not much to do . . . no jobs . . . everything requires
money . . . it's a boring place . . . no privacy.' As this quote suggests, the
first element is boredom, the belief that there is 'nothing to do'; there
are no desirable activities available for young people. Boredom narratives abound. Indeed they are a frequent knee-jerk and anguished first
response to inquiries about local life. 'Nothing to do' is associated with
'nowhere to go': no resources and available spaces to hang out with
friends, form new relationships, meet new people, build a biography
amongst one's peers. 'Nowhere to go' also means there are no desirable
spaces in which young people can gather and freely undertake activities of their choice away from the adult gaze of the community panop-
ticon that so oppresses the young in small places. This sentiment is
evident in the words of Seaneen MacInearny (age 15 from Renmark),
who complains that:

> Country life is so boring and you know, you don't have any freedom
> . . . you're basically under surveillance all the time, it doesn't matter
> who you are . . . you can't even walk down the street without
> someone seeing you that knows you.

Narratives about 'nothing to do' and 'nowhere to go' are also associated
with those about 'no-one here', no available like-minded people to share

activities with. The lack of varying spatial areas, harshness of the land-scape and climate and the sluggish pace of local life mean that few boys see Coober Pedy's spatio-temporal dead zone as a preferred space of identity. Nonetheless, boys' embodied masculine identities are, in many ways, framed around these territorialities. The ways in which time affects identity formation in out of the way 'dead zones' such as Coober Pedy is evident in the kinds of men that live there. The adult mas-culinities that are fashioned in the unhurried but harsh frontier land-scapes of Coober Pedy are usually, 'no rush, no problems' – relaxed, convivial, robust and resilient; within limits. Males who are not fash-ioned in this manner will be seen as out of place in Coober Pedy and may attract suspicion, derision and hostility – as the story of the drag queen in *Pricilla, Queen of the Desert* shows.

As young people grow older, their readings of place shift and so too do notions of live and dead zones. For older boys, relationships may 'stretch out', as Giddens suggests, to include other townships and cities. Such widening horizons may be accompanied by a sense of local inad-equacy, re-enforcing the notion of home as a dead zone. Jonathan Nichols, age 15 from Morwell, describes this age trap:

> If you are under 10, there is heaps you can do; places that you can go. For anyone over 10 or 15, there is just nothing to do. At least up at Melbourne, you can go to *Timezone* or something.

Stretching out in this case is accompanied by a sense of place being emptied out. And, this does not involve an increasing sense of world-wide and imaginary 'proximity' as Tomlinson argues (1999: 9); rather, the proximities are real and nearby. But another spatial paradox is that they may be near yet far away, or at least very hard to access. While '[m]obility practices are common for many people in contemporary individualistic societies and cultures, especially those with the means to be physically mobile, such as those with class, race, and/or gender priv-ilege' (Knopp 2004: 123–4), such practices are often unobtainable priv-ileges for young men without jobs, cars and money for bus fares. They can only escape from place in their imaginations.

What is considered a dead zone for some is not necessarily so for others. The Coober Pedy example shows that landscape can play a major role in the construction of dead zones but it can also be a feature of live zones. Some young people have a very deep attachment not so much to the scapes of the global cultural economy, but to the scapes of the local in which they live, be they land-, street- or waterscapes. Nick

Bradley, age 13 from Eden, describes with total delight his attachment to his local landscape:

> You go down the rock pool and we are all there. You bring your bathers and go swimming down the rocks and you can go around the other side where there is a beach and everything, and you jump off the rocks and swim into the beach and do it again and again.

Boys like Nick focus on their homes, street or neighbourhood. While they tend to know very little beyond, they often know their own place intimately and love the sight, smell, texture and taste of it. Their sense of place involves 'topographical intimacy' (Lippard 1997: 33) which is experienced kinesthetically. For them, it is alive and in their place they feel alive. Daniel Fitzsimmons, age 13, also from Eden, has a detailed knowledge of his neighborhood:

> It has got lots of beaches, it has got a beautiful river mouth that is good for fishing, good waves, good caravan park, good little shop there. It has also got a swamp out the back of my friend's place that has got lots of different birds – some bird-watchers go over there . . . There is heaps of walking tracks and motorbike tracks, a footy field. There used to be a bowling club there but now they are turning it into a school.

Daniel's description of his neighbourhood is also a description of how he spends much of his life. He and others like him are embedded in their immediate landscape and have little wish or thought for activities or relationships that are more 'stretched out' (Giddens 1990: 19). The ways in which they assemble space and time are connected, astute and their place feels light, populated and alive.

Even downtrodden and desolate places can be construed as live zones. What enlivens is the light, easiness and busy familiarity associated with place-based relationships. Morwell is a deindustrializing township that has suffered greatly. But some young people still construct Morwell as a 'live zone'. In so doing they draw on local family traditions, deep roots within the community and strong sense of home.

Take the case of Mark Thinley, age 15, who has lived in Morwell all of his life. He has a very strong attachment to it and would not consider living anywhere else. His family has lived in the town for three generations and he has a large extended family. He belongs here and feels sorry for anyone who does 'not have the satisfaction of living in a nice place like Morwell' or has not had the opportunity to get 'attached to any one place like I have'. Mark experiences Morwell as a live zone, a rich base for who he is and for what he wants to do. Others feel the same. Such feelings arise from local socioscapes; the connections between time, blood and belonging. Cherie Mathers, age 16, says she loves:

> the closeness with everyone. Practically everyone's parents have grown up here, and their parents have grown up here, and we have all just grown up with each other. That is probably the most special thing about it.

Friendship[1] is an important factor in perceptions of live zones and can attach both males and females fondly to a place even if there is 'nothing to do'. Indeed, doing friendship can be the only thing to do. Constructions of masculinity articulate strongly with local mateship and male connections and, for many, this is the traditional anchor of male identity. Andrew Morrissey, age 14, invests a great deal of his masculine identity in who his friends are and what they do together. Robert Godard, age 16, similarly expresses the importance of friendship for males in Renmark:

> You've got to have fun with other kids up here. You've got to have friends, especially as a boy. If not, it's going to make life difficult for you because you're classed as a loser.

Gendered assumptions often underlie constructions of live and dead zones and boys associate certain scapes more with males than females, often seeing non-city locations as dead zones for girls because there 'is not enough shopping' and because they associate outdoor lifestyles with masculinity. Girls are generally constructed as antithetical to the masculine landscape and are represented as inactive and passive in relation to it. For instance, with regard to the beaches at Eden, the boys say that the girls have 'got nothing better to do than sun-bake'. However, boys' readings of gender, through, and of landscapes, and of live and dead zones for the girls, are usually based on traditional constructions of femininity that some young women are challenging, especially around Eden. The case of 'surf chicks', 'snow chicks' and 'country chicks' illustrates this point. Eileen DeCarli, age 13, explains the differences she perceives:

I'm not really into the beaches and surfing and getting a tan. It is just not my thing. My best friend Rhianna is into all that. I'm more country, I get wood, I collect rocks for the garden, and soil and manure, and I'm just a country person. I'm no pretty girl that is afraid of breaking a nail. And I like skiing, I'm a country person, I've grown up there all my life in the snow. This isn't my scene down here, I'll always go back home . . . I'm not the kind of girl that is into bikinis and getting a tan and surfing and being cool.

This suggests that some young women do construct themselves in relation to the outdoors. Further, Eileen's statement that 'I get wood, I collect rocks for the garden, and soil and manure, and I'm just a country person' is perhaps an example of what Knopp (2004: 125) calls a 'humble ontology'. Such a way of being calls attention to the subtle connections people make with place and gender identities and identifications.

Spatial fictions and frictions

In suggesting that place is a web of social interactions that have a spatial form, Massey (1994: 120) argues that spaces are cross-cutting and intersecting. Such complex places are amalgams of existing relations of social paradox and spatial antagonism. There are many ways in which people, institutions and localities produce and secure the meaning and identity of their place and, indirectly, of themselves and others. These include the establishment of sensory and temporal boundaries and the invocation of binary spatial comparisons and rivalries in relation to neighbouring locales and places further afield. Massey argues further that 'the need for the security of boundaries, the requirements for such a defensive and counter-positional definition of identity, is culturally masculine' (Massey 1994: 7; see also Hooper 2000a).

The mediascapes of the global cultural economy – be they in the form of popular culture or news and current affairs – regularly construct images of place that mobilize a country – city binary. Additionally, they normalize and prioritize the city's mores and morals. Metropolitan and non-metropolitan places and people are often presented as the antitheses of each other and are arranged in moral hierarchies. For example, well-liked television programmes such as *Ahmish in the City* (UPN 2004), *The Simple Life* (Fox 2004) and *Survivor* (CBS 2004) each offer very restricted constructions of city and country spaces. *Survivor* turns the experience of living in the country into a nightmare. Indeed, the only reason competitors on this popular 'reality TV' show subscribe to their live-to-air sojourn in the wilderness is because of the ways their city life will be enhanced if they last the longest in their battle with the elements. A CBS concluding statement that reflects on a recent series of *Survivor* says:

> After 39 days of hard island living, the 39-year-old corporate trainer from Newport, Rhode Island, won *Survivor*. For his troubles and toils, he takes home a million dollars, not to mention a Pontiac Aztek. Viewers may recall Rich's prediction on Day 1 on the island: 'I've got the million-dollar check written in my name.'
>
> (CBS 2004)

The Rhode Island 'home' to which the aptly named Rich takes his million dollars in his Pontiac is clearly a different kind of island living from the 'hard' life endured for such great fiscal reward. In shows like *Survivor* and *The Simple Life*, the city is rendered a safe, commercial space and is contrasted with the rugged, 'unknown' and potentially perilous 'country'. An opposite reading of the country – city binary is offered in the UPN television programme *Ahmish in the City*. Country life is portrayed as pure and clean and the metropolis becomes a space filled with danger. According to one North American newspaper (Kennicott 2004), the Ahmish symbolize an anti-commercial culture best characterized by 'homespun simplicity on farms in the heartland'. Here commerce and its corrupting influences are seen as city menaces. Overall, such 'spatialised story telling' (Reville 1993) about country/city life illustrates some of the mediatized ways in which the metropolis and spaces beyond it are ascribed identities. But what of the practices and perceptions of those who live these spatialized lives?

There is much research on the sexualization and genderization of city spaces by youth and others (for example, Gagen 2000; Grosz 1995, 2001; Matthews, Limb and Taylor 2000). However, there is relatively little looking at the ways in which the young outside the city construct it as a gendered and sexual space, and the implications for their fixity and mobility.[2] Young people's 'chronotopes of the city' (Crang 2001: 188) have in common a view that involves an intense profusion of speeds, mobilities and rhythms. In contrast to the slow, substantial assemblages of life in out of the way places, city life is seen as fast-paced, superficial, random in flow and teeming with bodies and signs. Pro- or anti-metropolitan sentiments often hinge, in part, on such matters: speed and abundance can delight or deter. The speed of life for many boys in out of the way places is very different from that of the metropolis. As Bergson (1992: 93) reminds us:

> the living being essentially has duration; it has duration precisely because it is continuously elaborating what is new and because there is no elaboration without searching, without groping. Time is this very hesitation.

For those young men who have identity investments in the large, unbounded spaces they associate with non-metropolitan live zones, the 'hesitation' of their being, their time, is assembled in ways often fundamentally incompatible with the speeds of city life. They do not, and possibly cannot, connect with the very different ways in which time, space and the senses are configured in the city. Various configurations of time, space and the senses form the bedrock of country people's sentiments about the city. But there are additional views overlaying them. These quite frequently include two extremes – the city as a utopia of boundless opportunities, or alternatively the city as a fearful hellhole. Interestingly, quite a few of the boys hold the latter view.

One set of constructions of the city by the young men who live outside it revolves around notions of danger and depravity and the city here is largely understood as masculine. These interpretations are particularly associated with violence, crime and drugs. The city is seen as a menacing space to be feared, a place of perpetual hazard and the temptations of drugs – peopled mainly by criminals, bums and 'druggies'. Matt Garson, age 13 from Eden, typifies this view: 'Murders, there is more murders and all that sort of thing, kidnapping, getting punched.' Nigel Watkins, age 14 from Eden, proclaims: 'You can't go out at night because you would be worried about getting attacked in a dark alley.' As these remarks by John Lohner, age 15 from Eden, indicate, for some boys in out of the way places, there are no safe spaces in the city:

> I have heard a lot of disturbing things about the city like muggings and theft and everything. When my grandma was up there with mum . . . somebody broke into their house and then they took a few things. But my grandpa went over and belted them over the head, knocked them out.

There is little doubt that such views of the city are informed by the action and crime movies that many young males consume voraciously (Browne and Hamilton-Giachritsis 2005). These often produce a view of the city male as either degenerate, menacing, vicious and violent (Beltran 2005; Giroux 2001), or perhaps as a forceful and fearless defender of good order. Such films offer young males entry into a fast-paced reality and the pleasure of vicarious danger and heroic control. They also promote hegemonic masculinities that either evoke in their audience impossible identifications and/or fear and anxiety. The city comes to represent these affective intensities and speeds that are then mingled with the place myths of danger produced by peers and parents. As a consequence, many such boys feel that their masculinity would be put under severe pressure in the city, that while they might be 'the big man' in a country town, the city would expose their weakness and vulnerability and also potentially corrupt them.

However, some of those young males, who see the city as a dangerous and depraved place, proclaim they are simply not interested in ever moving to the city to study or work. Certain local girls see this as a masculine cover up. Brie Idleman, age 16 from Morwell, exemplifies this view:

> Boys from around here just couldn't get on in the city. They don't have enough sense. They haven't got the brains to be able to deal with city life.

While Brie is right, many boys from her community 'just couldn't get on in the city', this is not because they don't have enough sense, but rather that they have a different kind of sense – a kind that is specific to the places in which they have, and continue to, become themselves.

The contrasting view of the city is of a fabulous utopia, associated with the possibility of lots of new relationships and particularly with consumer desires. It is constructed as a spectacle of stores, products and images and of endless opportunities for desirable consumption and entertainment.

While it is seen as a place that can satisfy their shared desires for globalized youthful consumer culture, the city is seen by boys to have a particular appeal to the girls. As Paul Jones, age 16 from Eden, says: 'Boys are more into physical stuff, surfing and stuff, while girls are more into not physical stuff. Like just shopping. I reckon girls would fit in better in the city than the country.' More subtly, Seamus Doyle, age 16 from Renmark, observes that while girls and boys might see the city as 'the place to be', the expected thing for a lot of the guys in Renmark is to stay and work on the family fruit blocks. He implies that as there is no point in their being tempted by city life, the boys thus choose to refuse it.

Here, we are reminded of Berg and Longhurst's (2003: 351) suggestion that 'the assemblage of qualities regarded as characteristic of men' in context can be taken as providing local definitions of masculinity. For some young men in out of the way places, the spatio-temporal and spatio-sensual assemblages of family and home soil or the landscapes of the bush or the beach are what holds them in place and what they articulate their masculinity in relation to. They could not be who they are in the city or, to put it another way, they could not be sufficiently male in the metropolis ('mother city').

Scholarly discussions of place/space-based variations in the construction and reconstruction of gender include Matthews, Limb and Taylor's (2000) discussion of *The Street as Thirdspace*. To them streetscapes in the metropolis are not necessarily as 'feminine' as some boys living outside the city believe:

> Only 18 per cent of boys never used the 'street' [as a social space] . . . compared to 34 per cent of the girls . . . girls and boys often 'use' the street in different ways. For example, the main activity reported by girls was talking and chatting with friends (46 per cent), whereas boys are more likely to see the 'street' as a venue for informal sports . . . (50 per cent).
>
> (Matthews, Limb and Taylor 2000: 66)

Perspectives such as this lead us to contend that it's not just the physical busyness and fast pace of the city that some young men in out of the way places characterize as feminine. The feminization of city space is also a response to cultural difference. Metropolitan spaces are full of girls 'talking and chatting with friends', they are also shaped by flows of corporate signs which bring specific cultural significances and economies of relation into young people's lives. For some young men, these flows are welcome augmentations to the existing connections they have with popular culture. To others, they are senseless: disruptive, anxiety-provoking cultural mores. Such young men will often characterize city spaces, or places heavily populated with corporate presences, as girl zones.

A 'progressive sense of place' beyond the metropolis is not just constructed in city/country terms. It also involves other place/place relationships beyond the metropolis which may then link back to wider cultural and economic codes. Particular sorts of economic change have implications for particular understandings of place. Global economic flows and territorial spaces coexist and interrelate in a complex fashion, and can be experienced very differently even in places of close proximity.

Eden ascribes to itself an identity as a 'working-man's town'. This spatial identification has long roots in the fishing and logging industries. Additionally, place-based masculinities in Eden are produced through comparisons with the neighbouring town of Merimbula. The adult males in Eden consider themselves decent, down to earth blokes who work hard to 'make a quid' and who don't live a fancy life. They subscribe to a 'no frills' form of masculinity that involves more than a little contempt for any consideration of the aesthetic. In comparison, Merimbula is booming as a tourist location, its economy firmly rooted in the service industries and is considered feminine by Eden's working men. There is much rivalry and ridicule between these towns. Eden boys call those in Merimbula 'fairy-bread eaters', while Merimbula boys call those in Eden 'concrete munchers' (Senior Boys' Focus Group). Clearly these cultural constructions extend beyond oral characterizations.

It seems that these spatial rivalries are integral to the formation of youthful masculine identities. The story of Paul Jones, age 15 from Eden, illustrates how this place-based masculinity is produced. Paul has lived in Eden all his life, as did his father. He is very proud of his town and gets quite defensive if anything critical is said about the place. He also constructs his masculinity in direct contrast to his readings of Merimbula and especially Merimbula boys.

> I consider the Merimbula people to be wimpy and dickheads. The Merimbula people probably think it about us, but they are surfy people, and Eden is more like stronger people and we are into footy and stuff . . . Everyone from Eden thinks that Merimbula is sort of poofter people, we don't do the same things.

Paul's sense of his own masculinity is established through contrast and, at times, conflict with Merimbula boys, whom he derides as feminine and gay in contrast with the more acceptable masculinity of Eden males. He also observes that Eden and Merimbula boys do not mix at school. For him, and many other boys, they are working from a completely different identity base, they have nothing in common, and in fact they have a conflicting identity base. This spatial friction is often played out on the sports field, especially through football in the case of Eden, but also in the school grounds. Paul delights in talking about the fights between Merimbula and Eden boys, and is quite proud of the fact that the Merimbula boys are scared of his group of friends because they have beaten up several Merimbula boys in the past. Paul has big investments in the Eden–Merimbula enmity and clearly uses it as a resource for identity. Some older boys think that 'as you get older, you just get over it' (Simon Jackson). It is possible, however, that this is easier for the more privileged boys of Merimbula than for those in struggling Eden.

Young men in Merimbula are more likely to grow up connecting to the global flows of commodities, people and corporate signs and thus to more diverse gender identities. As such, Merimbula boys are also somewhat more accustomed to the ways in which spaces, cultural beliefs and people's occupations come to be reconfigured in relation to flows of capital, commodities and bodies. These boys are already part of spatio-sensual assemblages that are fast paced and accommodate random flows. The ontology of people occupying such positions is markedly different from those deeply located in the thick space of the country where, as Shaw (2001) explains, the slow life is understood as the good life.

Scapes of consumption

The images and imaginaries of 'consumer/media culture' (Kenway and Bullen 2001) flow through Morwell, Eden, Renmark and Coober Pedy in the form of global brands, music, TV, film, fast food and soft drink directly appealing to the young. Global brands are emblazoned on young people's bodies, the things they use, and on what they watch, eat and drink. These brands are usually carefully niche marketed to age or to the styles and artefacts of particular youth subcultures – such as those of skateboarders or surfers. As we explain in Chapter 7, such brands directly shape what some young people want and in so doing, they change who they 'are': what they do and do not connect to.

'We just go up to the shop and everything and drink Coke, because we are obsessed with Coke. We always drink Coke', says Emma Smith, age 13 from Morwell. In its own market-speak: Coke is 'the real thing'. For Emma, Coke is 'everything'. It's a catalyst in the ways her social network comes together and a defining feature of the space in which these friendship connections are made. Troy Collins is a 13-year-old boy who offers another good example of the cultural and financial reign of this transnational cola. He has been addicted to Coke for some time. It's his favourite drink and he likes some at least every day. In fact, for him Coke is more than a drink. It is a lifestyle. Troy's taste for cola is a testimony to the success of the corporation's marketing machine, a local example of the successful Company manifesto:

> The Coca-Cola Company refreshes people across the globe . . . we are meeting the demands of local tastes and cultures with nearly 400 brands in 200 countries.
>
> (Coca Cola 2004)

Coke does not just meet Troy's demands; it shapes them as well. The taste of the beverage connects him to a global community of other 'cool' young people who live a caffeine-paced life and make up global/local spatio-sensual and spatio-temporal assemblages through the shared enjoyment of a flavour and an imagined community of happy youth. The senses connect to cola as imaginations connect to fast-paced lives across the globe – and heartbeat rates increase. However, recently Troy has become very interested in computer games and has bought a Nintendo. He now wants as many games for this as he can get. With 1797 on the market (Nintendo Online 2004), Troy is 'giving up' Coke to buy Nintendo.

Here we see one of the ways in which the youth consumer market shapes not only what young people 'do' in space, but what spaces they occupy in and beyond their imaginations. Coke's marketing vision constructs an imagined community that comes together outdoors. Coke's 'life' is a sporty, sexy, outside life which happens on imagined beaches, freeways or pool-sides. In local terms, the life that Coke encourages is hanging around in public spaces; casually, but closely observing others' behaviour in these places and renegotiating individual senses of belonging in relation to these spaces.

The imagined community constructed by Nintendo games is notably different to that of Coke. Conceptually schizophrenic, Nintendo is marketed as a disparate community of disenfranchised, not so stylish young people in individual virtual worlds, but also as the virtual worlds themselves. The blurring of lines between bodies escaping the everyday and the fantastic game-worlds escaped into has become emblematic of the mysterious, and liminal, appeal that constitutes Nintendo. Spatially, the ways in which Nintendo invites young people to occupy places could not be further from those encouraged by Coke. Far from the hordes of young people cruising public spaces with cola in their hand, Nintendo users are indoors, publicly invisible, and the spaces they occupy are physically private and virtually determined by this multinational corporate giant.

There are many reasons why young men in country places might choose to plug into and occupy 'private' space over 'public' space. Such places can lack the signifiers of global youth culture. As we show in Chapter 7, such presences and affective communities are easily found online or through sound. Alternatively, young men can seek places of cultural significance, in localities away from the public spaces of the home, school or sportsfield. An example for Morwell youth is Mid Valley Shopping Centre containing many specialty chain stores – Sanity, Jeans West and Rockmans – and a cinema. It is considered a 'live' zone partly because it is saturated with the signs, images and sounds of consumer media culture, and it is thus filled with significances and meanings and makes available to them another kind of belonging that reaches beyond the locality. But, as we show later, such opportunities for belonging may be limited.

Places involve and evoke many senses; and sensory taste is also a kind of belonging; even a shared craving. Cosmopolitan café society has reconstituted First World, globalized notions of desirable public dining. Any worthwhile place must at least be able to provide a good cappuccino or latté. Such notions have led to a shift of ideas about what services and facilities small towns outside the city should provide. The more they have the signs, symbols and short black coffees of the city, the better, according to many young people. Here, the corporate power to dictate global tastes, and exploit local places, surfaces with a painfully ironic twist, as young people in the country leave local places in search of cosmopolitan flavour and those in developing countries destroy their local places for the meagre wages paid to them by multinational coffee giants. As one coffee culture watchdog reports:

> Children of coffee workers and farmers are being forced into harsher, more exploitive forms of child labor. Displaced coffee workers in Nicaragua, according to a recent news story in La Prensa, have congregated near the Costa Rican border, and reports of child prostitution have sprung up for the first time there, as families have been driven to desperate actions just to survive.
>
> (Tea and Coffee Net 2004)

In order to accommodate the cosmopolitan taste for coffee at an 'affordable' price, young peoples' labour and local ecosystems beyond the developed Western world are exploited. Certainly, the incorporation of cheap coffee into people's imaginings of desirable public dining has reconfigured many 'developing' places such as Ethiopia and Guatemala around coffee production.

Half a world away, other acts of disrespect, performed in the context of changing notions of what a town needs to have in order to be worthwhile, have also disenfranchised young people and emptied out the productive capacities of spaces in Eden. Not only has the local job market shrunk, but 'Eden is stuck in a time warp' an elderly female resident tells us. Eden has no big name supermarkets or fast food outlets, let alone any café culture. Its lack of corporate signs means that it is seen as old fashioned. This adds to its employment troubles. Many Eden residents, the young people in particular, feel as if they and their town are missing out. Indeed, the lack of the golden arches within Eden means the town's landscape has become symbolically inadequate for many of its young residents. As one young resident reflects, live zones for the young are places with the big M – and the most exciting thing that has happened to Merimbula, where he hangs out, is:

Probably the McDonalds going up. That is the biggest change that I have seen in Merimbula, its getting bigger and better . . . Unlike Eden – they don't have McDonalds. So people aren't going to go there as much . . . Eden just isn't as good.

(Aamon Baker, age 15)

Aamon's dissatisfaction reminds us of the Wal-Mart story that began Chapter 1. The *Store Wars* (2001) documentary illustrates that some Ashland residents were very keen to have a Wal-Mart in their town. One complained that 'the only people who don't want Wal-Mart is the rich people, and they've already got theirs' (*Store Wars* 2001). While demographically the percentage of people who wanted a branch of the chain store in Ashland was not solely divided along class lines, the desirability of corporate power and the effects that corporate powers have on public spaces are clearly evident in both of the above examples. For the young people who participated in our study, McDonalds is the global sign *par excellence*. Its arrival registers powerfully on young minds and signifies a change for the better.

The town of Renmark has only recently acquired a McDonalds restaurant. The town had to fight to be chosen as the new site, the Mayor explains:

The only one we've ever had walk in the door in the last ten years was Kentucky Fried Chicken. They said, 'We want to start a shop up here. Where would you suggest would be a good site?' But Macdonalds, we had to fight, beat off other places for that.

To the Mayor, and the young people in Renmark, the presence of McDonalds is a sign of economic success and renewal. Indeed, they think it will attract a lot of people and Lukas Dillon (age 13) even states that 'McDonalds is a tourist attraction.' Sara Clouser (age 13) explains that Renmark is the best spot in the Riverland because it has McDonalds and KFC and she thinks it will be significantly improved when it also has Pizza Hut and Hungry Jacks. Here we are reminded of Appadurai's (1996) 'ideoscapes', as for many young people corporate signs become ideoscapes of possibility and impossibility. Fusions of media and ideology are welcome extensions to both the spatio-temporal and spatio-sensual assemblages of boys who have access to a certain level of consumption across their childhood. Boys with X-boxes, who spend time online and hang out around McDonalds and other corporate fast food outlets, exist in fundamental relationship to speeds of cyberspace, virtual corporeal capacities of electronic games, and live their social lives through the mediation of corporate signs. They are often connected to others, feelings and possibilities through plugging into scapes of consumption.

In Renmark, McDonalds is a centre of social life for teenagers. It is defined as a youth spot, as young people staff it and it is focused on a youthful clientele. McDonalds attracts young people from right across the Riverland and it is part of certain kinds of 'boy behaviour' in space. For young men, Friday nights are spent doing laps of the town in cars and at various intervals pulling into the McDonalds' car park. Cars, loud music, loud talk and wound-down windows feature in their favoured ways of occupying what is affectionately known as 'Maccas' car park, which has become part of their spatio-temporal and spatio-sensual assemblage associated with speed and machines as we explain further in Chapter 7.

Flows of corporate signs also constitute flows of people in space, and trajectories of social possibility that are opened up in relation to place. Young people are attracted to the possible lives that corporate signs offer them. Dead zones are starved of certain kinds of possible lives for young people. There are exceptions, however; for example, the film industry in Coober Pedy has changed the face of popular images of the town and the nature of being a young person in the town. The searing heat and borderless red sand of Coober Pedy was recently transformed from the oppressive media of isolation to supernatural features of a world to come in *Red Planet*, a film, starring American actor Val Kilmer, about a man on a space mission to Mars. Other Hollywood reconstructions of place in Coober Pedy have included *Mad Max 3* (1979), *Red Planet* (2000), *The*

Adventures of Priscilla: Queen of the Desert (1994), and *Siam Sunset* (1999). The locals have rubbed shoulders with such super-celebrities as Tina Turner, Val Kilmer and Mel Gibson. Everyone seems to have a 'star' story to tell.

Toby, age 14, takes great pride in this. His father may not have a job, a regular income or be able to take his family on holiday (Toby has been stuck in the desert for the last six years) but he has met Mel Gibson. His father and 'Mel' worked together on *Mad Max 3* (1979). Although Toby's father was only an extra, he shared many an evening with 'Mel' and 'the boys' at the pub after a hard days 'shooting'. Mel was a 'good bloke', hanging out with the locals and sharing a good yarn, unlike the aloof Tina Turner who stayed locked away in her trailer. But you don't have to be in the movies to get to meet the stars. Many students from Coober Pedy have been able to undertake work experience in the movie industry. After the completion of the filming of *Red Planet* (2000) in Coober Pedy, the star, Val Kilmer, spent some time attending community events and visiting the local school. He even allowed himself to be interviewed by a couple of male students on the local radio station. Here trajectories of social possibility are transformed for young men through the ways in which films have reterritorialized their place. In the eyes of the young men from Coober Pedy, Hollywood changes the desert from a dust bowl to a mecca of activity. While the movie making lasts, the town is alive with new faces, new money and new opportunities in the heart of the desert.

Eventually, however, the filming ends, the cameras and equipment are packed up, the stars and crew move on to their next exotic location. The town loses its liveliness. The only visible reminders of the exhilaration are the remnants of old sets and props – space ships and manmade lunar landscapes. Hollywood trash joins the local trash in the street; old abandoned car-bodies, drums and heaps of twisted tin and metal. Unlike local trash, though, 'Hollywood trash' adds value to the local landscape. These material traces of possibility retain their significance, even once the moment of filming has gone, as the associated dreams live on in the local imaginaries.

The unique Coober Pedy landscape and lifestyle have become famous via the silver screen. International tourists come in busloads to see such an astonishing juxtaposition of remnants of Hollywood in the red desert. Indeed, the locals become an exotic bonus. Coober Pedy highlights the complexity of place in contemporary globalized circumstances. It is physically isolated and yet it has multifaceted connections with the rest of the world through global flows of signs, images and bodies.

The corporate reconfiguration of place

Spaces all over the world are reconfiguring themselves in response to increasing flows of corporate signs, products, services and institutions. These link places into global 'economies of signs and spaces' (Lash and Urry 1994) and reconfigure local spatialities and identities. Clearly the arrival of corporate signs in small, out of the way places usually signals a comprehensive reorganization of space. For example, Wal-Mart built major new roads in the town of Ashland, creating spatial routes that redirected traffic flows. By sourcing customers not just from Ashland residents but also from traffic running along nearby highways, the retail giant redesigned the lived environment of the town. There are also residents of Ashland who are drawn to the retail giant. While the majority of the town fervently opposed the reconfiguration of municipal space in relation to Wal-Mart's arrival, some inhabitants were pleased to see Wal-Mart take an interest in their township. Wal-Mart was a cheaper, easier one-stop shop. Indeed, Wal-Mart was where 'everyone' shopped, not just the people of Ashland.

Irresolvable incongruities lie at the heart of people's attachments to corporate signs. So often, large or multinational corporate signs politically represent exploitative labour settings, sweatshops, environmental degradation and a plethora of serious global social injustices. No consumer philosophically supports the weighty, unethical practices that usually constitute the rise of big corporate signs. However, as much consumer theory has so insightfully shown, relationships between consumers and corporate signs are rarely as simple as an 'aware consumer' versus 'ethically challenged corporation' (Kenway and Bullen 2001).

The complexity of relationships between consumers and corporations has particular inflections for out of the way places. Regional places are held up against cultural imaginings of uniqueness, peculiarity or inaccessibility. Alternatively, the narratives pertaining to out of the way places are those of nothingness, struggle against circumstance and confinement. Corporate signs are none of these things. The corporation is a collective body – it 'is' a kind of belonging. Corporate signs are familiar, rather than unique. Such images reterritorialize places in hegemonic ways – as one resident of Ashland reminds us in posing the rhetorical question: 'Where's the fun of travelling to other parts of the country if I'm just going to find all the same stores and restaurants that are in my hometown?' (Ann, in Public Broadcasting Service 2001).

Our research suggests that it is precisely this sense of 'all the same stores and restaurants' that makes corporate signs so appealing to certain non-metropolitan consumers. Some people choose to live in out of the way places, others do not. For those whose lives are embedded in regional spaces by chance rather than choice, corporate signs have the potential to open out the social horizons of their daily life, by connecting their practices of consumption to those of people in urban places and other non-city locations. They have pulling power and it is this that implicates them in the reconfiguration of space/place relationships and identities. People's life-worlds become commodified as they are connected with the desires and market needs of corporate giants.

The establishment of the new Mid Valley shopping complex in between Morwell and Traralgon illustrates this point. As both towns are small in population, there was much debate as to which town would be the most appropriate site for the new centre. The shopping centre itself is not a corporation; however, it houses many multinational and national corporate stores. Mid Valley was eventually constructed *in between* Morwell and Traralgon. Then over time, it drained custom from Morwell into its liminal zone of corporate selection, reconfiguring Morwell's identity and status. Morwell's story is strikingly similar to many other country towns – a point made well by Morris (1993: 313), who reflects on the corporate drain of another Australian out of the way place, suggesting that it is a 'a well-known law of development' to build on town fringes in ways that 'further fragment' spatial identities. In part, the success of Mid Valley has to be read as part of a global trend that involves the effacement of small towns' specificities. The dominant narrative here, Morris (p. 315) argues, is the notion that the changes are a result of the diminished town's inherent weaknesses. They are not the corporation's fault; the problems were there already.

Hubs of corporate consumption are restructuring uses of, and investments in, space across the world. The drain of business from Morwell directly contributed to the evolution of its town centre as a dead zone for Morwell youth, and to their loss of an affordable and accessible live zone. Traditionally, the young people of Morwell would walk into town and 'hang out', gathering in friendship groups, checking each other out. But the emptying out of Morwell's town centre has meant that the young no longer go there if they are able to get to, and fit into, more upmarket spaces. If they cannot, they stay home. 'I don't see the interest of going down the street and walking around when there is no one down there and nothing to do', says Jonathan Nichols, age 15. Mid Valley has shifted the centre of youthful emotional and aspirational gravity. But it does not necessarily welcome all local youth, particularly noisily loitering, not purchasing boys. As Matthews, Taylor, Percy-Smith and Limb (2000) point out, certain young people are often conceived of as problematic and inappropriate in shopping areas. Further, however, many young people in Morwell cannot afford to regularly 'shop till they drop', watch the films or play the pinball machines. Indeed, just getting to Mid Valley involves the cost and inconvenience of using a very irregular bus service.

Mid Valley shopping centre offers an excellent example of the ways corporate signs reconfigure place and speak to and effect local masculinities. This popular shopping location is the cause of much gendering and sexualizing of place. At the heart of the Mid Valley shopping complex lies the biggest 'Bunnings' to be found for miles. Bunnings is a hardware and gardening retail chain that began in England in 1886 and now owns sawmills and franchises across Australia. Open seven days a week, from 7 a.m. on weekdays and 8 a.m. on weekends, until either 6, 7 or 9 p.m. at night – depending on the day you shop – the Bunnings store in Mid Valley is designed to assist, and produce, 'the family man'. Handy around the house, motivated and competent, the Bunning's customer might not begin with a load of DIY home carpentry knowledge, but they can pick it up easily enough in Bunnings' regular skills-building workshops. Such commitment to crafting a particular kind of masculinity is a feature of Bunnings' (2004) corporate face that it displays with pride, stating:

> From educational workshops to face painting for the kids, there's something for the whole family. It's all part of our commitment to serving you better.

An image of a group of young men concentrating intently on an older man, who is instructing them on how to perform some kind of carpentry, clearly positions this statement as being directed towards men.

Arguably, the kind of men such marketing hopes to attract are heterosexual 'family men', who bring their wives and children along to Bunnings to consume with them. However, Bunnings is working to cultivate its female clientele, with special parts of its website dedicated to helping the 'Ladies DIY'. The introduction and advertisement of the 'Bunnings hardware café' and large Bunnings garden range have also targeted the female consumer by including women in promotional images and incorporating typically 'feminine' graphics, such as flowers, into the logos employed to organize the store.

In its active engagement with the community, Bunnings also develops a particular kind of community – an employed, respectable, home-oriented and aspirational community. As such, Bunnings is somewhat emblematic of Mid Valley shopping centre and its clientele. There are no *haute couture* boutiques or top-range specialty shops amongst its many retail outlets. Although it's not gourmet or exclusive, Mid Valley is big, popular, busy, bright and clean and full of every practical home-making item a family might need. Mid Valley sells much more than household commodities, consumables and clothes. There is motivation and self-improvement written into the semiotics of shopping at every second turn. It sells the privatizing notion that home improvement and household consumption equate with the good life.

A bus ride away from the mega-sized Bunnings and busy flavours of Mid Valley, the landscape of consumption in Morwell produces starkly different cultures of masculinity. As a consequence of major economic shifts in production, and the introduction of retail franchises in neigh-bouring locations, many small businesses in Morwell have closed. Deserted shop-fronts and rundown bargain, 'two dollar' reject shops are interspersed with the odd local business still struggling on, and a giant, cheap Coles New World supermarket. There are few places to shop for leisure rather than necessity, and those that remain do not sell excite-ment. Shopping in Morwell is as hard as life in Morwell is for many, and its streets serve many aged or working and welfare poor; many broken people. Many men of Morwell wear check flannelette shirts and faded tattoos as signifiers of class and character. Their culture of mas-culinity is not able to connect with flows of corporate signs. Corporate globalization has emptied the commercial colour from Morwell streets and fiscally drained its economy. Empty shop-fronts, few jobs and unfilled days have hardened such men against flows of corporate signs, and they have come to resent the ways in which these flows reconfig-ure places other than their home town. Here, class divides are produced by differences in place and articulated with the changing faces of con-sumption in Morwell and Mid Valley.

* * *

The manner in which place is deployed as a resource for masculine iden-tity and identification has been the central focus of this chapter. We have shown how young males and others draw on a progressive and global sense of place in selective ways to establish who they and others are, and how and where they belong. Landscapes, local socioscapes and the scapes of consumer-media culture feature. The ways that places and the spaces within them are ascribed identities and the possible lives and imaginings these make available were also elaborated. Overall, we have pointed to some altered configurations and rhythms of place, particularly those associated with the global corporate choreography of peripheral places and the speeds and senses they speak to, deny and produce. As a means to enhance understandings of the powerful entities that places are and the ways that they shape embedded and disembedded identities and fuel the imagination and emotional intensities, we developed the concepts of live and dead zones, spatial paradox, spatial fictions and frictions, and scapes of consumption. These are encapsulated in our broader notions of spatio-temporal and spatio-sensual assemblages. These concepts identify complex configurations of spatial, temporal, affective and sensual coordinates that in various formations shape masculinity in out of the way places. They help to explain when and why masculinity is in and out of place.

5
Scapes of Abjection

Until the miners' strike of 1984–5, these two young men were close friends. They have now been driven apart by choices that men should never have to make. Gary's family desperately needs his income. Shamed, labelled a 'Scab', he goes back to the mine for his weekly pay cheque. Tony will never forgive him. Spotting Gary in the local grocery store, and choking with rage, Tony throws Gary's trolley, screaming 'Got enough food there, SCAB?' Tony is hungry. His little brother is hungry. His dad's on strike. He's on strike. Gary should be too. Tony spits the remainder of his point. 'What ya doin' eh? EH? You're my best mate! First rule of the Union, Gary, you NEVER cross a picket line.' Flanked by his father, Tony throws Gary out of the store, accompanied by a verbal postscript: 'We're all fucked if you forget that.' But Gary reminds father and son of a truth they are trying not to see, replying: 'We're all fucked anyway.'

Set in a Northern England pit village, this story is from *Billy Elliot* (2000) the popular English film written by Lee Hall. It tells of the impending 'rationalization' of the coalmines under Thatcher, the (year-long) miners' strike of 1984–5 and the ruthless treatment of the strikers by the state. The National Coal Board eventually closed 20 pits across England. This not only meant the loss of 20,000 jobs, stripping these men of their income, identity and pride, it also led to deep and bitter divisions within the working class. Young Billy's journey to become a ballet dancer is played out alongside his brother's struggles on the picket line and the emotionally fierce dividing politics of working-class masculinities under the pressure of global economic restructuring. Billy's brother and his best mate are the two characters who are fighting in the scene above: a scene that resonates with the experiences of many working-class men and their families who lived through Thatcher's brutal Britain.

This film points to some of the costs of economic globalization for certain groups of males, the beginnings of the end of the social contract between labour and capital and the bitter emotional intensities involved. It highlights the divisions that can arise between males who are downwardly mobile – sinking towards poverty in an increasingly integrated global economy. Our focus here is on the noxious mobilities and immobilities associated with poverty, gender and race in places beyond the metropolis and the scapes of abjection associated with them.

Appadurai (1996, 2000) considers the cultural significances of mobility through his notion of scapes and it is this notion that provides our starting points in this chapter. Ethnoscapes, he says, are:

the landscape of persons who constitute the shifting world in which we live: tourists, immigrants, refugees, exiles, guest workers, and other moving groups and individuals [that] constitute an essential feature of the world and appear to affect the politics of (and between) nations to a hitherto unprecedented degree.

(Appadurai 2000: 95)

For Appadurai, the lived cultures of ethnoscapes are reconstructed and often reconfigured in global ideoscapes (moving political ideas) and mediascapes (electronic images and sounds). As we noted in Chapters 1 and 2, Appadurai's 'scapes' come together to form imagined worlds. Such imagined worlds are 'multiple [and] . . . constituted by the historically situated imaginations of persons and groups spread around the global' (1996: 2). Here, we extend the notion of ethnoscape and relate it to some 'moving groups' and some fixed groups who remain within nation-states, but whose lives have nonetheless been reconfigured by global scapes. We focus on two groups of people who are widely acknowledged as economically and culturally marginalized and stigmatized; the welfare poor and Aboriginal people. Our concern is the unjust politics of the interlaced scapes associated with them.

We seek to add a further political edge to Appadurai's, 'scapes' and his notion of imagined worlds through Fraser's notions of injustice, Bauman's work on 'global hierarchies of mobility', and particularly Kristeva's (1982) notion of the 'abject'. Collectively, these concepts assist us to think through the ways in which people made abject and living in peripheral developed Western places are characterized and constituted politically and emotionally, and how this is entangled with the broader circulation of people, ideas and images. Bringing such ideas into a relationship with Appadurai's global scapes assists us to foreground recent inflections of certain long-standing social and cultural rejections. Such ideas also help us to consider the emotional dynamics associated with globalization and how they have contributed to social and psychic divisions in out of the way places. We begin with a brief elaboration of what we call 'scapes of abjection'. We then examine the ways in which the working poor construct the welfare poor in the context of global ideoscapes associated with notions of welfare and the underclass, we then consider the abject dynamics of the ways in which tourist ideoscapes and mediascapes construct Aboriginal people. Throughout we note the implications of such noxious politics for masculinity and gender dynamics.

Noxious mobility and immobility

Fraser (1997) argues that there are two main forms of injustice, 'socio-economic' and 'cultural or symbolic'. The former refers to experiences of economic exploitation, marginalization and deprivation. The latter involves cultural domination, non-recognition and disrespect. She observes that although some social groupings suffer injustices that are primarily economic, these may also involve cultural devaluation; and the reverse. In globalizing circumstances in which 'the world is on the move', as Appadurai says, notions of material and cultural injustice are usefully complemented by ideas associated with the unjust politics of mobility and immobility.

Studies of globalization and of the associated flow of people, ideas and images have drawn attention to such noxious politics. Bauman (1998a, 1998b), for instance, talks of 'global hierarchies of mobility' and identifies two main typologies. First, he focuses on those who are constantly on the move by choice, usually the 'time-poor' but asset-rich winners of globalization and points to two of their main tendencies. The first is to float free from certain territorial matters. This involves disassociating themselves from the problems of grounded injustices and reframing such injustices as transgressions on the part of the victims. A second tendency is to spatially and/or emotionally segregate, insulate and fortify themselves when they are not on the move, thus creating their own insular geographies of plenty that, in turn, restrict their vision. They distance and disregard others' discomforts (Bauman 2002).

Bauman also points to the difficulties and anxieties that arise for those who are forced to move, and for those others who are forced to stay put. Both are losers of globalization. The former, he says, are 'pushed from behind' and 'not welcome when they stop' (1998a: 92–3). The latter find themselves in a situation of 'enforced localization'; they are tied to space in a period when the freedom to act is increasingly tied to the freedom to move (p. 70). These people are 'bound to bear passively whatever change may be visited on the locality they are tied to'. Space is an obstacle for them, it 'signals their defeat', 'their incomplete humanity'. Bauman stresses that these various meanings of mobility are linked and that 'Freedom of choice for capital descends as a cruel fate for others' (p. 93).

One of the ways that these meanings of global mobility, these hierarchical ethnoscapes, are linked is through global ideoscapes and mediascapes of abjection. In the early 1980s Kristeva (1982) theorized the corporeal, psychological and social processes associated with the abject. She identified three main forms of abjection, associated with food, waste and sexual difference. The abject has since come to be associated with those bodily fluids, people, objects and places that are couched as unclean, impure and even immoral. The abject disturbs 'identity, system, order' (Kristeva 1982: 4) and provokes the desire to expel the unclean to an outside, to create boundaries in order to establish the certainty of the self. It involves the erection of social taboos and individual defences. Insofar as the abject challenges notions of identity and social order it 'must' be cast out. Abjection involves the processes whereby that or those named unclean are reviled, repelled and resisted. But the 'abject' does not respect such expulsions and boundaries and so constantly threatens to move across boundaries and contaminate. It is thus understood as a threat to 'the pure and the proper'. However, as Grosz (1989: 71) points out, the abject 'can never be fully obliterated but hovers at the borders of our existence, threatening the apparently settled unity of the subject with disruption and possible dissolution'.

Scapes of abjection circulate globally and seep into national and local geometries of power and affect. They reinvigorate such things as the ugly history of colonization and geopolitical relationships between the metropolis and its othered spaces. They justify injustice, draw attention away from social suffering and thus deny the social reality of the marginalized. They can be woven through neo-liberal ideologies and help to legitimate the more insidious aspects of global economic restructuring, as was the case in Thatcher's Britain. They can, as we will show, provide a justification for the diminishment of state welfare support for those who suffer the economic and cultural consequences of the noxious politics of mobility. The associated social tensions come to be expressed in the language of disgust and it becomes accepted that certain social groups, the black and white welfare poor particularly, can justifiably be treated as trash. Scapes of abjection can also be entangled with the long chains of commodification associated with global ethnoscapes. In such cases, we go on to explain, the processes of abjection take on a more complex configuration as culture is navigated for profit.

Animating animosity

Amongst those who suffer the burden of the noxious politics of mobility are the increasing numbers of 'new poor' (Bauman 1998b), those who once had some predictable economic security in their lives, but who now do not. In developed Western nations, these include the working poor and the unemployed. The working poor 'sell their labour for bare survival' (Bauman 1998b: 34) and have no industrial bargaining capacity. The unemployed poor cannot even find buyers for their labour. Given its declining economic power and tax base and the escalating demands upon it, the nation-state is increasingly unwilling to meet the needs of the losers of globalization. It thus finds it convenient to rearticulate ideoscapes of abjection into the national and local vernacular.

There are particular inflections to being amongst the new poor in places beyond the metropolis. Ideoscapes of abjection draw from long histories that construct the poor as a 'source of pollution and moral danger' (Sibley 1995: 55). They also mingle with existing national and local moral suppositions about country life and poverty. While acknowledging the importance of local variations, Cloke explains the different ways poverty is 'othered' and thus 'explained away' in rural England and the rural United States (1997: 268). In England, dominant cultural constructions of the rural idyll help to keep poverty denied and invisible. The 'overriding cultural logo', he says, 'is one of problem freedom.' In contrast, in the rural United States poverty is 'accepted as an often naturalized facet of the pioneering and even backward life "out there"' (pp. 267–8), or as just a 'space on the side of the road' (Stewart 1996). But further, poverty is most often associated with the inner city, the visible homelessness on its streets.

The situation of the 'new poor' male in Eden and Morwell is interwoven with local ideas about masculinity and hard work. It involves denial and demonization, not only of the poor by those who are not, but also of the welfare poor by the working poor. Both Eden and Morwell once enjoyed periods of relative economic and cultural stability and predictability. For Morwell this came about during the 'golden years' of the State-owned power industry, at which point unemployment figures were as low as 4.6 per cent. Workers enjoyed a higher than State-average disposable income and jobs were secure, often for life. The affluent times for Eden occurred prior to the regulation of the fishing and logging industries, before environmental controls were put into place. But times have changed dramatically. As we discussed in Chapter 3, both localities have experienced dramatic economic change and along with this, rising numbers of 'new poor' in the locality.[1] Bauman (1998a: 86) argues that '[t]he mark of the socially excluded in an era of time/space compression is immobility and immobilization'. In Eden and Morwell, the excluded are those who have been 'left behind', constrained by space, and also those who have had no choice but to move into each township. These economically barren contexts with their emotional climate of vulnerability, uncertainty and anxiety have provided the perfect breeding grounds for the toxic emotional dynamics of abjection. Resentment has ricocheted through each town in relation to the unemployed on welfare support. They have been marginalized economically and stigmatized culturally.

For the most part, those receiving unemployment benefits, especially those enduring long-term unemployment, are written off as lazy 'wasters' and 'bludgers'. Rosemary Reagan, age 16 from Morwell, describes what she calls 'bludge culture' as being made up of:

> Slackers. People who sit around on their bums all day watching TV and eating and they say they want to get work but just don't do anything about it. There are more and more people like this in Morwell ... People on the dole should get out and do something with their life ... even if they had to move away from Morwell because there is not that many jobs ... They are just low-lifes, wasting their money on drugs.

Such views are quite widespread, even amongst those who might be considered the working poor. In short, the view is that '[t]he work is out there if people will get out and look for it' (Beau Knox, age 14).

Opinions such as this draw on neo-liberal social policy discourses circulated globally by such international organizations as the Organization of Economic Cooperation and Development (OECD) and the

International Monetary Fund (IMF) and nationally by many 'developed' nation-states. These mobilize discourses of derision to justify the reduction and privatization of welfare support and reframe and shame those who receive it (Mendes 2003). They construct unemployment as an individual problem that is due mainly to an individual's attitude to work and refusal to move to look for it. The logical conclusion to this proposition is that those in this predicament are there by personal choice. Bauman (1998b) discusses this sentiment in relation to consumer society and the notion of 'free choice' and it can also be related to the logic of public choice theory, which has infused governmental thought over the last two decades or so. Bauman argues that by constructing unemployed people as choosing not to extricate themselves from poverty, the state specifically and society more generally are absolved from any responsibility in the creation and resolution of this problem, thus negating the role of the globalized economy and its reconfiguration of the economies of place. But it is also the case that the derision has deepened to also suggest that accompanying the 'choice' to be unemployed is the compulsion to cheat and defraud the system. Disadvantage and dishonesty have become somewhat fused. This situation results in the 'demonization' of those living in poverty (Jones and Novak 1999: 26). Such demonization is evident in both Morwell and Eden, and is largely manifest in the negative attitudes to the payment of pensions and benefits by government bodies.

Unemployment benefits are perceived as a drain on the taxes paid by hard-working people who are forced to support those who have 'decided' not to work. The unemployed are understood as exploiting the system and by implication their neighbours, getting their daily needs met by the State rather than from their own work. Unemployed parents are blamed for cultivating cultures of laziness. These beliefs are made very clear by the remarks of Cherry Daigle, age 14 from Eden:

> I think the kids look up to the parents. If their parents are just sitting around all day doing nothing, then they probably think that it is acceptable to do that. But if they are up and working, then the kids think, 'Well, I have got to work then, earn money.'

Such views about 'just sitting around all day doing nothing' show no comprehension of the immobilizing weight of what Bauman calls the 'burden of abundant, redundant and useless time'. For him, those who are space tied and unemployed 'can only kill time as they are slowly killed by it' (1998a: 88). Time makes few demands on unemployed men, except perhaps via the programming of media culture that, in offering seductive images of life elsewhere, makes their perpetual present even more intolerable.

The view is prevalent that pensions should be scrapped as they take away any motivation to work. The welfare system is seen as creating dependency, reducing the local work ethic. Certain local residents worry that this declining work ethic is contagious, or what Jones and Novak (1999: 27) have described as 'cancerous':

> The town was a working-class area but it is now turning into a social welfare class area. There is a real loss in the Protestant work ethic because of the dole. As more beneficiaries come into the community it gets worse.
>
> (Rob Gravina, community member, Morwell)

In discussing the difference between 'abstract intolerance' and 'concrete tolerance', in his study of Australian people in some of its poorest locations, Peel (2003: 152) points to the fact that many people in such difficult circumstances will repeat such 'expressions of intolerance'. But he argues that these were 'almost always abstract and concerned people who were not known'. Further, he says, they 'were always contradicted by concrete examples of commonality'. While this was sometimes the case in our studies, such 'expressions of intolerance' nonetheless give local life to the global ideoscape that state welfare creates poverty and dishonesty by reducing individuals' motivation to work and by encouraging them to cheat (Mendes 2003: 42–3). And, Peel points out that such ideoscapes have become popular mediascapes; what he calls 'poverty news' which relishes threat, fraud, helplessness and incapacity (2003: 31). Probert (2001) calls this process of blaming the 'politics of grievance'. In Australia, when recipients of welfare appear, to some, to be better off than the working poor, this 'politics of grievance' is driven by anxiety and resentment which is fuelled by the press through what Gibbs (2001) calls the 'amplification of affect'; 'intensifying rage (and outrage), magnifying fear, and, not coincidentally, inciting hatred'. One consequence of this is widespread public support for more stringent welfare regulation and onerous eligibility criteria and more intense policing of entitlements (Mendes 2003). In carefully crafted processes of blame shifting, systems of welfare *support* are redefined as systems of welfare *dependency*; indeed, as creating dependency, irresponsibility and dishonesty. Social injustice is redefined as individual fault. What is left of the welfare state is blamed; the need for 'mutual obligation' policies is proclaimed and such policies are introduced (Mendes 2003). Fox (2000) shows that the introduction of such policies has had a marked impact on public attitudes towards welfare recipients. A striking convergence emerges with regard to the noxious politics of mobility. The well off, the comfortable and working poor blame the unemployed poor for the difficulties they encounter. Economic globalization is not usually blamed here; it is too vast, intangible and intractable. Rather, ideoscapes of abjection help to do its ideological work.

This process has notably gendered overtones. Earning an income and financially supporting the family are local masculine imperatives. Having a job is tightly connected to self-respect, while lacking one is shameful and attracts disdain. This view of masculinity is a key element in local social constructions of the unemployed and of the associated local politics of abjection directed at those who have been 'left behind' in place, but out of work and who suffer 'enforced immobility' (Bauman 1998a: 121). Unemployment and immobility are associated with laziness, weakness and submissiveness – in fact, with a lack of masculinity. Masculinity, 'breadwinning' and mobility are linked, as are dependency and femininity. To bludge (scrounge, scavenge) 'off your mates', even if indirectly via the tax system, is to sink beneath contempt in terms of historical working-class norms of male propriety. The bludger is akin to the 'scab' mentioned at the outset in association with *Billy Elliot* (2000). The scab is the sign of the pustule or wound and symbolizes the body's unending battle against offensive residues. The 'scab' and the 'bludger' have very different origins in terms of the working class, the former arising from the organized working-class worker (Fox 2000) and the latter from government discourses of derision with regard to those on welfare. However, they both signify the humiliated, defiled male who 'beckons the subject ever closer to its edge' (Grosz 1989: 73), and highlights the 'abyss at the borders of the subject's existence, a hole into which the subject may fall when its identity is put into question' (p. 72).

The economic and existential uncertainties associated with economic globalization have caused deep divisions among those who have been most disadvantaged by the global economy in developed Western countries. Those hanging on 'by the skin of their teeth' are 'convulsed by anxieties' (Bauman1998a: 67). Some who fear becoming unemployed and dependent vilify those who already are. People's anxieties about their own vulnerability are displaced on to those whose positions they fear, and such fear is converted into revulsion and rejection. As Kristeva (1982: 9) says 'abjection is above all ambiguity. Because, while releasing a hold, it does not radically cut off the subject from what threatens it – on the contrary, abjection acknowledges it to be in perpetual danger.'

Spaces of deprivation and denigration

The notion of the underclass entered the popular imaginary in the United Kingdom, the United States and Australia in the 1990s. Bullen and Kenway (2004) observe that there are two main inflections to this notion. The more astute commentators associate it with structural changes in the economy, marginal employment, reliance on state benefits, confinement to neighbourhoods of poverty, and structural and/or cultural separation from society (MacDonald 1997b). However, other discourses are much more malevolent and are infused by ideoscapes of abjection. These encourage the social 'mainstream' to view 'underclass' culture as a pathology (often racial), as dysfunctional, to deride its behaviours, values and survival strategies. Jones and Novak (1999: 26) argue that the processes associated with such malevolent constructions of a so-called underclass involve defining them as different, deficient, disorderly, deviant and disgusting. And it is such cultural pathological constructions that have colonized the concept, seeped into public consciousness and morphed into the language of disrespect and into 'contagious feelings' (Gibbs 2001) of disgust. Underclass groupings are seen as a form of 'social pollution' that contaminates the proper local order and brings about moral and social decline and decay. Containing the 'underclass' discursively and spatially and rejecting them emotionally are some of the mechanisms of abjection whereby their social exclusion and polarization occur in Morwell with regard to a government housing trust area, which the locals call the 'Bronx'.

The Bronx is a space of deprivation and denigration, a geography of abjection, which brings to mind Kristeva's links between abjection and waste and the lengths to which people go to externalize it. The Bronx is described by some of the local boys in the following manner: 'It is just where they have got all the commission houses, and where all the people who can't afford to buy real houses, they all go down there' (Jonathan Nichols, age 15). 'It's disgusting. It is the sort of area where you see long grass everywhere and parked cars, paint peeling off every single house, houses that have squatters in them' (Mark Thinley, age 15). While some adults tactfully describe the Bronx as place for the 'have nots', many of the young are less neutral and talk of it as 'a bum area where all the no-hopers live' (Mark Thinley). The young people who come from the Bronx are commonly described as 'Rats'. 'Rats have bad hair, look scruffy and don't wear deodorant. Rats are normally poor people' (Jed Duda, age 13). 'Rats wear grotty clothes, have grotty hair and they stink' (Deanna Marginson, age 15). The children of the local poor are associated with dirt, bad smells and the defilements associated with unclean bodily residues. They disgust their peers. Sibley (1995: 28) observes that the rat is a particularly potent 'abject symbol'. Rats, he says:

> are associated with residues – food waste, human waste . . . with spaces which border civilized society, particularly subterranean spaces like sewers . . . The potency of the rat as an abject symbol is heightened through its role as a carrier of disease, its occasional tendency to violate boundaries by entering people's homes, and its prolific breeding.

We will return to the matter of 'prolific breeding'.

The Bronx is also constructed as beset with rough and dangerous deviants. Stories of drugs and trouble requiring police interventions abound. Beady Crescent is the main street that runs through the Bronx. The local police target it for extra patrols for they view it as a high crime area. They tell us that it has a large number of young offenders, approximately 70 per cent of whom are under 25 years of age and many of whom are repeat offenders. One local service provider describes crime as part of the lifestyle in that area. When asked what the lifestyle is, he says, 'Unemployed, on the benefit, drugs, thieving and manipulative' (Gary Silva). Many young people who live outside the Bronx are not allowed in the area by their parents. It is considered unsafe:

> There are lots of rough-looking people there and it is scary. They sit around smoking, with big dogs, big guys, and the dogs wander free because people are not watching their dogs. So we have some restrictions on our kids here – they are geographical restrictions.
>
> (Mothers' Focus Group)

Among the young who live outside it, Beady Crescent has an alluring aura of danger. Stories about the risks of being there, and of its horrors, abound, and become quite extreme and fanciful. Such fantasies of expulsion are illustrated by the following young man's story:

> There is always somebody breaking into someone else's house. There is always the police down there. I remember a few years back mum told me that there was a big massacre down there or something, and

six people got their heads chopped off with a machete or something. And just outside of Beady Crescent, someone shot himself in the head while he was in his car. Because they are all really REALLY cheap houses, so all the people on drugs go there because they spend all their money on drugs, so they don't have enough money to buy a house.

(Frank Chigetto, 15)

Mobilizing such fictions of depravity and constructing prohibitions around them are among the rituals deployed by the 'pure' to defend themselves against the impure. Across the generations they reproduce the dynamics of abjection. MacDonald (1997: 19) explains that

> a key tenet of underclass theses . . . is that the young people of under-class locales are being socialized into the deviant cultures of their economically side-lined parents; that a distaste for work and traditional patterns of family life and a taste for crime and welfare dependence are being inculcated into the young so that the underclass reproduces itself down the generations.

With little in the way of disposable income, the poor, in a consumer-oriented society, are understood as economically and socially 'surplus'. It doesn't take much for those castigated as 'wasters' to become constructed as human waste, refuse or trash (Newitz and Wray 1996) and for them to be associated with the Hollywood films about 'white trash' and 'trailer park trash' such as *8 Mile* (2002) which we will discuss shortly.

'Degenerate' mothers and fatherless boys

In terms of the noxious politics of mobility, many of the single mothers in our study are an example of the set of people whom Bauman terms 'vagabonds', those who have no choice but to move and are unwelcome when they arrive; the 'waste of the world' (Bauman 1998a: 92–3). The common view is that the high cost of living in metropolitan areas (such as Melbourne and Sydney), and government policies, mean that increasing numbers of the cities' poor are 'being dumped' into low-cost rural housing. A Morwell community member elucidates the politics of this social choreography of city expulsion:

> There is a big waiting list in Melbourne for Housing Commission houses, and so the government literally shunts the single mums

and that over here. So there is a large influx of single mums and unemployed.

Such people are seen to bring undesirable values into the locality. Their so-called 'transience' is very negatively regarded in these localities, where belonging is often associated with length of residence. 'Lots of them don't want to be here, they are transient and don't settle into the community', a member of the mothers' focus group in Morwell tells us. They have 'no experience of rural life and find it extremely difficult', says a female community member, also from Morwell, noting that these 'transient people just drift in and stay for a while, then drift out'. They do not have 'a lot to give, and they take a lot of caring for'. Some local community members resent these new residents' perceived neediness:

> There is a lack of money in the area and it is already hard enough to provide the services that the community needs. But these beneficiaries are a real drain on community resources, especially the churches and Salvation Army.
>
> (Johnnie Manson, church leader, Morwell)

Single mothers on the move are seen as city waste draining out from the metropolis to contaminate the country. Their abjection powerfully disturbs *local* 'identity, system, order' (Kristeva 1982: 4).

Like all those on welfare support, single mothers are thoroughly resented and despised for their State dependency and are castigated as welfare freeloaders. They are seen to get pregnant in order to secure an income and a home, and to avoid working. Further, the state is seen to encourage their 'promiscuity'. Such views were expressed in our Community Focus Group discussion in Morwell:

> *Woman*: A young girl came in, she was our customer and she had two babies. It was obvious that she was having another one. Her mother came in and said, 'Oh well, when she has this one, she goes to the top of the list to get a Commission home.' So it seemed you had an extra baby and you were actually rewarded. I know girls that have married and had three children and their husbands are just on a production line or a low wage and they are actually worse off money-wise than their sisters who haven't married and have had three or four kids.
>
> *Man*: That's what it amounts to. I've heard the term used ... 'Oh, she's due in about three months. She'll get a pay rise.'

Clearly the mother with the working husband is pure and praisewor-thy, while the single mother on welfare is impure, scheming, manipu-lative and untrustworthy. Somewhat similar views are expressed by some of the young men in Eden. As one says 'It's "in" at the moment for young girls to have a kid . . . You know, they get knocked up because they think that's the way to go' (Senior Boys' Focus Group). Local males may cast out these young women, their pregnancy seen as their indi-vidual problem. Such girls are variously described as 'dead shits' and 'the used and abused' – in a sense as disposable female waste – who have failed to subscribe to dominant local standards of respectable feminin-ity and, in so doing, are implicitly seen as a threat to the local gender order. Siouxie Lang explains what it is like to be on the receiving end of this community prejudice. She is a single mother who has been living in Morwell for several years. She owns her own home and is currently in paid employment, yet despite this she is still not considered moral:

> There is an area around Beady Crescent, which has lots of single parents living in the cheap housing. It's a single-parent nightmare. I am a single mum and I live near that area. There is a lot of stigma attached to me because of where I live and because I am a single parent and I really don't like it. I was on the benefit, but I worked really hard to get a job and I no longer get a pension. But there is a lot of discrimination about being a solo parent and being a bludger living off the state. People would call me that even when I was working three casual jobs. I had lots of heartbreak before I got my job. Now I have it, but the stigma is still there.
>
> (Mothers' Focus Group)

In Morwell and Eden, certain local adults see single mothers as spear-heading the rise of a local 'underclass'.

Teenage and single mothers have been central figures in global ideoscapes of abjection and malevolent underclass discourses for some time (Bullen and Kenway 2004, 2005; Bullen, Kenway and Hey 2000). These draw on strong gender distinctions and traditional conceptions of the family. The single mother not only challenges notions of the proper family and respectable femininity; by her very existence she defies and defiles the view that women need men. Her abject fecund maternal body disturbs phallocentric forms of thought. Jones and Novak (1999) note that conservative social commentators actually blame the declining work ethic on the breakdown of the nuclear family. They claim that this breakdown takes away men's motivation to work.

Furthermore, single mothers are seen to be instrumental in effecting this process of disintegration. To the usual range of anti-social behaviours associated with the underclass (crime, drugs, violence) the single mother adds 'illegitimacy'.

A particular focus of this ideoscape of abjection is on the corrosive social consequences of illegitimacy and 'fatherlessness' for young males. Commenting on the work of Charles Murray (1990, 1994, 1998, 1999), a global propagandist of this view, Bullen and Kenway (2005: 50) argue:

> This orientation is reinforced by the key indicators which Murray selects to track the growth of the underclass: illegitimacy, criminality and unemployed young men. Criminality and unemployment among young men, it is implied, are an outcome of illegitimacy since the masculine role model for unfathered boys 'is the unconnected male for whom success is defined by sexual conquests and who sees the responsibilities of parenthood as a trap for chumps' (Murray 1999). They suffer further as a consequence of the correlation drawn between illegitimacy and 'intellectual, emotional, and financial deficits among mothers that in turn show correlations with bad parenting practices' (Murray 1999). Clearly, all roads lead back to the single mother's door.

Further, within this mindset, the particular 'illegitimacy' to which she is party constitutes the single mother as the 'abject womb' to borrow Creed's (1993: 43) terminology. She is seen to 'prolifically breed' the next generation of 'rats' and underclass social scavengers and thus reinforces the construction of the underclass as a threat or danger to the social order. Creed observes that the monstrous feminine is strongly related to 'women's maternal and reproductive functions' (p. 87).

Such cultural phobias are illustrated by a range of popular film texts, including Scott Silver's (2002) *8 Mile*. The film has been read as a contemporary reconstruction of colonial victory narratives, in which a white man reterritorializes black men's cultural property and makes a living out of this pillage. But it can also be read as an ideoscape of abjection with regard to single underclass mothers and families in places of deprivation and denigration. The film features a notably misogynist character depiction of a 'degenerate' single mother, Stephanie Smith (Kim Basinger), raising a young man and little girl in a trailer park on a city's outer limits. The mother's life is out of control, except to the extent that she controls her son through her neglectful mothering, forcing him to stand in for her and the absent father of his sister. She is irresponsible, needy, self-destructive and desperate for male approval. She drinks excessively in order to quell her overwhelming fear of male rejection. Her alcoholism is coupled with her foregrounding of her own sexuality over her role as a mother. Scenes such as her son walking in on her (having sex) on top of her boyfriend, and the constantly repeated fact that her son and her boyfriend went to school together, position Stephanie Smith as 'morally degenerate'; a monstrous mother whose sexuality is transgressive and excessive. Indeed, her deployment of her son as a surrogate father for his sister and her interest in young men her son's age hint at an incest impulse suggesting the violation of further taboos by the abominable underclass mother. Creed (1993: 25) points out that 'Kristeva discusses the way in which the fertile female body is constructed as "abject" in order to keep the subject separate from the phantasmatic power of the mother, a power which threatens to obliterate the subject.' The mother in *8 Mile* (2002) is portrayed as provoking in her son a sense of engulfment, a fear of the monstrous feminine swamping him. The anger and revulsion that Stephanie's son feels as a result, is ultimately what propels him to reject his mother and rescue himself by crafting his identity as a rapper. Only by escaping from his mother can he find success and escape abjection himself.

Abjectifying Aboriginality

Explaining the historical and spatial processes of abjection, McClintock argues that:

> the expelled abject haunts the subject as its inner constitutive boundary . . . Abject peoples are those whom industrial imperialism rejects but cannot do without: slaves, prostitutes, the colonized, domestic workers, the insane, the unemployed, and so on. Certain threshold zones become abject zones and are policed with vigor: the Arab Casbah, the Jewish ghetto, the Irish slum, the Victorian garret and kitchen, the squatter camp, the mental asylum, the red-light district and the bedroom. Inhabiting the cusp of domesticity and the market, industry and empire, the abject returns to haunt modernity as its constitutive, inner repudiation: the rejected from which one does not part.
>
> (McClintock 1995: 71)

The various processes whereby the abject is expelled, restricted to 'abject zones' and returns to 'haunt' are all evident in the complex history of the abjection of Aboriginal Australians. These processes of abjection are integral to Australia's colonial and neo-colonial history and have been rearticulated in recent discourses of 'downward' envy associated with the abject positioning of Aboriginal welfare recipients. They have also been rearticulated in the ideoscapes and mediascapes related to the tourist industry.

The noxious politics of mobility and associated processes of abjection are integral to Australia's colonial history and the treatment of Australia's original inhabitants by the British occupying power in the eighteenth and nineteenth centuries. Cast out and treated as non-human contaminants, Aboriginal Australians were dispossessed of their land, denied their laws and customs, refused citizenship and usually treated brutally and exploited by white settlers (Broome 2001; Reynolds 1999). Australia's colonial history involves the dispossession, denial and exploitation of Aboriginal peoples who continue to experience well-documented, indisputable economic injustice and widespread social exclusion, cultural denial and denigration. Such injustices are integral to their mobility which has included not just voluntary movement but also being forced to move (Haebick 2001).

The life chances and opportunities of Aboriginal males are severely circumscribed. According to the *National Strategic Framework for Aboriginal and Torres Straight Islander Health* (NATSIHC 2003: 10), significant numbers of Aboriginal men have very poor physical and mental health, suffer from alcohol and substance abuse, are involved in family violence, and 53 per cent die before they reach 50 years of age. Furthermore, such men commit suicide much more often than non-Aboriginal men and they are much more often imprisoned. They are less likely to have educational qualifications and employment than non-Aboriginal Australian men and their personal and household income is particularly low. These patterns for older males arise early in life for Aboriginal boys. Such boys have far less educational success than their non-Aboriginal peers. Indeed, completing primary and secondary schooling and attaining a higher education qualification are much less likely for Aboriginal boys than non-Aboriginal boys.[2] Twenty-two per cent of Aboriginal males are unemployed, compared to 8 per cent of non-Aboriginal males (ABS 2003: 25). Further, Aboriginal boys living in remote or regional areas do not have access to the same housing and environmental health facilities that other Australian boys take for granted. Such facilities include safe drinking water, continuous power supplies, effective sewerage systems, housing and transport (p. 35).

More than any other identifiable group in Australia today, Aboriginal people experience social deprivation in terms of housing, health, education and employment. Various forms of government welfare support seem little able to alter this situation and, equally, various approaches to reconciliation seem unable to end racist sentiment. Interwoven with this situation is a racialized version of the abjection processes we have already discussed with regard to the welfare poor, although in this instance the white working poor and the white welfare poor join forces to abjectify Aboriginal people, who come to be seen as privileged, unde-serving and ungrateful.

For example, there is quite a common belief in Coober Pedy that Abo-riginal people get it easy because of the government subsidies and allowances allotted to them. Take the case of schooling. Systems have been put in place to try to encourage Aboriginal young people to regu-larly attend school. For example, those school children living in the Umoona Community (a settlement outside the main township) are bussed to the school every day, while local students walk (most live much closer to the school). The State government also subsidizes school fees and the costs of extra-curricula activities for Aboriginal students. This extra financial assistance is the focus of much resentment. Indeed, the provision of State and Federal government benefits more generally is central to the local residents' abjectification of local Aboriginal people. Stefani Moulder, age 14, holds this dominant view:

> When school camps come up – we had to pay $200 and the Aborig-inals only had to pay $20. That is because the government pays for them, and I think that is stupid . . . They [Aboriginal people] think that they own this place but they don't.

Stefani's logic is that everyone in financial difficulty should be entitled to the same financial subsidies and allowances. At a 'common-sense' level this seems reasonable enough, but it denies the history and current dif-ficulties of Aboriginal people as a whole. Like most residents, Stefani does not agree that such benefits are a justifiable means of addressing the broader social, cultural and political denial of Aboriginal people in Aus-tralia. The common view is that the locally poor whites are more in need and deserving of assistance. Further, Stefani's comment that 'They think that they own this place, but they don't' is a rather poignant reminder that while they once did they now do not. Welfare benefits seem little compensation for the loss of their land and independence and the attacks on their identities and pride. Stefani's view is also that Aboriginal people should not be so pushy, should not act as if 'they own this place'.

Such assertions of Aboriginality have been 'shaped within a long-standing, but now vigorously contested subordination' (Cowlishaw

2004: 11). They include an assertion of self-respect and a denial of an 'ever-abject state of being'. This state of being is implied in the 'permanent victim status' associated with a politics whose 'central motif' is 'injured and suffering Aboriginal people' (p. 52). Who represents whom, how and with regard to what are central and highly contentious questions within and beyond Aboriginal communities. Cowlishaw (p. 129) explains that

> Characterizations of Aborigines have shifted over the years from primitive threats to useful stockmen, from town nuisances to inmates of missions, and from excluded inferiors to 'our Indigenous people'. Celebrated contemporary images include original inhabitants of this land from time immemorial, heroic survivors of oppressive history, and damaged victims of colonial crime.

The politics of the film *Australian Rules* (2002) illustrate this complex politics of representation. A small-budget production, *Australian Rules* (2002) is a fictionalized account of actual racial tensions that occurred in a rural Australian town, years prior to the film's inception. The film's story of small-town culture and the perpetration of racism in a closed environment offers powerful images of the politics of abjection, particularly as they relate to white and Aboriginal males living together in out of the way places. The film's makers saw it as an anti-racist statement in a right-wing political climate becoming increasingly hostile to Aboriginal people. However, their meta-political intentions were counteracted by the micro-politics of the film's production. Phillips (2002) comments on the tensions that erupted in the face of the film's release:

> Wilson, . . . a vocal black nationalist, alleged that Goldman and the film's producers did not adequately consult with Aborigines and had violated 'cultural protocols' laid down by the Australian Film Corporation, SBS Independent and other financing bodies. He also claimed that the film denigrated Aboriginal women, was racist and demanded that the murder scene be excised completely because it rekindled memories about the 1977 shooting of two Aborigines in Port Victoria, the town where scriptwriter Gwynne grew up.

In spite of protests by Wilson and others, *Australian Rules* aired at the 2002 Adelaide Festival of the Arts, and, through international film festivals, the images of racial tensions amongst males in places beyond the Australian metropolis circulated in a global context. The white Australian appropriation, intentional or otherwise, of Aboriginal stories led Aboriginal people and Aboriginal film industry members to feel denied and abused. Their outcry was an instance both of an Aboriginal refusal of an 'ever-abject state of being' – a refusal of refusal, and of the haunting return of 'the abject' to disrupt and disturb.

The tourist glaze

The cultural and economic dynamics of abjectifying indigenous peoples now feature prominently in global tourist ideoscapes and mediascapes. Bauman calls people who are on the move by choice, and who accept few territorial responsibilities as they travel, 'tourists'. 'They stay and move at their heart's desire. They abandon a site when new untried opportunities beckon elsewhere' (1998a: 92). Bauman's notions of the tourist is one of many 'metaphors of mobility' (Urry 2000: 27), in current social thought and his tourist metaphor is applied largely to the mobile winners of globalization, 'the global businessman, global culture managers, or global academics', for instance, those who are 'emancipated from space' (Bauman 1998a: 89–93) because of the resources at their disposal. Amongst Bauman's 'tourists' are actual tourists – those who combine leisure and travel in search of 'experience' (MacCannell 1999).

Tourism has become a key economic renewal strategy among many non-urban communities around the world. It involves, as we indicated in Chapter 3, branding place. It is about the identification and promotion of difference, where differentiation marks a place as unique. It is also about the construction and promotion of marketable differences within places. Aboriginal culture has become a highly marketable feature of the Australian tourist industry, particularly to those sorts of tourists whom Cohen and Kennedy (2000: 219) call 'alternative tourists' (as opposed to mass tourists). These people require adventure, contact with nature, spiritual renewal or experiences of authenticity. As Cohen and Kennedy (p. 221) observe, they yearn to 'sample exotic cultures', seek the 'curative properties of wilderness, remote regions', the 'off beat' and 'unusual'. They 'are disposed to interact directly with locals and show interest in traditional culture'.

The contemporary ideoscapes and mediascapes that frame our discussion are certain global, national, state and local tourist texts constructed to tantalize the palate of such tourists. As we will show, these texts and some of their associated spatial practices involve complex abjection processes of *selective recognition and erasure*. Aboriginality with all its complexity (Cowlishaw 2004) is denied and instead split in two; certain aspects become cultural embellishments to the tourist industry while other aspects are denied. Denials and erasures occur when features of Aboriginality are found lacking in market value or when they detract from the image of place. These are eliminated to abject zones beyond the 'tourist gaze' (Urry 1995). Alternatively, marketable aspects of Aboriginal identity become tourist 'zirconia': culturally fabricated gems – the tourist glaze.

Aboriginal Australians have their own disparate and evolving cultures and histories, which continue to be significant despite past and present injustices. But it is highly selected aspects of Aboriginal culture and history that have become Australia's cultural tourist zirconia. These aspects are the acceptable and commodifiable parts of the abject split. Included here are Aboriginal cultural knowledge, ancient art, connections to the land and experiences of spirituality. These are allocated a tourist patina. Such processes of commodification and exoticization can be understood as contemporary examples of Aboriginal abjection. They involve a stage-managed set of comfortable images that white populations want to see. They suggest that Australia has now exorcized the ghosts of the trauma of white invasion and injustice and become reconciled. Take the example of the opening ceremony of the Sydney Olympic games in 2000, with its Aboriginal segment 'Welcome to Country'. This involved over 1000 Aboriginal and Torres Strait Islands people from various communities and was hailed by politicians as a testimony to reconciliation, harmony and hope. But more importantly for the Australian state and the tourist industry, it was seen as a statement to investors and tourists worldwide that domestic tensions around Aboriginal issues are in the past. Admittedly such images are ambiguous. However, a case can be made that they erase many other aspects of Aboriginal culture, identity and agency, including those fusing the contemporary and the traditional. As culturally objectified zirconias, Aboriginal identities become bound to a colonial past and a neo-colonial present.

In appealing to the tourist demographic noted above, marketing Australian places beyond the metropolis often involves the historical and spatial fixing of Aboriginal Australian people. They may thus, for instance, be conflated with Australian bushscapes; as if that's all there is to them. They may be used to make non-metropolitan places seem especially interesting and profound. But marketing is likely to ignore the fact that many present-day Aboriginal people live in the metropolis and that urban Aboriginal people and sites might be of tourist interest (Hinkson 2003). The consumer-driven psychology here is that tourists will feel there is something tantalizing, almost sensual, about Aboriginal histories. In order to relate to such ancient powers, one must travel and get close to the land, as the soil holds traces of such mythical peoples. Subtly implied within these ideoscapes are particular tropes of Aboriginal masculinity. 'Authentic' Aboriginal masculinity is sutured to timeless ideas of the wise tribal elder, the purveyor of spiritual wisdom, the skilful hunter and tracker with spears or sticks in hand, the pensive player of the didgeridoo, the semi-naked, body-decorated and scarified ceremonial dancer. Such cultural character is, in its very synthesis, simultaneously put forward as fascinating but ultimately impractical. It is a reason to visit a place, but not a way of life that will be useful for 'getting on' in an economically driven world. Many examples of such temporal and spatial fixity and exotic imagining can be found in online tourist mediascapes. The examples to follow are collectively emblematic of abject splitting processes.

Texts produced by The Lonely Planet publishers are a significant feature of contemporary global tourist mediascapes and ideoscapes and have important implications for out of the way places around the world. They support 'adventure on demand' (Friend 2005: 20). *Journeys to Authentic Australia* is written as a guide to what the Lonely Planet suggests is 'Authentic Australia'. The Lonely Planet has declared the left-hand side of Australia is its 'authentic' region. From Mount Gambier in South Australia, via Alice Springs in Central South Australia, to Darwin and the top of the Northern Territory, and down along the coast of Western Australia via Albany and Esperance back to South Australia, the Lonely Planet maps out the 'heart and soul' of the country. Indeed, according to their advice, travelling this land is a way of 'accessing Australia's heart and soul' (The Lonely Planet Online 2005a). A key aspect of this 'authenticated' Australia is ancient Aboriginal culture, which lends the land particular desirability:

> Away from Australia's eastern seaboard lies a treasure-trove of superb beaches, mind-blowing natural features, authentic outback experiences, world-class wines and gourmet fare, ancient Aboriginal cultures, rare and precious fauna, and, of course, the resilient and welcoming people who have made this part of Australia the intriguing and unforgettable place that it is.
>
> (The Lonely Planet Online 2005a)

Through the use of the word 'ancient', Aboriginal culture is positioned as temporally distinct from 'the resilient and intriguing people' (some of whom are Aboriginal) 'who have made this part of Australia the intriguing and unforgettable place that it is'. Here, ideoscapes of abjection deploy what McClintock (1995: 37), drawing on Foucault, calls 'panoptical time'. Panoptical time is an 'image of global history consumed – at a glance – in a single spectacle from a point of privileged invisibility' (p. 37). Panoptical time makes invisible the full history of colonized peoples but also makes hypervisible, indeed turns into a tourist spectacle, those historical features that can be exoticized.

The Lonely Planet also publishes a guide to 'Aboriginal Australia' (Lonely Planet Online 2005b) that offers a more politically sensitive attempt to engage with contemporary Aboriginal people and culture. This book, with its contributions by major Aboriginal leaders, indicates how they wish the tourist industry and tourists to operate:

> Use this practical companion guide to find organized tours, festivals, indoor and outdoor art galleries, films, literature, Internet sites and other points where Indigenous people share their culture. Also included are tips and protocols for interacting respectfully with Indigenous people, recommended retailers working with Aboriginal communities and detailed information on the permits required to enter Aboriginal land.

Increasingly since the 1970s and 1980s, as part of a more general refusal of the 'ever-abject' images that batter them, Aboriginal people have been taking charge of their own representations and rekindling their own language, stories and customs – a 'cultural renaissance'. For instance, many dance companies have been founded which recognize 'culture as the touchstone of Indigenous well-being' and which aim to 'promote a strong sense of heritage and identity amongst Indigenous populations' (Australian Dance Council 2005), in part through traditional/contemporary fusions. Some of these have been directed towards males. The internationally renowned Bangarra Dance Theatre performance *Skin* premiered at the Sydney 2000 Arts Festival alongside the Sydney Olympics. This was a 'double bill comprising a work for the female dancers, entitled *Shelter*, and *Spear* which explores the challenges for Aboriginal men in urban and remote communities' (Australian Dance Council 2005).

Sadly, such Aboriginal sensibilities do not play a major role in most tourist constructions of Aboriginal Australia. They certainly do not resonate with Coober Pedy's construction of itself as a tourist destination. Coober Pedy's District Council's promotional online site is aimed at showcasing Coober Pedy to a 'World Wide' audience. The District

Council invokes a selective past tense notion of Aboriginal people that imagines them only in relation to landscape. Indeed, the following quote is one of three past-tense references made to Aboriginal people or communities on this particular page of the website. There are no present tense references to Aboriginal peoples on this page. It reads:

> For thousands of years Aboriginal people walked across this area. Because of the desert environment, these people were nomadic hunters and gatherers who traveled constantly in search of food and water supplies as well as to attend traditional ceremonies.
>
> (District Council of Coober Pedy Online 2005)

According to this website, the land around Coober Pedy is steeped with the sacred significance of ancient nomadic knowledges of Aboriginal people. But no connection is made between these 'nomadic hunters and gatherers' and the existing, large Aboriginal population in Coober Pedy. It is as if contemporary lived cultures of Aboriginal local people are being imagined into extinction. By focusing only on the past, it is easier to erase them from the present. Further, at the time of writing (2005), the Coober Pedy Tourist Centre was not aware of any Aboriginal owned or operated tourist businesses in Coober Pedy.

Alongside the construction of Aboriginal people as spirits that infuse the landscape with qualities of desirability, they are positioned as charming zirconias to be consumed alongside fine local produce, live art and scenic tours. For instance, the South Australian Tourist Commission (SATC) suggests that tourists with 'special interests' in backpacking or four-wheel driving may like to sample some indigenous culture. The backpackers' page of the South Australian Tourist Commission's website (2005) features images of didgeridoos and a link to the Commission's page on indigenous culture, which also discusses Aboriginal people mainly in historical terms, or positions them as the special ingredient that makes Australian landscape worthy of tourist consumption. This retrospective/consumed by landscape discursive continuum is broken by a single reference to seeing the 'city through the eyes of the Kaurna people' and learning to play the didgeridoo. It is interesting that none of the Commissions' 'special interest' tourist groups are Aboriginal people – nor are there images of Aboriginal people deployed as representations of 'special interest' groups, which include Family, Gay and Lesbian, with Pets, Disability, Backpacker and Self-Drive.

The SATC (2005) publicity website suggests the tourist might like to:

> See Aboriginal middens in sand dunes by the coast and ancient rock paintings in caves throughout the Flinders Ranges. Or visit Ngaut Ngaut Conservation Park on the Murray River to discover one of the most significant archaeological sites in Australia.
>
> In Adelaide, see the world's largest collection of Aboriginal artifacts at the South Australian Museum, get tips on how to play the didgeridoo at Tandanya, or take a guided Tauondi tour to experience the city through the eyes of the Kaurna people.
>
> Coorong National Park, south of Adelaide, was declared a Wetland of International Importance in 1975. For thousands of years it's been home to the Ngarrindjeri Aboriginal peoples – their ancient middens (rubbish and fire mounds) strewn with cockle shells and heating stones can still be found at sheltered spots throughout the sand dunes. The Ngarrindjeri gave the region its name of Karangh, meaning 'long narrow neck', and today share their culture at Camp Coorong on Lake Alexandrina. Stay in simple accommodation and learn about the environment, food, traditional life and Dreaming stories of the Coorong.
>
> In 1929, a 7000-year-old skeleton of a young boy was discovered on the Murray River in Ngaut Ngaut Conservation Park. Today, you can take a guided tour of the archaeological site and listen as tribal elders unearth Dreamtime legends of the region.
>
> (South Australian Tourism Commission Online 2005)

No mention is made of who these 'tribal elders' are. Contemporary Aboriginal creative practices or art forms, and contemporary Aboriginal engagements with the ways their cultural histories are commodified, are also excluded from this discussion of Aboriginal culture. Neither is any reference made to where the proceeds of these cultural tours go, who owns the land being promoted, and who owns the companies that facilitate tourists being able to 'stay in simple accommodation and learn about . . . Dreaming stories of the Coorong'.

Erasure and spatial purification

Another example in which historicized imaginings of Aboriginal Australians are deployed to market place can be found in the media corporation Fairfax Digital's international tourist website. This website is called the *Walkabout Australian Travel Guide* (2005). 'Walkabout' is the name given to the nomadic wanderings of Aboriginal people and has deep cultural resonance. But what we see here is the deployment of the concept as a linguistic gimmick rather than a comprehensive engagement with contemporary Aboriginal cultures. Indeed, in relation to Coober Pedy, the *Walkabout Australian Travel Guide* textually erases the town's Aboriginal people. It does so via a discussion of the town's multicultural population:

> At the moment there are about 4000 people living in and around the town and over 45 nationalities are represented. The majority of the population is Greek, Yugoslav and Italian (the town has a remarkable similarity to a dusty Mediterranean village) with many Chinese buyers of opals.
>
> (Fairfax Digital Online 2005)

Aboriginal people are not mentioned here even though they constitute 11.8 per cent of the total population of Coober Pedy (ABS 2001a). This is a notably higher percentage than the Greek population (4.0 per cent ABS 2001a) and the Yugoslav (2.8 per cent ABS 2001a) population. Only 1.4 per cent of Coober Pedy residents were born in China. The Italian population of Coober Pedy is so small that it is not listed by the ABS.

As this example suggests, tourism results in the development of artificial authenticities. These conceal those things that are seen to detract from 'best face', including place-based divisions, stratifications and conflicts. The packaging and selling of place by the tourist industry is not just about mobilizing marketable differences but also about willing away certain unpalatable differences. In Coober Pedy such willing away has involved a form of 'spatial purification', an attempt to provide a 'clean space' (Sibley 1995: 77) for tourists. Here local Aboriginal people are made invisible in order to attract tourists.

The development of the Coober Pedy tourist industry has resulted in an increased focus on the image of the town. Even some young non-Aboriginal people see the presence of Aboriginal people in the main street as detrimental to this image. Pailin Rieflin, age 13, observes 'They [Aboriginal people] make the place look messy. The street is ruined by the drunken Aboriginals.' Chuck Clinton, age 14, agrees:

> They look like flies hanging around. They used to drink booze up and down the street, and I have even seen them throw bricks at each other . . . A bit of that still goes on. It is not quite as bad but you still

do get the occasional people who hang around the streets and do bad things and make Coober Pedy look bad.

Like rats, flies are also an abject symbol. Aboriginal people in the street are marked as dirty and dangerous. Their public alcohol consumption is seen as a particular issue. Indeed, Aboriginal people are often constructed as a constantly drunk public spectacle. 'It is not really something you want to see or you want your children seeing everyday' says Mario Ciccone, age 16. Steps have been taken to remove them from the main street; the establishment of a 'dry zone' being the most notable.

The town applied to the Attorney General's office to make its streets alcohol free. Anybody caught drinking in the street could be moved. Given that it is mainly Aboriginal people who drink outdoors, this change was racist in its intent. It also came to mean that any Aboriginal residents who were found drinking in town were dumped in Umoona whether they resided there or not. This caused such subsequent problems as increased violence and property damage. It also led to a clash between what Cowlishaw (2004: 191) calls 'respectable and disreputable Aboriginality'. The Umoona community then applied to become a dry area. This move was met by significant opposition from other Coober Pedy townspeople, who realized that they could not so easily sweep public drunkenness out of view to the abject zone of Umoona and neither could they use this excuse to create a 'clean space' for the tourist gaze.

Kristeva explains, 'that word, "fear" . . . no sooner has it cropped up than it shades off like a mirage and permeates all . . . with a hallucinatory ghostly glimmer' (1982: 6). The deployment of abject splitting keeps Aboriginal identity and culture both erasable and marketable. But it also means that the tourist industry constantly 'shades off' into a 'hallucinatory ghostly glimmer' of fear that the erased will return to 'haunt' the industry. A particular fear is associated with what we call 'abject agency' (drawing on Cowlishaw 2004). Such agency arises from 'chronic discontent' and 'continuing and unresolved rage and resentment which has resulted from past injustices' (Cowlishaw 2004: 75, 189). It is derived from the derogatory symbolic codes used to abjectify the group in the first place. 'Abject agency' involves 'taking up an abject position' (p. 158), mocking and exaggerating it through defiance and disrespect, and hurling it back at the original perpetrator. Cowlishaw talks of the ways in which some young Aboriginal men participate in this process. As a result, say, of being noisy or fighting in the street or throwing stones at shop windows, or drinking or chroming (sniffing petrol), many come into direct contact with the white legal system. She explains how:

> Anger and abjection are performed in the court and in the street, using language which confounds, disconcerts and embarrasses the white audience. . . . [and] seem to confirm the grotesque images of deformed Aboriginality
>
> (Cowlishaw 2004: 74)

'Experiences and actions that whites despise can be displayed as triumphant defeat of attempted humiliation' (p. 192). As a consequence, such young men may be treated 'like champions' with cries of 'Good on you brother'. This form of 'desperate excess' (p. 163) is designed to evoke extreme discomfort, disgust or dismay in the dominant white population. It can thus be argued that 'spatial purification' for the tourist gaze may create precisely the sorts of behaviours it seeks to hide. Kristeva explains:

> abjection is elaborated by a failure to recognize its kin . . . hence before they are signifiable – [the subject in question] drives them out . . . and constitutes his own territory edged by the abject. A sacred configuration. Fear cements his compound . . .
>
> (Kristeva 1982: 6)

The splitting of abject Aboriginal people and culture into 'compounds' of the desirable and the undesirable can be read in Kristeva's (p. 6) terms as a refusal to let a population solidify and become fully recognizable to itself and to others; to be understood and to understand itself in all its complexity and ambiguity. So, for Aboriginal boys growing up in Coober Pedy, tourism has a range of different significances, not the least being its abject refusal of their full selfhood.

*   *   *

In this chapter we have sought to add further political and spatial density to Appadurai's notion of global 'scapes'. We have shown how global scapes intersect with local geometries of poverty, gender and race. Apparently minor mobilities and immobilities within the nation-state are, we have argued, modulated through noxious global ideoscapes and mediascapes. Further, we have illustrated how ethno- and mediascapes abjectify 'local' populations in highly contradictory ways. In sum, we have put further flesh on ideas associated with the disjunctive flows of the global cultural economy, by offering examples of such flows in and through marginalized places, and the implications they have for embedded and embodied social and cultural groupings. Further, we developed the notion of 'scapes of abjection' to show how affect and abjection work on and in the imagination and have flow-on effects upon particular economically and culturally marginalized and stigmatized populations in non-metropolitan, developed Western places. We have shown how long-standing injustices are rescripted and reinsribed through their links with contemporary scapes of abjection and some of the implications for masculinities and gender dynamics.

6
Everyday Knowledges

In 2000, a furore erupted following the publication of the dramatically titled *The War Against Boys* (Sommers 2000). The book begins with an alarming analysis of an apparently life-threatening 'war' being played out in America's schools:

> It's a bad time to be a boy in America. As the new millennium begins, the triumphant victory of our women's soccer team has come to symbolize the spirit of American girls. The defining event for boys is the shooting at Columbine High.
> (2000: 13)

Sommers qualifies her deployment of the Columbine High School shootings by noting that most of the boys present that day behaved honourably and describes a 'new and . . . corrosive fiction that boys as a group are disturbed' (p. 15). Undeterred however, she identifies a 'crisis' facing American boys, and claims 'too many of our sons are languishing academically and socially. The widening education gap threatens the futures of millions of American boys' (p. 15). Sommers's analysis of the 'war against boys' and the manner in which 'the truth about boys has been both distorted and buried' (p. 16) resonated in many developed Western world countries, featured prominently in news media and morphed into debates about the 'gender gap' and boys' 'underachievement'. For example, the UK National Literacy Trust reported on 'a yawning gap between girls' and boys' achievement' and the fact that 'boys' underachievement in reading is far greater in England and Wales than other developed countries' (National Literacy Trust 2000). The *Guardian* reported that 'the underachievement of boys in

reading at British schools is part of an international malaise
... Far from being confined to the UK, the 'gender gap' in
reading scores appears to be universal. Girls had higher reading
scores at 15 in every one of the 43 countries surveyed in [a]
report by the Organization for Economic Cooperation and
Development and UNESCO' (2 July 2003). In Australia, reports
called 'The Trouble with Boys' appeared in both *The Australian*
(19 June 2000) and the *Sydney Morning Herald* (17 June 2000),
both reflecting on the apparent decline in boys' educational
achievements. This narrative about boys performing and indeed
behaving badly at school has gained a high public profile in the
press and in public and political sensibilities in Australia, the
United Kingdom, Canada and the United States and there is
now a widely held belief that boys are 'in crisis' and 'at risk' in
and out of school. A common claim is that boys are increasingly
disengaged, disrespectful, disaffected and distrustful.

Emotive declarations regarding 'the war against boys' and the crisis
in the gender order[1] have inflamed public opinion and sparked debate
in many developed, Western countries around the world. Ultimately
however, they are hysterical and hyperbolic and unable to contribute
to understandings of the complex current connections between boys
and schooling in different places and spaces.[2] Collins, Kenway and
McLeod (2000: 20) argue: 'The model of gender equity often implied is
that of a see-saw or pendulum, in which achieving "equity" is a deli-
cate balancing act between potential "winners and losers".' Most serious
scholarship in the field explicitly avoids simplistic gender comparisons,
engaging instead in a more nuanced analysis of 'the effects of significant differences within (i.e. not only between) each gender group'
(McDowell 2003: 20). A common theme, is the need to progress from
broad, general discussions of 'gender wars' to more detailed analyses of
particular masculinities and of the ways in which they intersect with
schooling (e.g., Adams and Savran 2002; Martino 2003; Youdell 2003).
In seeking to advance both the debate about boys' schooling and the
scholarly literature, we offer a different perspective that focuses specifically on the links between knowledge, identity and spatiality.

Our starting point in this chapter is the discussions about identity
and reflexivity that we introduced in Chapter 1 and developed in
Chapter 3, where we linked the notion of reflexivity to the changing
nature of work, pointing to the implications for certain groups of male

workers and unsettling notions about the de- and retraditionalization of gender. Here, we further consider the notion of reflexivity as a characteristic of contemporary biographies that involves the imperative to self-consciously and reflexively construct one's own identity (Giddens 1994). Our thinking starts with a notion of schoolboys as knowledge seekers, reflexively constructing their identities and reflexively responding to the demands and dilemmas of their everyday lives. But we do not focus particularly on the institutionalized knowledge of the school curriculum. Our focus is on the sorts of knowledge-based identity work that is going on in, around, in opposition to and outside of school. In other words we make diverse knowledges central to our discussions of boys and schooling. We identify the multiple knowledges and sources of expertise that boys deploy in their identity work.

We also seek to enhance Giddens's and others' notion of reflexive self-making through de Certeau's (1984) signature concepts, 'the strategy' and 'the tactic'. De Certeau's concepts assist us to highlight the knowledges boys pursue, resist, cling to and relinquish in relation to the shifting knowledge imperatives of their lives in the globalizing local. We begin with a brief elaboration of de Certeau's notions of strategies, tactics and spatialized knowledges as ways of knowing the everyday. We then deploy these concepts to assist us to understand how schoolboys purposefully and profitably mobilize knowledges to invent themselves and others. There are two main sets of knowledge that boys deploy in their reflexive self-making; knowledge about life chances and lifestyle. As we will explain, each involves diverse strategies and tactics.

Ways of knowing the everyday

For de Certeau (1984) spaces are trajectories of knowledge as well as physical and social areas. De Certeau explores the ways that knowledge is spatialized and does so from two main perspectives – above and below. Knowledge from above is achieved through the 'map' and the 'tour', and is the space of strategic knowledge. Knowledge from below, is not readily mapped or steered and is the space of tactical knowledge. It is:

> Beneath the [cartographic, strategic] discourses that ideologize [sic] the city, the ruses and combinations of powers that have no readable identity proliferate; without points where one can take hold of them, without rational transparency, they are impossible to administer.
>
> (de Certeau 1984: 93)

Strategies and tactics are everyday knowledges. Strategies are knowledges of spatial and embodied control and tactics are knowledges of embodied, embedded and temporal resistance. Strategies and tactics constitute each other, as the strategy is the exteriority of the tactic (de Certeau 1984: 37). Strategies and tactics are different ways of knowing, as de Certeau explains:

> I call a *strategy* the calculation (or manipulation) of power relationships that becomes possible as soon as a subject with will and power (a business, an army, a city, a scientific institution) can be isolated. It postulates a *place* that can be delimited as its *own* and serves as the base from which relations with an *exteriority* composed of targets or threats (customers or competitors, enemies, the country surrounding the city, objectives and objects of research, etc.) can be managed.
>
> (de Certeau 1984: 35–6, original emphasis)

A strategy draws directly on map knowledge; on the grids of knowledge laid down by those with the power to map space. Maps involve the mastery of space, the capacity to name and frame, to control ways of being and seeing. They are teleological; they entail control. Strategies follow the grids of power. But they are more than this. In de Certeau's (p. 36, original emphasis) words:

> It would be legitimate to define the *power of knowledge* by this ability to transform the uncertainties of history into readable spaces. But it would be more correct to recognize in these 'strategies' a specific type of knowledge, one sustained and determined by the power to provide oneself with one's own place.

For de Certeau (p. 36) then, a strategy can also be understood as 'the establishment of a break between a place appropriated as one's own and its other'. Making 'one's own' place involves spatializing knowledge. It involves the construction of readable spaces and of one's place in such spaces. The strategy, then, is also concerned to establish a relationship between boundaries and belonging, insiders and outsiders. Indeed, strategies involve thinking in powerful packs. They involve pack knowledge – how to belong, differentiate, patrol. Strategists speak from, and to, collective subject positions. The strategist is the friend of stability and command.

According to de Certeau (p. 119) strategic thought involves two orders of engagement, the map and the tour or 'itinerary'. 'The first [the map] is of the type: "The girls' room is next to the kitchen." The second: "You turn right and come into the living room".' He continues by stating that 'tour' style descriptions of places and spatializations of knowledge 'are made for the most part in terms of *operations* and show "how to enter each room"' (p. 119). Tour knowledge is 'how to' knowledge; it steers people along predetermined routes and shows them how to behave along the way. Both maps and tours control the ways in which spaces are utilized, thought about, seen and moved within. Here the body, its surroundings and interpersonal relations are coded in terms of pre-established ideals of power. Such ways of knowing and of spatializing knowledges in terms of established, static power relations can be likened to the scholarly standpoints canvassed in Chapter 1 that conceptualize processes and dimensions of globalization from above. This is a mode of knowing that abstracts the lived politics of spatial relations in order to consider aerial global images of cultural terrains. We think about 'map' and 'tour' knowledges as embodiments of views from above (de Certeau likens knowledges of the tour to gazing from the summit of the World Trade Center: a metaphor for detached scientific/scopic representations of place).

The map and the tour regulate knowledge and power. De Certeau contrasts these with less or unregulated knowledges that arise from below, through the intimacies of the immediate, the body, the street, the day by day, the corporeal. De Certeau places more cultural value on tactical knowledges and views from below than above; he celebrates the 'poets of the streets', those whose movements subvert map and tour knowledge in the everyday. De Carteau summarizes the tactic (1984: 37) by saying: 'The space of a tactic is the space of the other. Thus it must play on and with a terrain imposed on it and organized by the law of a foreign power.'

A tactic is 'a manoeuvre "within the enemy's field of vision"' (p. 37). Tactics are timed and positioned in relation to a dominant power and are inventive, often spontaneous responses to the exercise of control. They have little or no capacity to amass power:

> [the tactic] . . . must vigilantly make use of the cracks that particular conjunctions open in the surveillance of the propriety owners. It poaches in them. It creates surprises in them. It can be where it is least expected. It is a guileful ruse. In short, a tactic is an art of the weak.
>
> (de Certeau 1984: 37)

For de Certeau, then, tactics involve the spontaneous development of guileful ruses. They require crafty ways of getting away with actions that go against the grain of dominant cultural formations. A guileful ruse may be a disguise or mantle of invisibility donned by the tactician in order to escape the scrutiny of the strategist's all-seeing eye.

Tactics are at once spatial and temporal. In a space that is not their own, tacticians articulate alternative moments and power relations. Such occasions of dissent occur at opportune times. Indeed, to play a tactic is to bet on time (p. 39). Tactics might involve a quick escape, fleeting alliance or temporary imprint. They may involve novel juxtapositions that undercut dominant narratives or 'facts' and produce something original and politically minoritarian. Overall, tactics are moves of response to strategic acts within a space defined as 'other' by those with the power to 'other'. Hence, they invariably also involve knowledge of ways to protect oneself from the forces of an outside that threaten to consume a person, cultural group or body of knowledge.

'What knowledge is of most use to me?' is an ongoing question for schoolboys. Indeed, it is a common question for many in what Giddens calls 'a runaway world of dislocation and uncertainty' (Giddens 1994: 83). But it is made particularly pressing by adolescence, locality, employment vulnerability, and by the proliferation of resources for youthful identity building in globalizing times, many of which we discuss in other chapters. The school is an important place, in relation to which boys play out their gendered narratives about useful and useless, acceptable and unacceptable knowledge as they engage in their reflexive project of self-making. It invokes and involves multiple narratives. De Certeau's concepts assist us to understand the patterns of power in young male's different orientations to school and other knowledge, and to identify the multiple knowledges, and sources of expertise they deploy in their identity work.

Young males at our schools have a primary emphasis either on knowledge that relates to life chances or to lifestyle. This is not to say that one excludes the other. Their orientations to knowledge can be mapped along a continuum, at one end of which is an emphasis on life chances and, at the other end, an emphasis on lifestyle. Some boys sit at the extremes of this continuum and others sit at the centre, keeping life chances and lifestyle in balance. Further, at different times and in different places in their educational biography, knowledge for and about life chances or lifestyle may become a primary aspect of their reflexive self-making. We include certain boys in one orientation because this is their primary orientation, but they may also adopt aspects of the others. Each case entails a somewhat different relationship to school knowledge. Indeed, very different sorts and sources of knowledge are mobilized in these boys' reflexive self-production.

Leveraging life chances

'Official' school knowledge can be likened to de Carteau's (1984) map knowledge. It is an atlas of knowledge trajectories, a command geography. It identifies a set number of knowledge grids and shows how they intersect. But official school knowledge can also be likened to the tour, for it sends students along these predetermined grid lines. Indeed, it conventionally sends certain social class groupings of students along particular lines. It also ascribes more merit to certain lines on the grid than others, and in so doing it distributes students' life chances.

Of course, how students respond to the atlas or the tour guidebook varies. We show later in this section that some boys don't live their everyday lives according to either, and seek to maximize their life chances off the map. But the first two sets of boys we discuss ascribe in one way or another to map and tour knowledge. They see it as determining their life trajectories. With regard to their futures, they take a strategic view of knowledge. These boys have an affinity with what Deleuze and Guattari (1987: 20, 24) call 'tracing': methods of knowledge reproduction that support established determinations of power.

Some such knowledge strategists have what we call aerial vision; they see school knowledge from above and they also see it within a broader and somewhat fluid socioeconomic context. They strategically chart their own tours through the full range made possible on the maps in the atlas. They are scopic strategists. Other boys only read certain maps, take local tours and cannot, or do not, see the complex geometries of possibility seen by those with aerial vision. They only tour the maps of their socioeconomic place, and cannot read these maps as fixing them in their place. Trajectories to other places are not part of their life. While they are on the map of strategic knowledge, they are grid-locked. Some other boys refute the strategies associated with aerial and neighbourhood vision. They go off the map of school knowledge, and tactically make their life chances from their out-of-school experience. Because they refuse to surrender to map knowledge, they are beyond the command of the school. Their knowledge arises from the micro-worlds of intimate community; it is from below, inventive, sensory – in a word, haptic. Let us now unpack these knowledge narratives of boys who focus on their life chances.

Boys with aerial vision

Boys with aerial vision are highly reflexive about their life chances. They are scopic strategists who are preoccupied with what they need to know,

do and have available to them in the present to be secure and successful in later life. Whatever specific knowledge they, the school and sometimes their parents think they need, they subscribe to; and more besides
in some cases. Formalized and credentialized knowledges are understood as central to their biographical projects of getting on. In a sense
they help to put in place:

> an immobile and stone-like order (in it, nothing moves except dis-
> course itself, which, like a camera panning over a scene, moves over
> the whole panorama).
>
> (de Certeau 1984: 118)

Frank North, age 16 from Eden, and Mick Dean, age 15 from Renmark,
are typical scopic strategists. They have a strong sense of the particular
knowledge they need and value and they trust their school to give them
the support they need to get where they want to go. Each has crafted
an identity around being smart and skilled according to map knowledges. Frank says, 'I should be able to go to Year 12. I am pretty confident that I would be able to do that.' He wants 'something to do with
plants. I was thinking National Parks and Wildlife, or just working in
the Ministry of Health.' He is making sure he chooses the right subjects,
is using 'work experience' to further his ambitions and making the most
of both his father's and the school's support:

> Oh, I saw . . . our head of placements this year, and got a sheet of the
> electives we would need next year, and I should be doing biology,
> agriculture, geography, and I will probably do French still. I might
> do drama because I need another elective.

For work experience he and his father rang up National Parks and
Wildlife and booked him in. He has already got a 'mini biology degree
certificate, which doesn't really mean much, but it still looks good', he
chuckles, and explains the science excursion camp at which he gained
this degree:

> Well, they had a science festival, and we had a few lectures . . . futur-
> istic things, just normal scientific things. And there was a plant
> section where you could do leaf cuttings and stem cuttings, and that
> was pretty good stuff. To actually do the mini degree course, it was
> pretty simple like microscopes and bacteria and germs and stuff, and
> a little DNA quiz.

Mick is one of a number of boys in Renmark and elsewhere for whom information and communications technologies (ICTs) have become quite central to who they are and want to be. He says:

> Work Education is probably one of my favorite subjects; you get to use a computer and that. Technology, I like designing things; same with Art and Design, you get to design things.

Along with his friends, he has ICTs at the top of his priorities. Mick's friend Bob Parker, for example, didn't go to school on the sports day so that he could spend the whole day at home working on the computer. He is making a power point presentation for his Work Ed. class. He hopes to get into the computer industry after school. This industry is understood as The Future.

As Frank and Mick demonstrate, boys with aerial vision understand the macro-geographies of knowledge and plot their best routes to success on the grids of knowledge/power. They can think geometrically; they observe intersections, trends. They have foresight. Their life-lines are connected to future opportunities through the logic of 'if' – 'if I do this now, then . . .'. They understand cause and effect, and operate in terms of actions and consequences. Boys with aerial vision are thus often good readers of the economic trends in their locality and these are also becoming part of these boys' knowledge narratives. As we noted in Chapter 3, in Renmark and Coober Pedy tourism and service indus- tries are on the rise. Robert Godard's family run a successful houseboat business and he talks very knowledgably about the boom in the tourism industry. Tommy Logan from Coober Pedy has a part-time job at the Breakaways café, but will stay at school through to Year 12 when he hopes to get a local apprenticeship to become a chef. Both boys know what kind of knowledge is a good investment if they wish to continue to live locally. Collectively, then, boys with aerial vision are also multi- map thinkers. But of necessity, they must also have some knowledge of the 'streets' of the school.

Knowledge about how to survive in an intellectually hostile climate is vital for these boys. They are often taunted by the school's 'street poets'. 'Boys have two choices', says Dawn Clarentine, age 13 from Eden, 'to be smart, do their work and put up with being teased', or to 'join the tough kids, drop out and have less of a future'. To scopic strate- gists, toughness and coolness are not important for their life chances and so they try to refuse the guileful ruses of the tough tacticians. Such tacticians will often denigrate the boys who stick to the grid. Jonathan

Nicholls of Morwell, for example, explains how his friend Mark Thinley, is too linguistically strong for their friendship group:

> His words sound different to ours . . . our sentences are three words and his are a dictionary long. Instead of just saying, 'It is a fence-post', he has to put something else in there, and it doesn't sound right. We try to make him sound like us so that he doesn't sound like a mad professor – he is slowly picking it up . . . He is very, very intelligent; he has just got to try and not act so intelligent around us. I don't know, you could probably put it down to a jealousy sort of thing that we pick on him because he is smarter than us. But when he is around us, he drops down to a lower level.

But such pressure to adopt a view from below is not the biggest worry of boys with aerial vision. Tom Frank tells us the smart boys worry most about how well they are going at school. He worries about assignments, the time he has to complete them and about getting good marks; not much else. Mark Thinley, age 15 from Morwell, explains that 'Sometimes, they will say that I am square and stuff like that, but I am thinking "Yeah, I can imagine seeing you in 20 years time, what are you going to be?"'

Grid-locks

There are various ways in which boys become grid-locked on schools' map knowledge. One set of grid-locked boys knows the doxa about the value of aerial vision, but can't work the grid. While they try to adopt aerial vision, they know a great deal less about the expert and abstract systems associated with education, training and employment than do the scopic strategists. These grid-locked boys know that they need to stay at school, work hard and 'get an education'. Indeed, such notions have an almost mantra-like status for them. They place a high degree of trust in the education system and in the capacity of qualifications to translate into work. However, they are not quite sure of the knowledge value systems that exist, of what knowledge they need to secure their futures, or why such knowledge is important.

Shawn Rodgers, age 13 from Morwell, is typical of such boys. He says: 'You have got to do the work to get a good job.' He is scathing about his friends leaving school early, saying: 'You know exactly what they are going to be. They are going to be a trolley boy or something like that.' Shawn is aware that qualifications are important in securing work. He explains:

> Like, if you have a degree as a mechanic, they would get jobs in Morwell just like that . . . On the TV it says jobs are so hard to get and stuff like that. It is because people haven't got degrees or anything like that, or they don't know anything about their jobs.

Shawn has radically diverse ideas about what he wants to do when he leaves school:

> I want to work on a big building, or be a mechanic, or something like that. I am trying to, I don't know. I probably want to be a professional guitar player. I am really good at that, or a professional golfer. But for job work, I want to be a mechanic or a lawyer.

In order to encourage him to stay at school, Shawn's father has him on an incentive scheme. He explains this as follows:

> None of my brothers, nobody in my whole family – my dad's family and my mum's family – they haven't gone past Year 11. So I am going to try and beat that. And Dad has given me a deal. If Ken, that is my older brother, had gone past it, he would have got $600, and Bruce, if he had passed, he would get $900, and if George had passed, he would have got $1200, and then if I pass, I get $5500. So I am going to try and pass.

The trouble for Shawn is that neither he, nor his family, knows much about school knowledges or how education systems work.

Knowing the geography of school knowledge is essential to leveraging life chances. These grid-locked boys recognize the commands of the map, but the operational knowledge in the educational tour guidebook is far too coded for them. It requires the sorts of cultural capital they and their families do not have. These boys' spatial stories are social class stories of a command geography that keeps them in their place. Most often, they and their families simply don't occupy a place that allows them to take an aerial view of knowledge. For instance, Beau Knox from Merimbula says his father fell through the cracks of the educational system and can't really read. He has thus had to take on menial jobs and wants much more for his son. Beau has obviously been very affected by his father's frustration and wants to succeed for his sake. But sometimes he 'slacks off' at school, gets behind and has difficulty in catching up. His family does not have the educational resources to help him. Nigel Watkins, also of Eden, tells us his father's story of educational grid-lock:

He left in Year Ten and he was really disappointed because he had worked to be at university. He had the scores, he was really high up and he could have done a hell of a lot of things, but his granddad said, 'Oh, don't go to university, I work with university people and they are all useless.' So dad goes, 'Righty ho', and he didn't go. He has regretted it big time. He has thought about going back all the time, but it is just too late. He says he couldn't get back into the study.

With his father's encouragement Nigel may not repeat his fathers' spatial story.

A second, overlapping set of grid-locked boys, who we mentioned in Chapter 3, is only willing to invest their intellectual and emotional energy in highly specific curriculum spaces. These are usually directly related to further training, paid work or sport; they are usually practical, technical or physical knowledges. For these boys, worthwhile knowledge is not often associated with what they call paper work; with 'too much' writing, 'too much' theory and/or with being indoors. Charlie Belew from Coober Pedy associates these with a 'sit down and shut up and write' approach. One difficulty for such boys arises when they become aware that the school does not necessarily value and reward highly the knowledge they like and the things they can actually do. Indeed, some observe that although they have skills, the school sometimes has no idea about them and assesses them according to tests that cannot demonstrate their skills. For instance, Nigel Watkins of Eden explains that 'A mate of mine is useless at schoolwork' and fails all the tests. But, 'he knows every part of a motor, you just can't imagine it, he knows everything.'

Boys who are grid-locked in maps of practical knowledge often think schools don't give them enough 'hands-on', practical, job-related knowledge. Indeed, much of the time, schools are seen to dispense useless knowledge which can really only be tolerated if it is at least enjoyable – like physical education, for example. A difficulty for the school, of course, is the boys' withdrawal of consent in the subjects they do not approve of or enjoy. This can be accompanied by an 'I don't care, I don't want to try, don't push me' attitude. A vicious retracing of a worn, narrow road may arise: the less they care, the worse they do and the worse they do, the less they try. As we suggested in Chapter 3, there may be a causal paradox of relevance here. It is possible that some boys want the school to prepare them for the jobs that are in fact dwindling or which require additional skills that these boys do not have and are unprepared to gain. Yet, having locked themselves into particular knowledge grids, these boys find it difficult to take up other/othered knowledges that they may have previously stigmatized, but which may have more 'pay off' in the longer term. These boys do not understand the logic of 'if'. Rather, they think in terms of 'there is'. To revisit de Certeau (1984: 119), the 'path' of their knowledge is a 'series of units that have the form of vectors that are . . . "static" ("to the right," "in front of you," etc.)'. They only tour the maps of their socioeconomic place, and cannot read these maps as fixing them in place. The choices these boys make only occur within the neighbourhood knowledges they understand. They don't read the atlas.

Haptic tacticians

Some boys make their own life chances off the map of school knowledge. Such boys seek instead to build life chances outside school or below the school's scopic visions. These boys hold the view that 'you have to make your own future'. They are intent on invention through the use of their own social, sensory sensibilities. They feel out possibilities, follow hunches, create intimate spaces of engagement. We call them haptic tacticians.

Haptic knowledge is based upon, or expressive of, the sense of touch. The term 'haptic' as a signifier of sensory knowledge is derived from the Greek *haptikos*, which itself is derivative of *haptesthai*: to grasp, touch. Haptic tacticians grasp the complexities of 'below', the intimate and immediate, they grasp opportunities. These boys are sensible and sense-able: they know how to read for practical possibility. They generate – and live in – 'actions that multiply spaces' (de Certeau 1984: 118). They distrust the singularity and abstractions inherent in school map knowledge.

There are two main overlapping ways that haptic tacticians seek to enhance their life chances; through part-time work undertaken whilst at school and through building networks and reputation. Terry Vincent, age 14 from Morwell, is not waiting for work, he cannot afford that luxury. He is out hustling for work experience and generating his own part-time paid work. Terry is the sort of boy who evades the all-seeing eye of the school, he does just enough work to get by and teachers overlook him. But outside of school he has adopted some highly successful tactics of necessity. His parents are in dire financial circumstances and the money he gets from part-time work is an important component of the family income. He believes strongly in the importance of 'experience and references' in getting further work. He has even established his own 'small enterprise':

I have got tons of references from past jobs. I used to work at the Shed, used to do a paper round. There was several things that I did. I even did my own things like cleaning wheelie bins and stuff, and I did that for about a year. Yeah, I used to charge $4 per bin. For a spray, a wash and everything.

Terry has a host of ideas about how the locals might provide work experience for local kids:

Probably just offer small jobs. Like, the bowling alley could say 'Oil the lanes, $2 a night' or something like that. It is 20 lanes up and down with the machine, pretty easy, and say $2 each time you go up and down. Do that everyday. Just small things to get kids going.

According to Terry, you need to know how to create opportunities in your own immediate spaces. 'Poaching in the cracks' of entrepreneurial knowledges, Terry crafts sources of income from features of the day by day:

My paper round, the original delivery boy, he wanted to quit because he was old enough to get another job. So when he left, this other kid Bill got the job, and not everyone liked him. He never kept up. So the boss gave me the job as well. So Bill got put on three nights and me on two, so he gets a rest, and if Bill leaves, I get the three nights and someone else gets the two.

Some boys who refute school map knowledge are busy in and outside of school building up their life chances according to the age-old premise: 'Its not what you know but who you know.' These boys invent opportunities through 'know how' about 'know who' and in a sense they subvert map and tour knowledges which are normally about 'know how' and 'know what'. Sport and extended families play important roles here, as Paul Jones and Nigel Watkins, both from Eden, argue. 'I reckon if you play footy, or if you are in the footy or the soccer club or some club like that, if you know heaps of people it would be easier to get a job because you just ask everyone if there is any work going', says Nigel. Paul adds, 'If you don't know people you could have trouble getting jobs. My brother, all the jobs he lost was because the people he has applied to get jobs from employed their cousins, nephews, brother's friends, brother's stepsons.' Simon Jackson, also from Eden, is deliberately tactical about leaving his personal imprint. He thinks getting ahead for boys is about actively networking and deliberately seeking to get a good name through part-time work. He works part-time at the local news agency and consciously seeks to get a good name by:

> Being polite to people, they really appreciate it. Then it goes on to someone else, they tell someone else, and it goes on. People come in and they actually know you and they talk to you by name. It is a way to get your name around so that you can get a job later on. Oh, some days you just feel like staying at home, but you have got to do it, so you put your mind to it and go to work. You can't just do a no-show. It is sort of really hard [to get work]. It depends on if you have got a name around the town. If you haven't then you've got no hope. But if you have got a good name and your name is around then, yeah.

Haptic tacticians know about the power of artful social contrivance in intimate settings. They craft their life chances through the materials immediately on hand in the spaces they know how to manoeuvre.

The Krakouer brothers are haptic tacticians *par excellence*. Australian Rules Football (AFL) legends, they grew up:

> Living next door to a railway line in effectively an old humpy, reserve life . . . an incredibly difficult situation which was brought about . . . through the policies of the time, which only wanted Indigenous Australians . . . around things like the sanitary depot and the rubbish tip.
>
> (Gorman 2005)

Much of their childhood was spent kicking goals, leaping and catching (marking), bouncing and balking, ducking and weaving; refining their skills. From such a shockingly marginalized position, Jim and Phillip Krakouer rose to the pinnacle of Australia's aggressively competitive athletic arena and reconfigured popular imaginings of the ideal football player:

> The [media] hyperbole just would be amazing, and some of the quotes were that 'They transcend the way that the game is meant to be played', 'They are the Pele and Maradonna of VFL football'. . . [they] took the game to another level, and gave non-Indigenous Australia . . . an appreciation of the way the game can be played.
>
> (Gorman 2005)

Phrases such as 'Krakouer Magic', 'Black Magic' and 'the Silky Skills' are now part of the language of AFL culture and fandom. Two indigenous boys' pleasurable childhood efforts led them to the peak of their sport and changed the cultural imaginary of an entire industry (O'Regan 2005). These brothers' biography illustrates how exceptional dedication and commitment can choreograph unique life chances, even against incredible odds, indeed perhaps at times in response to a lack of viable other options.

Lifestyle logics

Lifestyle is about the 'identification of self in material things' and about viewing such things as 'extended expressions of "self"'' (Featherstone 1992: 83). The term 'lifestylization' refers to the ways people's lifestyles express their politics through aesthetic choices (p. 35). To focus on students' lifestyles is to see what erupts on the 'street' level of the school where student cultures and subcultures of lifestyle performance proliferate. While for the school this bustling space is 'impossible to administer' (de Certeau 1984: 93), it contains its own micro-geographies of strategies and tactics. And lifestyle-thought often involves boys thinking strategically in packs; or tactically, in relation to dominant and dominating packs. This everyday, localized thinking in packs is also connected to broader social and cultural maps of meaning. It articulates locally global geometries of power.

For schoolboys, a focus on lifestyle involves the elevation to a high order of priority such things as the image, the look, the pack. Boys who focus on lifestyle refuse to privilege the education system's map or tour knowledge in their reflexive identity production. Instead, they draw on the knowledges necessary to accomplish valued forms of embodiment, display, sets of social connections and disconnections, ways of occupying space, linking to leisure. These boys may still complete their schoolwork and think spasmodically about their futures, but such matters do not have the affective lure of lifestyle knowledges. Lifestyle boys are more interested in the present than the future, immediate than delayed gratification, lifestyle now, rather than life chances for later.

Understanding cool codes is everyday lifestyle knowledge embedded in place. Cool is a contextually defined rhythm of life and spatialized regime. All places have their cool spaces, activities, modes of speech, styles of relation, ways of seeing. Cool boys own these locations and mores. Other kids either implicitly or explicitly position themselves in relation to the coolest kid's unwavering sense of ownership and right.

Cool logic is hegemonic. It's about drawing a firm line between acceptable and unacceptable behaviour, and it is about entitlement. Cool is a territorialization of freedom.

In all the schools in our localities, there are hierarchies of cool masculinity and different subcultures of coolness. Knowing what cool masculinity is and where one fits in relation to cool hierarchies and subcultures is an important aspect of school knowledge. Boys are expected to be able to read the signs of distinction. Those who are fortunate can also perform them, apparently effortlessly:

> Power is bound by its very visibility. In contrast, trickery is possible for the weak, and often it is his only possibility, as a 'last resort': 'The weaker the forces at the disposition of the strategist, the more the strategist will be able to use deception'. I translate: the more the strategy is transformed into tactics.
>
> (de Carteau 1984: 37)

Here de Certeau imagines a continuum of power, along which the 'pure' strategist loses his connection to visibility and power, and instead becomes the invisible tactician: the master of guileful ruses. In this section, we move along a similar trajectory of power relations. We start with the boys who are the school's cool cartographers. These dominant boys normalize their own versions of cool and enjoy the visibility of their power. We then consider the boys whose practices of 'cool' are contextually contingent, focusing on the subcultural spatial and corporeal controlling behaviours of second- or third-generation migrant boys and Aboriginal 'Homeboys'. Homeboy culture and cool Greek boy culture involve strategic cultural practice, the mobilization of grid logics, operating through the construction of firm boundaries. While profoundly controlling and inflexible, both these cultural strategies are at one and the same time tactical responses to the boys who normalize hegemonic cool. We then discuss the un-cool boys, those who invent their lifestyle beyond the cool boys' lines of vision and who deploy spatial tactics of survival. We conclude with an illustration of the problem of pack logic as everyday knowledge.

Cool cartographers

Determining what is, and is not, 'cool' is a sociocultural politics of corporeal inscription and gendered performativity. Coolness is embodied, spatialized. It's a style of walking, talking, wearing clothes. It's the places where young people do or don't hang out. It is a temporal rhythm, a pace of speech, movement, contact and response. Its defining features require certain kinds of knowledge. Knowing what is or isn't cool fuels an impetus amongst boys to change their life in order to 'be' cool or to have a position on various incarnations of cool. Some young men position themselves against dominant local ideas of cool. Others try hard to fit into a cool pack, but find coolness easier to recognize than reproduce. They hover on the margins of packs. Whatever a boy's take on cool, it's hard knowledge work. Cool is a powerful ideal, not soft or insubstantial:

> The 'proper'... allows one to capitalize acquired advantages, to prepare future expansions, and thus to give oneself a certain independence with respect to the variability of circumstances.
>
> (de Certeau 1984: 36)

Hegemonic coolness in a school constructs the 'proper' kind of cool, the one right mode. It is about knowing, owning and overseeing lifestyle thought and practice. Boys who are the school's cool cartographers are usually big, good at prestigious sports, well liked by the 'prettiest' girls, sociable 'party guys' who ooze independence, control and certainty. Heterosexuality is almost always a defining characteristic of youthful cool and the dominant logics of cool may also intersect with heterosexually aggressive, but socially sanctioned behaviour amongst boys. We return to this. Cool cartographers implicitly construct cool itineraries that guide other boys' aspirations and behaviour. One way in which such strategies are exercised is through scopic vision, through panoptic control of pack behaviour and through always mapping the pack as a 'whole' (p. 36), its interiors and exteriors.

Cool binds boys together in culturally and socially coded packs of insiders and outsiders and encourages them to think in packs. Frank Chigetto (age 15) notes the links some of his peers make between cool and commodities:

> I had a girl come up to me yesterday, and she goes, 'Where did you get them from?', and I go, 'Target', and she goes, 'Oh, you are so NOT cool'. And I go, 'Well, what shops do you go to that are COOL?', and she goes, 'Oh, sports shops', and I go, 'Why are they cool?', and she goes, 'Because they have good stuff', and I go, 'What's cool?', and she goes, 'I don't know'.

Sports shops sell label clothes, global brands (Adidas, Nike, DC, Globe, Reebok). Target supermarket only stocks its own range of clothing. In economies of cool based around brand labels, Target clothes are mortifying material deficits.

'Cool' commodities involve envisaging an 'authentic' (yet paradoxically commodifiable) state of cool. They are often items that well-off, mainstream young men have access to; items that are put forward as markers of their wearer's supposed individuality and autonomy. However, they are more appropriately read as markers of ascription to brand label aesthetics and their links to pack culture. Knowledges that reflect or express the commodification of cool, capitalize on the existing advantages of the boys who can afford cool commodities. These knowledges normalize the 'cool' boy's privileges and suggest that their ontological superiority will lead to further success and supremacy as their life moves on. Simply put, the commodification of 'cool' is a strategy, a knowledge system that is put to work mapping aesthetic, geographical and social spaces in order to support the interests, and advance the egos, of the young men who have the privilege to choose cool commodities. But the perverse indignity here is that while money and things can be a big part of being cool, they don't make cool altogether. To imagine that cool can be purchased and assembled is to misread the map. Hegemonic coolness is likely to involve cool commodities but it also involves the invisible and apparently effortless stitching together of various dominant forms of capital – financial, cultural and social. The status of the hegemonic cool cartographer is not easily acquired. Indeed, to try is to fail.

Cool contingents

There are also many subcultures of cool masculinity in our different schools. These tend to consist of young men who do cool differently from those in the mainstream. They have their own cool codes. We explore subcultural relationships in greater detail in Chapter 7. For now, we are concerned with ways in which cool is contextually contingent. Sociocultural and geographical contexts produce culturally 'majoritarian' and 'minoritarian' ways of being cool amongst young men. The 'majoritarian' (average, standardized) is a demographic not measured by physical mass, but by cultural power (Deleuze and Guattari 1983: 340). 'Minoritarian' social groups are demographics made up by those without much social capital or cultural power.

The coolest boys are usually members of a dominant sociocultural grouping; Anglo or Greek in the case of Renmark and Coober Pedy, Anglo in Morwell and Eden. In Coober Pedy, for instance, there is a strong Greek population. Greek traditions and festivals feature prominently in the town. The school has a Greek language programme, funded by the Greek government, to teach Greek to its large Greek population. The town also celebrates Greek festivals such as Glendi and Greek Easter, and has a social club where local Greek men come together to drink coffee and ouzo and play backgammon. This strong Greek cultural presence has a significant impact on youthful masculine identities and relationships. At school there is a large group of Greek boys who consider themselves 'the best' at soccer and attracting girls – the important things in life for these young men. According to these football enthusiasts, other boys, envious of their soccer skills and panache with girls, 'wannabe Greeks'. This desire for Greek ethnicity illustrates the ways in which cool can be related to ethnic cultural groupings. Boys in Coober Pedy wannabe Greek because it means being incorporated into a cool, heterosexually active, culturally endorsed social sphere.

The social ascendancy of Greek families in Renmark also assists the cool ascendancy of Greek boys. Young Greek males are known as Wogs and are considered the 'coolest' group in and out of school. The girls find them the most attractive. The other boys criticize but also envy them – although they are reluctant to admit it. Gem Johnston's envy is dressed up as critique:

> Up-themselves, Wogs, that's all I know. They are just in-love with themselves . . . They fancy themselves, they look at themselves in the mirror all the time. No offence or anything, the Wogs here, some of them are just arrogant and I get sick of it.

The cool hierarchies that Gem is so critical of are mapped on to youthful hangout spaces. 'Wog' areas are segregated off and marked as more prestigious. There are two main examples. 'Wog Corner' is an area in the school where the cool boys from Greek backgrounds and their friends hang out. 'Wog Wharf' is an area by the river where mainly young Greek men go to park their cars when they are doing laps of the town on Friday nights. The two main youth gathering points in the town are the 'Wog Wharf' and 'Feral Wharf'. Nicola Pitts, age 16, discusses the difference in status between these spaces:

> If you're hanging around with the Wogs, you're at the Wog Wharf and you would not be seen dead at the Feral Wharf. It's not exactly a Feral Wharf, it's just where other people park, you know. And if you're hanging around with those sorts of people, you park there and you would not go near the Wog Wharf, not a good idea! The Wog Wharf is older people, older guys, better looking. The other place is just everyone else. They're not as good as the Wog Wharf, not a high

enough standard. And the Wog Wharf they wouldn't go low enough to go down to the Feral Wharf.

The Ferals are the local poor, and the cool ascendancy of Greek males in and beyond school involves clear demarcations from them. Cool sub-cultures usually have an antagonistic relationship to each other. Indeed, one of the main sources of anxious pleasure for young males is the fighting that goes on between cool and other packs.

Another example of a socially contingent cool culture, this time from a minoritarian social group, can be found in Coober Pedy's 'Homeboys'. Hip-hop music and hip-hop cultural aesthetics have been marketed effectively across the developed Western world and appropriated by diverse cultures (Feitas 2005: 151–64). According to Christian Young, there is a group of Coober Pedy boys who watch so many 'black African American movies', they have come to 'think they are Homeboys' and behave badly at school. Homeboys draw their knowledge about cool-ness partly from American TV but also from Hip-Hop and RnB culture. This knowledge is aural and kinaesthetic – rap music, baggy pants and bandanas. Being a Homeboy requires specific ways of moving (a sloping walk, using expressive hand gestures), specific ways of talking (vocabu-lary such as: 'dope' [good]; 'yo' [hey]; 'bitchen' [excellent]). It involves subscribing to quite specific ideas about girls, evidenced by the use of nouns such as 'bitches', 'hoes' and 'babymommas'. In all these respects Homeboy culture can be seen as an aesthetically didactic strategy asso-ciated with the commodification of cool; no less grid-like than the school curriculum, or the prisons, armies or cities that de Certeau asso-ciates with spatial control from above (1984: 36).

But as Riley Stephens (Coober Pedy) explains, the Homeboys in Coober Pedy are mainly Aboriginal boys. This particular articulation of cool is about being black, minoritarian and challenging white author-ity through the use of a defiant black culture of masculinity. Homeboy culture involves the art of the black tactician, for being a 'Homie' is a means of protection from the attacks of other 'cool' boys, particularly the Greeks. Tactics are ways of coping with dominance. De Certeau (p. 38) explains the 'dialectic of the tactic' as 'resulting from combat at close quarters, limited by the possibilities of the moment, a tactic is determined by the absence of power just as a strategy is organized by the postulation of power' (p. 38). Homeboy culture is grounded in an 'absence of power' and aims to counteract this fundamental absence. It has evolved from the resonant image of the angry, hard-done by young man, rhyming with his mates to pass the time. This is a nihilistic, reactionary culture, but it is also a mantle of resistant visibility for the individuals it enfolds. Homies in Coober Pedy are fighting back against dominant, white, better off kinds of cool. It is this 'combat at close quarters' (p. 38) that binds them.

All our schools include cool tacticians who deliberately construct themselves through a form of anti-school and anti-majoritarian cool. These minoritarian cool tacticians seek to undercut dominant narratives and provide alternative moves and meanings for the disenfranchised, sometimes 'bad' boys. According to Frank Chigetto of Morwell, the 'cool kit' for these boys in his class is to 'sell drugs, have spray on deodorant (because it is banned at school), wear a white polo shirt, get into fights, pierce an eyebrow, write your name on school desks'.

Peripheral vision

Friendship is most important to all boys. Without friends at school, they feel very exposed. Certain knowledges are central to making and keeping friends, the more vulnerable the boys, the more fundamental or urgent their need for some such knowledge. Friendship groups usually adopt a standpoint on cool – they are cool, they try to be cool, they don't care about cool and so on. These positionings in relation to cool involve choice, chance and necessity, and relate to what boys think they can or must do in order to have a liveable life at school. Terry Vincent (age 14 from Morwell), for instance, describes his 'un-cool' lifestyle and friends in relation to dominant cool school codes:

> We are not really like . . . most groups down at the canteen end [who] usually play sports or go running and things. We just sit way up the back, up there, and don't worry about nothing.

Some boys are only peripherally on the cool radar; and then only negatively. These include boys who have no apparent aspirations to belong to any cool pack or who may have tried and failed. They may be loners or rejects. For example, Charlie Belew, from Coober Pedy, does not join in the sporting norm, and is somewhat marginalized by this, but he also enjoys his relative invisibility. It is clearly a lifestyle choice for Charlie, who hangs out with the 'bad boys' and crafts a life quite ulterior to those of the cool boys in his school. The boys peripheral to the cool radar have usually mastered the art of protecting themselves from the pack, and have probably needed to do so in order to survive socially. These young men have, in effect, built their school lives around 'the polemology of the "weak"' (de Certeau 1984: 39). They are the artful peripherals.

Such boys are not tacticians who master the critical arts of timing and articulating fleeting, contextual power plays. Rather, these young men are too vulnerable to think on their feet with such efficiency. They have quietly, gradually built their lives through 'clever tricks of the "weak" within the order established by the "strong"' (de Certeau 1984: 40). Yet the art of these boys' tactics is in the slow, silent, unnoticeable ways that they carve out an inhabitable space for themselves. The computer boys of Eden are an example of such slow-motion tacticians. Their daily movements at school are determined by their knowledges of spaces of survival – a cultural, rather than economic kind of survival. These boys hang out in the library and use the library computers during lunch hour. They are safe from judgement, abuse or attack there, as it is well and truly outside the cool kid's line of vision. Such spatial positioning is the guileful ruse. Young men whose lifestyle knowledges pertain to computer technologies, gaming, Internet use, and online cultures are happy to be considered library 'squares'. Such discursive constructions keep them safe from the imperatives to be 'cool' and, protected from the cool kids' field of vision by their irredeemably 'square' identity, they enjoy their computers in relative peace. The example of the 'library squares' illustrates how complexly intertwined relations of space and social status are, and how implicated ideas of 'cool' are in such economies of space.

If they are without companionship, life can be lonely for young men outside the cool kids' line of vision. Frank Chigetto, who described the idea of the 'cool kit' earlier, is another boy who says he doesn't fit in with the 'cool' boys. Frank, like a number of other young men we spoke to, talks about hanging out with the girls because it was easier to fit in there. The kind of 'hanging out with the girls' that Frank is talking about is not the highly sexed 'ogling' undertaken by the boys who patrol 'Wog Wharf' and that is an important part of Homeboy culture. This gender relation is based on safety and it is notably non-sexual; boys look to girls for a space where they are not bullied. While girls can be just as ferocious as boys when it comes to bullying, often girls who are not invested in cool will befriend boys who have similar values. These groups have easy-going approaches to aesthetics and each other. Yet, the cool boys can see this disregard for cool as offensive. Frank is bullied a lot. He talked about bullies and the ways in which they try to exert power over him, and attempt to make him do whatever it is they want him to do. Frank is very aware of the ways in which power and cool-

ness are spatialized. He has constructed a lifestyle in which he is protected from spaces where the strategies of cool kids are brought into
play. For example, Frank doesn't go to the 'Karma hall' because it is full
of 'mean' cool people. He talked about being beaten up, but carrying
on his peaceful approach to life, he refuses to hit back because he does
not believe in violence. Such acts of resistance are brave feats indeed
in the context of hegemonic cultures and the pack logic of school cool.

Violent behaviours are often supported by, or are performances of,
pack logic. The power and velocity such logic holds is illustrated with
disturbing proficiency in the Australian film *Blackrock* (1997). *Blackrock*
is based on a true story (Carrington 1998). Adapted from a play written
by Nick Enright, the film recounts the gang rape and murder of a 15-
year-old girl on the beach in Newcastle, a working-class deindustrializing Australian town. The rape is witnessed by a friend of the gang, who,
unbeknown to them, is sitting on a rock not far from the scene of the
murder. The witness' name is Jarred (played by Lawrence Bruels). He
does nothing to stop the rape or the murder. He does not tell the police
what he saw. He is silenced by pack logic. Majority rules. Even when
the pack is rotten with anger and acts out mindless violence, it holds
such power over Jarred that he sees no reason for the killer to be made
accountable for his actions. Images of the mutilated body of the brutally murdered girl prompt Jarred to eventually offer some information
to the police. Pack logic also determines the actions of Jarred's closest
friend, Ricko who kills himself in response to Jarred talking to the police.
The act of naming Ricko as the killer fractured the pack's reality of the
victim's deserving death. The pack implicitly justified their actions
through their belief that the murdered girl was a slut. They spray
painted the word on her tombstone. But it was not her supposed sexual
appetite, or her sexual availability that killed her. It was Ricko, who
believed that as a leader of his pack, he could do anything.

* * *

There is no 'war against boys'. Boys cannot be thought of as all of a
piece and as all lacking in agency with regard to schooling or everyday
life. Further, formal school knowledge is not the only knowledge that
boys mobilize or reject in their processes of self-making. Boys engage
most intensely with the kinds of knowledge that they think best suits
their needs in time and place and which they hope will advance their
own particular agendas and interests. Such knowledge is diverse and
quite often is not the knowledge that schools set out to teach or what

they officially value. It involves many everyday knowledges, some about life chances and some about lifestyle. We have argued that these two main forms of everyday knowledge each involve strategic and tactical knowledges and that schoolboys are knowledgeable strategists and tacticians. Those who focus on life chances, we have classified variously as boys with aerial vision, grid-locked boys and haptic tacticians. Those who focus on lifestyle we have called cool cartographers, cool contingents and artful peripherals. Each of these involves a different configuration and mobilization of knowledge and power, and is directed towards different temporal end points as boys respond to the situations they confront and seek to invent themselves. In short, their reflexive self-construction is situational, temporal and spatial.

7
Wild and Tame Pleasures

When you think of 'soccer fans' who is it that springs to mind? The most probable image is a rowdy collection of young men in their club scarves, swaying and chanting in a soccer stadium somewhere in Europe. A community of seemingly innocent, young Buddhist monks in Tibet – heads shaven and dressed in burgundy robes – is an unlikely image. Yet, as the film *The Cup* (1998) suggests, soccer is desired by young men even in the most out of the way places. Boys taking pleasure in football is a global phenomenon. Soccer culture and the ways in which it has become enmeshed with media technologies and the international marketplace offer rich examples of a global culture of masculine pleasure. Such pleasures are often experienced in virtual communities. Yet various local circumstances inflect these virtual communities of masculine pleasure in different ways.

Norbu's atmospheric feature film *The Cup* illustrates these connections. Beautifully set in a Tibetan monastery in the foothills of the Himalayas, *The Cup* sensitively (and humorously) illustrates some of the ways in which globalization, masculinity and pleasure are connected. It tells the story of a young monk's quest to watch the World Cup soccer grand final live on television. The conflicts between tradition and youthful masculinities that arise as he seeks to fulfil his wish, speak to tensions across the globe. These are drawn into focus when the community of young men he lives amongst all seek to actualize their connections to virtual communities of soccer-loving pleasure. People from different places like different teams, and virtual 'team connections' can be as strong as local friendships.

The Cup suggests that even local contexts that are firmly connected to history and tradition are grappling with disjunctions between local specificities and virtual communities of pleasure. Such local fractures and virtual communities constitute an integral part of youthful masculinities. For, as an independent UK film journal (*Film Inside Out* 2004) has noted, even a Tibetan monastery is not immune to global hysteria: 'Ronaldo rules here, too.'

One way in which young men craft their identities is by folding together leisure and pleasure. As they plug into diverse forms of local/global leisure by 'having fun', fun becomes serious business. How can pleasure be read as anything other than a critical practice when the art of crafting one's self is a primary purpose of leisure time? This chapter explores the connections between leisure pursuits, the pleasures they generate and practices of crafting youthful masculine identities in out of the way places.

In exploring the ways that spatialized leisure/pleasures inform the production of masculinities in remote places, we examine three (broad) kinds of amusement and three accompanying shades of masculinity. First, we consider spatially embedded and culturally endorsed leisure/pleasures. These involve locally entrenched, culturally sanctified activities. The masculinities they favour are sacrosanct. As we will show, the collective pleasures associated with car cultures and football typically entail the inscription of sacrosanct gendered identities. Further, they usually (re)produce sacrosanct masculinities across the generations.

The second set of leisure/pleasures we consider is also spatially embedded, but is simultaneously both culturally endorsed and unendorsed or ambivalent. We refer here to surfing and skateboarding. They can, but do not necessarily, involve the reproduction of sacrosanct masculinities, and usually entail certain forms of cultural defiance across the generations. While the masculine identities involved can be somewhat individualized and subversive, they nonetheless still subscribe to certain local codes of masculine embodiment. Indeed, the physicality of these leisure/pleasures speaks to a traditional, valorized hegemonic construction of masculinity and thus offers the possibilities of certain levels of local social acceptance.

Third, we contemplate those leisure pursuits that tend to be spatially and culturally disembedded and unendorsed. These are associated with music, computers and the creative arts. As we will show, these can also be culturally ambiguous. While they involve scorned masculinities they may also, indirectly, invoke the sacrosanct.

Overall, while we argue that these three different sets of pleasure pursuits can be traced to sacrosanct, subversive and scorned masculinities, we also make clear that these are impressions, not mappings. Each involves diverse masculine hues that animate varying degrees of affective gender intensity. Further, as we will show, although some pleasures are more territorial than others, many nonetheless involve elements of deterritorialization as local leisure/pleasures and masculine identities become entwined with global flows of brands and imaginings.

Pleasure, order and global flows

Different practices of leisure/pleasure involve and invoke different masculinities and these masculinities link boys to the social order in various ways. Barthes (1975) helps to explain these links. He conceptualizes *plaisir* as a pleasure that is derived from the recognition of a group's distinctive values and aspirations. Indeed, *plaisir* 'produces the pleasures of relating to the social order' (Grace and Tobin 1997: 177). In contrast to the socially bounded enjoyment of *plaisir*, *jouissance* is a pleasure that 'knows no bounds' (p. 177). It is a far more voluptuous pleasure than *plaisir* and involves a 'momentary loss of subjectivity'. It tends to produce the pleasures of transgression.

Through experiences of *plaisir*, young men enjoy the pleasures of conforming to the gender order of their locality and/or to those of their particular subcultures or affective communities. Further, their experiences of geographically and culturally bounded leisure/pleasures can also link males across the generations and help to reproduce gender codes and conventions. Alternatively, *jouissance* is associated with activities and spaces that transgress adult as well as community cultural codes. These pleasures evoke risk and 'the irresistible aura of power and danger' (McDonnell 1994: 42). Through some experiences of *jouissance*, the male body may become 'a site where the meanings, limits and excesses of contemporary masculinity are tested, defined and redefined' (Iocco 2003: 1).

Of course *plaisir* and *jouissance* are alternate ends of a continuum. A vast interiority runs between them. This means that leisure/pleasures include those that quite neatly reinscribe existing gender power relationships, those that are unbounded and thus risky and dangerous to the gender order of the locality and also those that are fluid and liminal. As we will explain, many leisure activities blend *plaisir* and *jouissance*, affirming dominant means of performing masculinity and also etching out new choreographies of gender. Further, some such blends affirm relationships between the generations. These pleasures involve fathers and other adult men and offer young males the pleasures of intergenerational contact, conformity and constraint. Others negotiate new intergenerational power dynamics and yet others directly overturn adult codes. These pleasures exclude adults and provide opportunities for young males to form and perform their gendered identities beyond the limits adults impose. They thus provoke adult anxieties and this is part of the pleasure they evoke.

Boys' practices of enjoyment are intimately linked to place and space. Many of the leisure/pleasure configurations practised by young men in out of the way places are deeply embedded and embodied in local scapes – the sea, the bush, the farm, the town streets, country roads and the school oval for instance. But also, in globalizing circumstances, the prospects arise for the respatialization and re-embodiment of leisure/pleasure. Even out of the way places are immersed in the global flow of commodities and images. Many pleasures are now associated with deterritorialized forms of leisure – with images and sounds, bits and bytes, brands and logos. These are little constrained by space and time and circulate among the world's young with ease, creating global 'communities of affect' (Hebdige 1988: 90) or what Maira and Seop (2005) call 'youthscapes'. Global marketplaces and mediascapes (Appadurai 1996) have become part of localized leisure/pleasure scapes and imaginings. What they have to offer may be rearticulated in the local male vernacular or may provide opportunities for local boys to perform youthful masculinities that are literally and figuratively *out of place*. Deterritorializing pleasures may thus alter the relationships between people and places. Many inquiries into masculinity and leisure lack a spatial analytic lens and thus fail to see the significance of locally leisure-based masculinities and their connections to the globally inflected fantasy backdrop of commercialization. This chapter catalogues the many ways that the local and the global are manifest in boys' leisure and pleasure cultures beyond the metropolis in globalizing times.

Sacrosanct masculinities and embedded and endorsed leisure/pleasures

The kinds of pleasure young men glean from motor vehicles and football drew us to Barthes's (1975) notion of *plaisir*. *Plaisir* is a qualitatively and politically specific kind of pleasure, an experience of satisfaction that 'hints at an easygoing enjoyment, [more] stable in its re-enactment of cultural codes' (Rabaté 1997: 8). Yet such *plaisir* has varying intensities – some bordering on and, indeed, eventually invoking *jouissance*. For example, boys who work on cars with their dad in the shed enjoy the relaxed pleasures of participating in an established gender and generational order. Boys wildly drag-racing down the main street of their home town also experience the pleasurable fusion of the machine with the masculine. Yet the velocity, risk and defiance of adult codes that they draw into such manic machining produces an intense affect that shades into *jouissance*. Nonetheless, despite such intense defiance, these pleasures still support and reproduce existent models of masculinity, as we will now explain. We will then show that similar claims can be made about football. The point here is that while the pleasures of gender and those of generation may not always be in tune, they may nonetheless both ultimately confirm sacrosanct masculinities.

Machine accessories

My boyfriend was recently in a car crash . . . Yeah, he was a passenger . . . the car crash happened at 12.35 in the morning . . . Oh, they were going along and another girl I know was in front of them. They were about a metre still behind her, his tyre blew out and he nearly lost control. Then he lost control when they went over that hump in the road and he went up the gutter and all the windows shattered, he hit a 60 km sign. Yeah, and then that made them slide and they slid into the stovvie pole.[1] With the Ute, like the cab came away from the back of it and the back of the Ute was wrapped around the stovvie pole and the cab, like in front of the Ute, went flying, they got airborne and hit side-on to one tree and went smack bang into another tree and the tree got ripped out by its roots.

My boyfriend has got a broken rib and three stitches in the back of his head and he walked out of it, he was fine; and the driver, he just had a huge swollen collarbone and shoulder . . . He can't see, he had to have a big piece of glass dug out of his eye . . . Yeah, the police had bodybags and all and they walked up to the car and no one was in there and they go, 'Who's dragged them out? Has the ambo's come and taken them?' Rod and Sam walked up and like, 'We're the guys in the car', and straight away the cops go, 'Go and buy a lottery ticket'. [Laughter]

Joanna Norbert, the narrator, later points out that Rod Halliday and Sam Hamilton now 'have got the biggest skid [in town] . . . it was something like 20 metres long when they hit the brakes'. Such wild leisure/ pleasures clearly have their dangers and their rewards. This particular case is now a local legend and the two survivors are local heroes.

Often investigations of youthful masculinity and cars focus on the high injury and mortality rates of young men (Spriggs 2000; Hartig and Dunn 1998) or the high instances of drink driving (Roeper and Voas 1999). These constitute a significant and often tragic backdrop to youthful car cultures beyond the metropolis. Car accidents and injuries are especially an issue for young men. We heard many dreadful stories about young people being badly hurt, killed or killing others in car accidents. But our focus here is on the meanings and symbols attached to car/machine cultures, their implications for youthful masculine identities and the pleasures, not the pain, involved.

For young males in many places around the world, the motor vehicle is imbued with desirability:

> Motor vehicles and their use offer boys and youth engaged in the construction of masculinity a number of experiences that many of them very much want: a sense of technical mastery, a realm that is symbolically masculine, a forum for friendship and peer recognition, thrills, laughter, and a certain amount of danger.
>
> (Walker, Butland and Connell 2000: 159)

Cars, trucks, Utes, motorbikes and even pushbikes and go-karts occupy an important place in the lives of young men outside the cities. This is due in part to the distances they need to travel, the basic practicalities of getting from one place to another when there is no public transport. It is also due to the fact that various vehicles are integral to many local worlds of work. Further, such machines are layered with different meanings and evoke different pleasures depending on the activity, space of use and time of day.

For many young men outside the city, cars are a normal aspect of everyday life and they evoke everyday pleasures and offer many positive opportunities for intergenerational contact and learning. Lots of boys spend time 'mucking about' in the sheds with their fathers or family friends as they work together to fix up cars, bikes or other farm machinery. Michael Ammerlaan, age 16 from Renmark, likes it that

> We've got buggies, motorbikes and an old car that we are fixing up ... When we go home we either drive the buggies or work on one ... My next-door neighbour, he's helped me with putting a motor in the buggy.

A shared passion for machines is sometimes a key point of interaction between males within and across the generations. Take Trent Finck, age 13, also from Renmark. Trent has great respect for machinery. He loves 'just the power of it, you can do so much things with it and create all this energy, like for electricity, and coal, build things'.

Trent's father used to own his own trucking company, but was forced to sell it and now drives a bus. Trent's best memories are of buying the first truck in his father's fleet; it was a Kenworth and a very fine piece of machinery. Trent misses the trucks, and being able to go on the long-haul journeys with his father. He also misses being able to show off the trucks to his friends; buses are definitely not as impressive. Large machines are often read as a masculine status symbol but they are also a source of great pleasure. Trent's lament over the loss of his father's trucks has been echoed in research elsewhere. Discussing the extent of the influences that father's cars have on their son's lives, Walker (2003: 51) notes that a number of young men in her research claimed that: 'cars are in my blood'. She expands:

> For boys and young men, car culture is a medium for emotional bonding between fathers and sons, as well as for affective relations with other male relatives . . . affective relations with brothers, uncles, brothers-in-law and cousins . . . were mediated through motor vehicles.
>
> (Walker 2003: 53)

The embedded pleasures associated with a love of machines are often also associated with part-time work and career plans and thus the tinkering alongside fathers or other adult males takes on another meaning. These activities are transformed into a type of training both for the mechanical aspects of the work, and intergenerational training on how to be suitably male. Riley Stephens, age 14 from Coober Pedy, wants to be a diesel mechanic like his father. He works as a 'grease monkey' part time at his father's firm. He has to do all the messy jobs like cleaning the oil out of the pit. But he thinks it is good experience for the future, 'I'm learning heaps', he says. He also enjoys hanging out with his dad and the other mechanics; feeling 'one of the boys' – even if he doesn't always understand the jokes: 'I pick up heaps of stuff and the guys are really good. They tease ya a bit though, but that's OK.'

Many young men in Renmark work on family owned and operated fruit blocks. In the course of this work most drive the farm machinery – Utes, motorbikes and tractors. Further, some families pay their children for working on the block in the form of an old car. Other boys buy one themselves, and with the help of older men do up these 'bombs' and drive them around the block. Within enclosed spaces and familiar places, the collective nature of such assemblages of machines and males, produces deep group-based experiences of *plaisir*. By owning and operating machines, boys connect to other boys and older men, as well as to the broader intergenerational masculine order.

But what happens when the enclosed spaces and familiar places open out and when the male–machine assemblage speeds up and breaks apart in intergenerational terms? It is at such points that *plaisir* intensifies. Unbounded space, heavy machines and speed can amplify *plaisir* as is the case of Trent's fantasy about the days when he is old enough to get his own licence and truck and move to the Northern Territory where the landscape is more open, where bigger trucks are allowed and where there are no speed limits. But high velocity, public space and corporeal risk can also produce *jouissance*. Take the case of 'bush bashing', a favourite activity of Renmark boys. Simon Barnes (age 15) explains:

> Bush bashing is when you go in your car, out on bumpy tracks and just go fast around them. Like you just do it in an old dump of a car so you don't have to worry about wrecking it.

Bush bashing involves the pleasure of reckless and risky driving; of speeding, skidding, sliding, swerving and stopping suddenly in swirls of sand, dust and mud. Often cars are bogged, crashed and written off. The young men who indulge in these leisure/pleasures are often under the legal driving age. They get away with it because it occurs on private property. To these boys, dangerous driving signifies freedom and masculine prowess. This intense embedded leisure/pleasure can be characterized as an 'addiction to affliction' (Iocco 2005) in which a 'lack of corporeal integrity ... is meaningful within the social context of belonging and membership'. This 'addiction to affliction' transgresses adult codes of safety, and such dangerous transgressions are part of the pleasure – the wild pleasure of *jouissance*.

Gaining a driving licence gives young men access to new pleasures. So too does getting their own car. Cars are status symbols and as such are paraded around the streets and inspected and assessed by peers. But more importantly, a licence and a car mean an end to reliance on adults, and taking charge of their own movements. It invokes the *plaisir* of gaining certain adult freedoms. Boys can legally drive out the shed, off the farm and on to the open road and 'adulthood'. Gaining a licence is often discussed as a rite of passage, a leap into the adult world (Walker

1988). 'Basically if you have a car you are free', says Jonathan Nicholls (age 14, Morwell). It also means access to wilder pleasures associated with greater speed and new spaces. Charlie Belew (14, Coober Pedy) explains; 'I think driving around pretty fast is cool, it's good fun . . . It makes you feel good, just being able to control something.' He especially likes doing 'burn-outs' and leaving his mark on the landscape. He likes to return and look at his skid marks and say, 'They're mine, I did them.' It is a way of remembering the pleasure of control; the pleasure in registering his presence in the local landscape for all to see. Joanna Norbert, age 15 and a keen and astute observer of the local male car culture, discusses the 'burn out' and girls' disdainful attitude to it:

> *Joanna*: A lot of teenage guys try and show off and do burn-outs and stuff. It's really pathetic, but, [laugh].
> *Anna K.*: Why do they do that, what's the appeal?
> *Joanna*: Who can do the biggest burn-out, who can get the biggest mark? It's just a thing with them, they love to do it and make a lot of screeches. I don't see why because it ruins the car badly – bald tyres and all.
> *Anna K.*: So there is a kind of competition to have the longest skid marks?
> *Joanna*: Yeah. Every time you hear them bragging about it, 'Oh, I did this wicked burn out on Mackers' corner and left this huge mark. Just go see it.' They're always carrying on about it. Most of the girls just sit there, 'Oh wow!' [sarcastic laughter] you know, 'Who cares?'

Whether girls approve or not, cars, velocity and jeopardy are a feature of the young males–machine–pleasure assemblages in non-city locations. Campbell and Phillips's (1995) analysis of rural leisure sites includes a discussion of dangerous driving through the example of 'circle work' at Bachelor and Spinster balls – formal 'black tie' events for young singles often held in shearing sheds. They describe this combination of speed, danger and skill as a specific characteristic of the performance of youthful masculinity. Campbell (1993) in her work on dispossessed working-class city youth in Britain finds similar linkages between cars, speed and gaining a 'macho' reputation. Walker (1988) argues that this involves a form of protest masculinity and is a rite of passage into manhood – which is denied to certain young men because of their exclusion from the labour market and the academic curriculum; 'hyper machismo protest', he calls it. Transgression, risk, danger and pleasure are important features of the youthful male–machine assemblage. Charlie Belew, from Coober Pedy, likes to ride motorbikes and to taunt the police, delighting in illegal rides on the road. 'Yeah, it is pretty good fun', he says, 'It's even better when it is someone else's motorbike and they don't know it's me.' The most intense affect arises from brazenly breaking the law and taunting authority.

Friday night is 'laps' night in the town of Renmark. Young people, particularly young men, come from all over the Riverland district to participate. They come in their cars and drive repeatedly and noisily around town. The cars are usually congested with passengers and the music is on 'full-blast'. Here the kinaesthetic affects of *plaisir* are inflamed as boys' practices of embedding themselves, mechanically, in local landscapes and experimenting with speed are coupled with sonic force and close bodily contact – the noise of cars, the thump of accompanying music, the rush of the wind in their faces. Through sound and speed they inscribe their identities in local space. Sometimes they hold competitions or speed around the back roads outside of town trying to test their skill against the tight bends and dirt roads. The aim is to show control of the vehicle, to see how far they can push it without rolling the car or having an accident. As Simone Mucovich (age 16) observes about her male friends:

> Being cool is overwhelmingly associated with cars here. Boys have to be tough, have a flash car, and have money to be cool. They do the laps around town. Some girls do it as well but not as much as the boys . . . The boys get into drag racing and doing burn-outs. It's a P-Plate tradition.[2] As soon as you get your Ps you have to get a car and smoke it out. Boys do it to be tough, to be manly.

Driving and doing 'laps' of the town are intricately gendered performances for males and females and it is important to get it right symbolically. For instance, status is associated with where you sit in the car. Whoever sits in the front passenger seat is second in status to the driver. Joanna Norbert elucidates:

> My boyfriend, he's close to getting his licence. He's already got a car and he's doing it up. Everyone knows that when he gets his licence, I'll own the passenger seat. If you've got a boyfriend and they drive, then you own the passenger seat. You're the one that sits in it. [So his best mate, will have to sit in the back?] Yeah. Oh, some don't like

it, like my boyfriend's best friend, Freddy, he kind of thought HE owned the passenger seat and then Frank said, 'No, Joanna sits there', and he'll kind of share it. When I'm not in the car, he owns it; when I'm in the car, he sits in the back. They don't really mind as long as they're actually IN a car, driving around.

Young women are important machine accessories. Much cachet is attached to a car full of girls. Here is Joanna again: 'It just seems like you have a car and you're noticed. The guys just love to drive around with all girls in their car. They look special. Yeah, like top notch: "Oh look, I've got a load of five girls in my car." ' As Jones (1999) has shown in her study of gender and identity among young rural women, girls add to the intensity and voluptuousness of *plaisir*.

Football and fitting in

Outside the cities much leisure time is structured around sport. It is a central part of the lives of many young men in Eden, Renmark, Coober Pedy and Morwell and includes swimming, tennis, golf, table tennis, badminton, ten pin bowling, basketball, hockey, volleyball, cricket and various forms of football; soccer, rugby and Australian Rules. Most boys play many sports. Aamon Baker, age 15 from Eden, is a typical boy in this regard. He states plainly: 'I have got sport, which is the main part of my life, and everything sort of revolves around that.' Many boys' lives centre on team sports, especially football, and so it is football that we largely focus on here.

Around the world, no matter what the code or location, football is generally read as a setting where males learn how to perform culturally revered masculinities. It is widely understood as a site where certain males can demonstrate their superiority to and difference from other, lesser males. It calls into play what Simpson (1994: 72) says is a process of 'subjective elimination' whereby that which does not measure up psychologically or socially is stigmatized and weeded out, and where what remains is culturally valorized through intergenerational and peer approval. Such lines of argument are so widely acknowledged that we will not pursue them here except to say that football beyond the metropolis is little different. It is certainly a locally entrenched, culturally sanctified leisure activity. It also conscripts young males to sacrosanct forms of masculinity.

The kudos associated with sport, and football in particular, in non-city localities makes it an important social structuring device. As our discussion of the Krakouer brothers (ABC Radio 2005) in Chapter 5 showed, Australian Rules football offers a large-scale example of the social power of such sports. As a particularly high-profile sport within Australian popular culture, success on the 'Aussie Rules' football field can make team members national heroes. In small town terms, football skills can be just as valuable. They are the making of local heroes.

Indeed, football creates exclusions and hierarchies, as Susan Dorkins from Renmark (age 14) indicates. 'Everyone plays', she says, 'Like if you don't play a sport, you're usually counted as square because you're into the books more than you are into sport. Sport is a big issue around here.' Such views have significant implications for boys who do not want to play sport, as is the case with Gem Johnston, the young music enthusiast we meet later in this chapter, who says with great indignation: 'There's a lot of sports freaks around here who don't like me and my friends a bit, because we hate sport.' We indicated at the outset that *plaisir* involves the feeling that one's distinctive values and aspirations have been recognized and affirmed. Another side of this is the cruel pleasure of excluding others. It is thus pertinent to notice how frequently boys argue that girls have no desire to engage in sporting activities. The following remarks are typical:

> Girls do not want to play sport because they don't want to get sweaty.
>
> (Jed Duda, age 13 from Morwell)

> Girls are afraid of making a nonce of themselves. 'Oh, I will mess my makeup up' and stuff, and guys are like, 'Who cares, if you get dirty you get dirty?'
>
> (Frank Chigetto, age 15 from Morwell)

While there are less sporting opportunities for females than males outside of the cities, many girls and women play sport and some do very well in the boys' domain of soccer. Boys who construct girls as too fearful and fastidious to play sport enjoy the pleasure of such 'subjective elimination'; of the disavowal and disapproval of the feminine. At the same time they also gain the endorsement of many of their peers.

Clearly sport is a major source of the pleasure of prestige but it is also a source of other pleasures. Football, for instance, provides access to the pleasures associated with specific ways of embodying space – it provides a fusion between body–skill–speed–space, which is exhilarating. It is also associated with the pleasures of social belonging and acceptance. Playing team sports provides social contact with peers and, in general, eases the way socially:

There are a couple of new people playing in our rugby league team. As soon as they got here they had a whole group of friends, because they play footy . . . If you play sport; you have friends straight away.

(Paul Jones, age 16 from Eden)

Intergenerational connections are a prominent feature of local sport. In many instances, interest in sport and sporting involvement have been passed down from parents to their children. Sport offers an important opportunity for intergenerational contact and mentoring. Parents are usually involved in one way or another in local youths' sporting activities – as coaches, trainers, spectators, drivers and even as active participants on occasions, as Shawn Rodgers (age 13 from Morwell) explains:

They have father and son days. Last year the sons were winning, so the fathers just started cheating. It was pretty funny. We had it in the bag, and they started pushing people over and things.

Non-city sports require parents to convey their young to different sporting venues across the region, sometimes quite frequently and over quite considerable distances if they are in major competitions. Generally, the rituals associated with weekend sport and weekday training bind families and communities together across the generations.

The *plaisir* assemblages fashioned by young men through playing sports come in other guises too. At times *plaisir* arises for young men through their connections to the disciplined, regularized and collective routines of team training sessions, reaching full fruition when their team wins a tough match or triumphs over an entire league. Training requires young men to behave according to adults' rules and routines. They are disciplined and are also expected to be self-disciplined. Some resist but others enjoy the synchronicity. Take Peter James, age 13 from Coober Pedy, who says: 'If you want to be tough, then get tough friends, but if you just want to have fun then you go for people who play sport.' Team sport can even extract such social discipline from 'wild boys'. For example, Marshall Buckley, age 17 from Eden, has recently dropped out of school and is unemployed. His usual appearance is scruffy and unkempt. He regularly uses drugs and alcohol as a form of entertainment. But Marshall is a very good rugby league player and when involved in football his transformation is dramatic. When he plays he is dressed smartly in his uniform and is focused and professional throughout the match. He dreams of becoming a professional football player and is quietly proud of his skills and abilities. He regularly attends training and trains hard.

But *plaisir* is not only a tame pleasure. It also involves dangerous pleasures that nonetheless still link those who enjoy such pleasures to the social order. Many observers, including Connell (2000a), argue that the competitiveness and status attached to organized male sport encourages arrogant, aggressive and violent behaviour on and off the field. It could thus be argued that one of the pleasures of football involves conforming to such dominant and dominating codes of behaviour. Patrick Thompson (age 15 from Renmark) exemplifies this point. Patrick hates school, does no schoolwork, is always in trouble, but is passionate about football. He says that the only reason he comes to school is so he can be in the school football team. Patrick only plays to win: 'It's great when you slaughter the other team, run rings around them.' He is very disciplined at training, and works hard to hone his skills. However, his passion for winning leads him to transgress the acceptable codes of the game, his desire for intensity pushing him beyond safe body–skill–space assemblages. If Patrick's teammates are not listening to the coach or training hard enough, he physically threatens them. This aggression also moves on to the sports field: Patrick threatens his teammates if they are not playing well enough. The compulsion to invoke aggression and physical violence into his *plaisir* assemblage is part of Patrick's masculine identity and football its full expression.

Other dangerous expressions of *plaisir* involve the drinking rituals associated with sport. Country sports clubs are an important location for intergenerational 'piss ups'. Campbell and Phillips (1995: 114) observe of rural golf clubs that the post-game drinking rituals involve 'alcoholic solidarity and mateship'. As Scott Whalley, age 17 from Eden, says: 'There's always been alcohol with sport.' And some sports, particularly football, are particularly associated with alcohol. Scott continues, 'Football in this town's pretty big and everyone that plays it and supports it, drinks. They're all sponsored by the pub.' Also, some sports clubs have a stronger drinking culture than others:

At my club they drink beer and that. They would rather drink beer than play cricket . . . At St Vincents, they are all drunks. At La Trobe there is probably only one drunk, but he doesn't drink while he plays cricket because that is illegal, but at St Vincents they do. They drink, then go out to bat, then come back in and start drinking again.

(Shawn Rodgers, age 13 from Morwell)

Key occasions for drinking in sports clubs are after the match, particularly after a win. Aamon Baker, age 15 from Eden is an exceptional young sportsman who has been promoted into the senior cricket and football teams and thus has a lot of contact with the older guys in these sports clubs. After matches his teammates 'get into the grog' and celebrate. Aamon is under the legal drinking age and his parents don't want him to drink. But Aamon feels a lot of pressure from his teammates. 'You get pushed into alcohol because everyone around you is drinking', he observes. He recognizes that drinking is a normalized pleasure associated with local male sport, that it is also associated with acceptable masculine identities, and that if he is to fully relate to this particular social order, he will need to violate the laws on under-age drinking. As this example suggests, the under-age alcoholic consumption associated with local sport involves dangerous *plaisir* for young males; some, like Aamon, deal with this quite sensibly, others deal with it by 'getting pissed and legless'.

And now a few words about ethnoscapes and mediascapes – particularly the inward flow of people, sponsors, brands and images. It is these that are disembedding what has long been a highly embedded sport and are also invoking a new sense of possible lives. Australian Rules football is the main game in Morwell. A lively competition exists between the different clubs and towns in the region. Rivalries are fierce; teams want to win the game and they also want to win sponsors. Team uniforms are paid for by corporate sponsors who are normally local businesses such as the pub, as we noted earlier. A successful team has an easier time attracting sponsors, thus having better uniforms and club support. Of course, the best sponsors are those that have the most money to spend and these are often local franchises of global corporations. A corporate sponsor is entitled to put their name or logo on the uniforms they pay for. Thus, different teams are emblazoned with a range of global signs. McDonalds is a popular sponsor, often the most generous: the golden arches are a common site on the uniforms of Morwell teams. The national supermarket chain – Coles – is also highly sought after, as is Telstra, the national Australian telecommunications company. Corporate logos vye for attention on the football field in places beyond the metropolis, just as they do in the virtual world of televised sport.

Sport is immersed in the global flow of corporate signs and images. Global brands and logos saturate the world of sport and as we indicated at the start of this chapter, this global flow is not restricted to the upper echelons of sporting culture.[3] Small-town teams are also connected to the intricate 'world-wide web of branding' (Klein 2000: xi–xxi).

Sporting bodies are branded and commodified (Fitzclarance 2005). Indeed, the globalized world of sport is intricately tied up in what Shilling (1993) calls the 'body project'; that is, the production of a 'desirable' body for purposes of ego and social exchange. Notions of desirable male bodies, fit, muscular, controlled and controllable, circulate globally in a deterritorialized fashion along with multinational brands. Conceptions of desirable male bodies and the products of multinational companies resonate and hybridize locally in the form of embodied biographical projects (Shilling 1993).

An example of the sprawling reach of this 'world-wide web of branding' can be found in Coober Pedy. Watching the boys on the soccer pitch, you might think you have stumbled upon a junior league for the Soccer World Cup. Young male bodies are dressed in the soccer shirts of a range of nations – Greece, Italy, England, Spain. Who would believe that these international sporting rivalries would be played out in the middle of the Australian desert? The boys in Coober Pedy love their soccer and support their favourite European teams with ardour and vigour. Shouts of 'Go Greece' and 'Italy forever' echo across the oval. Nicholas Moody's family emigrated from England when he was only four. His loyalties lie with the English Soccer League; his heroes are all English soccer players. He still has an English accent even though he has been in Australia ten years. He proudly wears his English colours. Indeed, all the boys on the Coober Pedy oval wear the shirt of 'their' overseas team, even though they play on the same team locally.

This local–global football connection speaks to Appadurai's (1996) powerful work on possible lives opened up by media representation. For example, the globalized broadcasting of World Cup soccer has allowed isolated South Australian country boys to think of themselves in relation to David Beckham and other such superstars of the soccer stadium. In these young men's 'possible lives' (Appadurai 1996), fame, fortune, prestige and recognition are somehow achievable – or at least imaginable – through the lived connection of playing soccer on the Coober Pedy oval and watching international, globally televised soccer on 'the box' at home.

A popular filmic example of the possible lives made available through media representations of football can be found in Gurinder Chada's 2002 film *Bend it Like Beckham*. This small-budget film was a global box-office success, arguably because of its capacity to speak to a community united by soccer culture and international soccer media. This film tells of Jess Bhamra (Parminder Nagra), a young, first-generation English Indian woman who escapes the confining realities of her cultural location by playing soccer. In so doing, Jess hacks into a global virtual community of soccer (and soccer fandom) and mobilizes this virtual, cultural power to transgress the gendered, racialized and firmly embedded expectations of her family and immediate community. While *Bend it Like Beckham* speaks to the valiancy of possible lives opened up via media representation and illustrates the affective communities brought together through such media texts, the kinds of transgression of the social order mobilized by Jess are not often accessed by football boys in out of the way places. The allure of football is intensified, boys' fantasies become more global, but the 'body projects' of football's heroes and sponsors, be they local or global, do not usually invite the pleasures of transgression. Earlier, we mentioned Nicholas Moody from Coober Pedy. His athletic body is his project and the primacy of sport is emblazoned across it not just in the form of his English soccer shirt, but also in the form of his Nike sneakers and Adidas pants. He spends all his spare time on the school oval, resisting school through sport and using sport to express his anti-authority sentiments. Conforming to local and global sacrosanct masculinities through football is his route to respect locally and his ticket to his 'possible life' out of town and back to England.

Subversive masculinities and embedded and unendorsed leisure/pleasures

Individual and unorganized, as opposed to team and organized, sports are becoming increasingly attractive to young males around the world (Evers 2004; Wheaton 2000). These sports include surfing and skateboarding. Surfing is popular amongst young men in the small seaside town of Eden and skateboarding is a boy subculture of some size in Renmark and Morwell. The rise in popularity of such sports has provoked many to speculate about their appeal in comparison with those leisure/pleasures that very obviously invoke sacrosanct masculinities. Drawing from their study of urban skateboarders, Karsten and Pel (2001: 327) argue that 'skateboarding can be seen as a way of experimenting with new forms of masculinity'. Beal (1996) claims that skateboarding is implicitly a critique of organized sport with its associated adult control, conformity and competition. Skateboarding, she argues, explicitly values the participants' control and self-expression. She suggests that as a consequence, skateboarding invites counter-hegemonic ways of being male – despite its exclusion of girls. This implies that skateboarding involves a form of cultural defiance with regard to sacrosanct masculinities and their reproduction across the generations. It is our view that the pleasures of skateboarding involve a form of *jouissance,* 'a violent, climactic bliss closer to loss, death, fragmentation, and the disruptive rapture experienced when transgressing limits' (Rabaté 1997: 8). The transgressions involved here are generational. However, while the masculinities involved are to some extent subversive, they are nonetheless also in sympathy with certain codes of masculine embodiment.

Boys skateboard in spaces away from adult surveillance and regulation, in specially provided skateboard parks, but also anywhere with the right surfaces and challenges – footpaths, stairs, malls, driveways, walls and empty swimming pools. These spaces provide a forum to act independently of adults in increasingly regulated times for the young, and to 'do' maleness somewhat differently. They 'colonize public spaces', observe Karsten and Pel (2001: 327), who also say: 'Groups of skateboarders are continuously putting public spaces in and out of use. In a sense, skateboarders can be considered the nomads of the city.' Skateboarders delight in the impertinent and transgressive use of public space and in the defiance of associated polite adult codes. Zac Field, age 16, describes the wild pleasures of skateboarding:

> Me and a couple of friends, about 15 of us, we'd just skate all day every day, 24/7 if we could. After school, weekends, we're all skating . . . Every day after school, just let it loose and just hang in, chill and do anything you want to. It's heaps of fun, just being together and having fun and doing things you want to do. Security tells you off for going through malls and stuff – but like not *really* . . . You don't really have anyone telling you off. You do, but only old people, security and people like that, but not much. It's not your parents . . . who only tell you off if you hurt yourself. It's just like freer and you skate, skate, skate.

Skateboarders do indeed get in the way of the public in Renmark and Morwell and in some instances risk knocking people down in the street, but nonetheless their behaviour is unregulated. This relative freedom from adult control and the transgressive use of public spaces are central components of skateboarding *jouissance.* So too are the deployment of dexterity and the challenges of embodied risk. Young men who skate for pleasure relish the thrills and skills of speeding down streets and of weaving precariously through the obstacles of people and posts, of accomplishing complex jumping manoeuvres and leaping down hazardous stairwells. These young men's athletic performances connect to these unbounded spaces in creative ways. There is a 'bodies on the line' mentality enjoyed and fostered within skateboard culture. Shilling's (1993) notion of the 'body project' is of limited analytical value here, as body reflexivity is overshadowed by a disregard for safety and by the importance of taking embodied risks. Status and pleasure are accrued through risk and dexterity. Zac has a blatant disregard for bodily concerns. He talks nonchalantly about skateboarding injuries, but has fire in his eyes when he talks about 'doing ten stairs':

> I'm known to be, like, heaps reckless on a skateboard. I don't know how many bones I've broken: my arm, twice, broken a disc and a shoulder, dislocating my wrist, done my leg. I was nearly paraplegic, done my left sciatic nerve . . . just pulled it a bit but it didn't snap, so I was in a wheelchair for about a month, just couldn't walk. That was lucky . . . Yeah, we are heaps wicked skaters. . . . When I first broke my arm it was like, 'Oh no, I broke my arm!', but now when you break your arm, its like, 'I just broke my arm'. Yeah, you don't really worry . . . my mum and dad are heaps worried about me because when I break stuff, they go, 'Hey you broke your leg again', and I really don't care and like they're going, 'You should do, it's your life. If you hurt yourself really bad you're going to hurt for the rest of your life.' I really don't care. Yeah, but they just worry too much . . . If you saw the way we skate! We do all ten stairs – I can do ten, Fred can't do ten, he can only do eight – but I'll leap ten stairs and like it's heaps high.

Surfing also invokes the sorts of pleasure associated with *jouissance*. It has an irresistible aura of power and danger and also involves the allure of transgressing the social order to some extent. This is partly because, for some local adults, young men who spend most of their waking time surfing rather than getting a job and treating surfing as a part-time hobby violate the traditional local codes attached to hard physical paid work. Further, the subculture that goes with surfing is regarded as rather deviant, particularly as it is associated with trendy dress codes, drugs and wild beach parties.

Like skating, the leisure/pleasures of surfing are known to young men in terms of embodied affect (Evers 2004). As Evers (2004) contends, 'fibreglass meshes with flesh, wax, fear, excitement, economics, sweat, politics and representations'. In choreographing such an enmeshment, young surfboard riders create 'radically different spaces that take us in unexpected directions' (Healy and Muecke 2004), challenging certain theoretical paradigms for thinking about masculinity and pleasure. Here masculinity is articulated in terms of sensations, in acts of boundary crossing. Such acts have meaning that exceeds the situation in which they are produced.

A startling illustration of the boundless pleasure young men get from surfing can be found in the ensuing description of the sport. In this quotation, taken from the Australian newspaper *The Age*, the surfer, his surroundings and the spectator become melded through the unbounded joys of surfing and watching surfing. The observer struggles to adequately represent his experience in words:

> What I can't explain is the way he looked as he came upright on the board, and hitched back, and drove upwards, dragging a white line through the blue. The way he twisted and flicked downwards, feet planted, toes flexing. I couldn't see his toes, of course. But I could feel them, the way you can sometimes feel a musician's fingers in his music. Toes, torso, eartips: a whole person tucking and stretching on a little lip of liquid on the wet skin of the world. It was like watching God surf.
>
> (Hooton 2005, 40)

This spectator could feel what it might be like to be in the surfer's body. His pleasure as an observer exceeded his visual field and crossed into his sensory and kinaesthetic awareness. He had become enmeshed with the act of surfing that he was beholding.

For the young men in our localities, both skateboarding and surfing mean living in the moment, making their own rules and pushing themselves to see how far they can go. They risk their bodies, and indeed their lives, in order to make the most breath-taking performances possible. The heightened experiences of risk that come with increased technical prowess are, as Zac explains, a pleasure that lies in feeling 'like you really don't care' – it knows no bounds. Even so, to the extent that skateboarding and surfing depend upon desirable male bodies – fit, muscular and controlled, and on competitive physical performance and reputation – they still partake of the sacrosanct masculinities associated with the affective fusion of body, skill and speed and the control of space that we noted earlier in this chapter. Both invoke the modalities of masculinity so frequently valued beyond the metropolis. They are outdoors, involve risk, are highly physical and require perseverance and endurance. The point, then, is that skating and surfing involve rather ambivalent forms of masculinity; they are unendorsed but also to some extent endorsed.

Corporate brands and images are not restricted to the sports fields in out of the way places. Streetscapes and seascapes also offer many a blank canvas on which to paint global signs. The youthful streetscapes of Renmark, for example, are globally marked. Boys' skateboards, bikes and scooters are branded with a plethora of popular labels such as BMX, Fox, Diamond Back, ABC, Zero, Toy Machine, Huffer and Circa. Here the street ironically reconstructs a 'global marketplace' via the young men's performances of subcultural leisure/pleasure. Surfboards, boats, surf skis, windsurfers, wetsuits, sunglasses, and T-shirts, trousers, hats have all become surfaces for branding. Any day in Eden sees the young men and women of the community covered in surfing logos such as RipCurl, Billabong and Quiksilver – labels that began as Australian brands and then went global. Part of these trade-marked garments' identity utility is to brand the wearer, to announce their subcultural membership and with this, their brand of masculinity – locally dissident, globally ascendant.

Quiksilver, for example, offers streamlined, quick-drying, comfortable surf shorts. However, Quiksilver board shorts are much more than their lightweight fabric. They give life to particular masculine identities. A global marketing fable, developed to sell Quiksilver online, reconstructs the brand's early success in terms of masculinity and pleasure. Quiksilver was and remains successful, so the story goes, because of an instinctive masculine prowess that has evolved through the hard labours of pleasure. This 'marketing fable' informs us:

> So Greenie and Law put them [their shorts] on and went surfing. Hard at it, all day, every day. People notice what works. They also pay attention to individuals who devote years to chasing a dream. Soon other riders would do anything to get one of these elusive newfangled board shorts. This was the birth of Quiksilver, the genuine, original, functional choice of the hard-core participant.
>
> (Quiksilver 2004)

This extract invests Quiksilver with vast amounts of masculine bravado, a desire to inhabit unbounded seascapes around the world ('individuals who devote years to chasing a dream') and a kind of pleasure that is enmeshed in physical labour. 'Hard-core' surfers are those who, apart from wearing Quiksilver, devote most of their physical, emotional and financial resources to furthering their skills on a surfboard and to chasing waves wherever they are – to pursuing 'Endless Summer' around the globe. The technical prowess required to catch a wave or 'drop in' on another surfer's, is a performance of skills that takes years to develop.

This extreme dedication and physical dexterity all fuel the emotional velocity that Quiksilver harnesses in marketing itself as 'the genuine, original, functional choice' (Quiksilver 2004).

Quiksilver illustrates the ways in which the global world of branding can endorse locally unendorsed masculinities. The brand can be deployed as a sign of local defiance and also used to stake a claim to alternative masculinities that transcend the local.

Scorned masculinities and disembedded and unendorsed leisure/pleasures

Cultural and subcultural studies of youthful masculinities, such as the recent work of Connor (2003) and Homan (2003), frequently consider the role of music, computers and film in identity building. But rarely do they consider what engaging in such leisure pursuits means for males in isolated places where such pursuits may be marginalized or even stigmatized. Enjoying such leisure/pleasures can mean that young males feel locally lonesome. Yet they can offer these young men a means of escape by disembedding them from their local loneliness. Global communities of affect that come together through music, film, popular culture, new media, fashion and computer games offer isolated young men the possibility of imagining themselves in relation to different places and communities that are filled with the possibilities which their embedded lives cannot provide.

In the form of international bands, albums and songs, global consumer culture is ever present in the soundscapes of most young men who live in remote locations. While most take pleasure in these, only a few in our localities make music a central feature of their lives. For the occasional boys who do, pursuing their enthusiasm for making sound is difficult. Take the example of Gem Johnston, a 14-year-old boy from Renmark. Gem has one passion: heavy metal music. He belongs to a global community of 'metal heads' that he's plugged into via such sonic aesthetics as heavy, overbearing vocals, power chords and loud, driven grunge. Like many global metal fans, Gem craves the raw rock' n' roll sounds of heavy metal blasted full volume from the best speakers he can find. Gem also plays guitar and has a makeshift band made up of a few friends, though they can rarely get together to jam. Gem is full of frustration because the drummer in his band has recently gone overseas and will be away for some time. The band now has no rhythm keeper and no one else is available locally to take his place. So Gem fills his spare time in the local music shop, 'Flipside', poring over CDs, listening to and discussing new bands and songs with whoever is around, mainly the shop owner. Gem seeks the bliss – or *jouissance* – of producing his own music, but is confined to consuming that of others.

There are very few local boys of Gem's age who are as much 'into music' as he is. Dominant constructions of masculinity within his school reject those who actually play music, often describing them as 'poofy' (Seamus Doyle, age 16). Gem observes bitterly:

> It's pretty hard to find the people to be a member [of the band]. Nobody is really interested in music round here. They're more interested in sport, so there's not really a lot of people to choose from . . . Some of them tease you because you like music. Some of them call you faggot.

The dominance of sporting masculinity within the town means that Gem is forced to look elsewhere for like-minded others and he has thus made contact with local adult musicians. Gem explains that the owner of 'Flipside' has 'done lots for the music scene':

> He's had these jam sessions at the footy club where everybody gets together. Usually about a hundred people go there from all over the Riverland, they all bring their instruments.

These jam sessions sadly came to an end when the football club refused the use of its premises due to 'costs'. The club thus effectively closed down live local music. Gem says, 'I feel rotten, like they do nothing here for anybody like me and Joe [his friend]. They only care about sport.'

The example of Gem offers an insight into the many complexities of globalization and youthful leisure, for while Gem is able to consume the deterritorialized soundscapes of the globalized music industry and to imagine himself somewhere else, fulfilling his yearning to play music with others is problematic in this small community. There is no music subculture in the town as the population is too small and Gem cannot easily access his affinity groups in nearby towns. Age and distance are insurmountable barriers. He states: 'I met somebody who was from Waikerie [a small town over an hours drive away from Renmark]. He said, like, "Come and jam if you want to", and I said, "No, no you're too far away man. I'll *never* get there".' Globalization has not worked to reconfigure time and space here, there is no implosion of space into time for Gem. Quite the opposite; his lack of mobility means that

Waikerie 'may as well be on the other side of the world'. Gem, like many young people beyond the metropolis, endures 'enforced localization' (Bauman 1998a: 70); they are 'space bound'.

Non-city localities offer little room for the development of alternative male subcultures. Those pursuing different modes of expression and different interests can experience difficulty fitting into small communities, to the point of marginalization. Some hold out anyway, as does Gem, some conform and some seek a haven in the worlds of their imaginations. Take two more examples. Christian Young came to Coober Pedy from Melbourne. In Melbourne he enjoyed living a punk lifestyle: the music, the embodied adornments as well as his large group of punk friends. When he arrived in Coober Pedy, the other kids treated him as a freak and teased him for his outlandish appearance – his spiky, coloured hair, studded collar and multiple piercings. Punk is way out of place in Coober Pedy. In his isolation and in his desire to be accepted, he stripped himself of all his adornments. Now, nine months later, Christian looks like all the other local boys, but he has lost a sense of himself. Philip McPherson is a 16-year-old boy from Eden, whose core identity revolves around his pleasure in drama and especially scriptwriting. His main ambition is to write and produce films. All life experiences are potential story-lines according to Philip. But he feels a lack in his life. He wants more 'experiences' – to enjoy excess, so he dabbles more and more with alcohol, drugs and sex:

> I started to realize that we had had some pretty wild nights, but not wild enough. I needed something wild, and needed more experiences and such. I wanted to be with three separate girls in a row. And so I did.

Such exploits have alienated him from his friends, especially one girl he had strong feelings for. Philip laments:

> She found out [about sleeping with other girls] and then she went off with some big guy. It was a pretty stupid thing. I had slept with her. I really liked her, and when she found out I really liked her, she really liked me. But then she found out. It's just like the people off *Dawson's Creek*.

Dawson's Creek is a popular North American TV soap. Philip not only uses such experiences as fuel for his creative writing, imagining himself as a tragic/romantic hero, he tries to create the sorts of wild pleasures that he thinks might be worth writing about.

Part of the difficulty for Gem, Christian, Philip, and other young men like them, is the scorn their personhood attracts when compared with sacrosanct and subversive place-based masculinities. Here the 'great outdoors' is valorized as a masculine space. Life indoors is feminized with the implication that males who pursue indoor leisure pursuits are less 'manly'. Such views are often held by adults, many of whom are strongly attached to these traditional views of the links between gender, space and place. However, increasingly many young males are wishing to engage in indoor activities, especially watching TV and DVDs and playing on computers. Interestingly, computer use, especially computer games and cyberspace, have become a key point of concern and conflict between parents and sons.

Many parents express concern and even anger over the amount of time that their sons spend in front of a computer. This concern is expressed thus:

> The advent of the computer has had a large influence over the actual interests of young people. So many of them, they'll shut themselves inside their computer room as soon as they get home from school.
>
> (Mothers' Focus Group, Renmark)

The sense here is that computers mean that young people are beyond parental supervision and enticed into a little known and rather hazardous world. In addition, as this father's comments indicate, computer use contests two aspects of traditional local masculinity – outdoor activity and mateship:

> That's one of the problems, them being inside all the time. And yeah, the other factor is, I guess, television and computer games and all the information technology business that goes on means the kids are more isolated from their mates. They don't need their mates like they used to.
>
> (Fathers' Focus Group, Renmark)

Far from isolating them, computers may provide young males with opportunities for virtual mateship. Further, cyberspace offers many young men a place to conduct non-hegemonic masculinity safely, away from the scorn of their peers and parents. McNamee (1998) suggests computers allow certain male youth subcultures to move into the safety of the home. Beau Knox, age 14 from Eden, does not have many friends and gets bullied at school. He says he has two main friends, but that even one of these 'friends' subjects him to teasing. Beau feels he has to hide what he is thinking and doing for fear of being called names. But he does not feel isolated. He has a computer at home and uses it as his main source of social contact and has what he calls 'pen pals' living in the United States, India and even Antarctica.

'Cyberspace offers a new space . . . without the fears attached to public space and indeed without undue interference from adults: it is adult-free, unknown and unsupervised' contends Walkerdine (1998: 6). Computers offer the possibility of constructing assemblages of *jouissance* in that they are away from adult control and surveillance.

Computers and cyberspace also provide boys with an opportunity to perform different facets of masculinity, for example, by taking up aspects of aggressive hyper-masculinity in the form of violent computer games. Some boys who rate poorly in local youthful masculine hierarchies use computer games and the Internet to perform online the sorts of masculinities that oppress them in the flesh. While cyborg masculinities may contest aspects of outdoors masculinity, if they are focused on violent computer games they confirm competitive, aggressive and violent aspects of the sacrosanct. For as Connell (2000a: 151) and many others argue, video and computer games circulate highly stereotyped images of violent masculinity and require players to enact such forms. But the matter does not end there.

Cyberspace allows people to reconfigure their gendered identities and offers the opportunity for other assemblages of *jouissance*. This intense, online moonlighting can be found in those who indulge in 'flaming' (Dery 1994) – the practice of generating hyper-aggressive, argumentative text in cyberspace. 'Flaming' has emerged as a kind of live cyber rage which is akin to the well-known phenomenon of road rage (Dery 1994). Young males who are not usually argumentative or aggressive and who might even seem quite shy offline, develop thoroughly angry and short-tempered alter egos online, in order to 'tear down' the opinions of others, either in chat rooms, on discussion lists, or on bulletin boards. Flaming is pernicious, aggressive and often malicious. Young people who indulge in the unbounded *jouissance* of flaming derive pleasure from their power to hurt others and to act outside of established mores. The embedded nature of their everyday offline identity requires a certain amount of congeniality if they are to get along – at school, home and socially. However, the freedom afforded by cyberspace, which allows users to radically reconfigure social behaviours and to refute behavioural norms, is literally taken up by some young men as a licence to go wild. Boys who are into flaming are often the most socially radical pleasure seekers, for it is often an embodied, socialized shyness that leads to the appeal of life online. The pure pleasure of flaming is that of being out of order – socially, morally and behaviourally. These young men are also out of place, venting their disconnection from the 'real world' through their virtual identities. The spatially and culturally disembedded and unendorsed leisure pursuits associated with scorned masculinities may, thus, ironically invoke the sacrosanct. This example illustrates the subversive joys of scorned masculinities, of how socially abject masculinities can bite/byte back.

We have catalogued various sacrosanct, subversive and scorned masculinities and their associated leisure pleasures, pointing to their intergenerational textures and tensions. We have explained them as localized affective performances that are variously embedded and disembedded. We have suggested that these masculinities involve different assemblages of body–space–time–skill–pleasure and that these intersect at different points and in different ways with assemblages of the commodity, the image and the imagination.

*   *   *

We introduced this book with a proclamation and an invitation. We said we would bring studies of masculinity and of globalization into creative dialogue. The conceptual and methodological terrain of each was laid out in Chapters 1 and 2. In both chapters we facilitated this conversation largely through the literature on gender, place and space. In the subsequent chapters, we performed the poetics of place-based global ethnography. We offered global, yet situated, analyses of masculinities in peripheral places and their imagined communities of affect. Drawing on diverse analytical trajectories and developing some new conceptual configurations, we showed how young males (individually and as groups), and others, negotiate global forces, connections and imaginings. Such negotiations are, as indicated, threaded through work, place, abjection, knowledge and leisure. Becoming masculine in place is not pre-given with regard to any of these, but neither is it totally optional. It involves much manoeuvring, much disassembling and assembling.

At the start we invited you to accompany us on an intimate travelogue through places outside the city. Our hospitality had a purpose, as we said. Globalization has brought many places into greater proximity. Given the ubiquity of the mediascapes and ideoscapes we have discussed, this sense of proximity is highly mediated. While this means that we have a sense of the places beyond our own, it does not mean that this is necessarily sensible or sensitive to the complexities of othered places or to the political issues associated with them. Our hospitality was designed to bring the beyond up close and through this, to provoke you to consider, in ways perhaps you have not done before, the predicaments, pleasures, power, perversities and ultimately the politics of places and people beyond the metropolis.

Notes

Introduction

1 The place names have not been anonymized, but all the people referred to have been.

Chapter 1 Globalization, place and masculinities

1 An earlier version of this section is Kenway's contribution to Singh, Kenway, and Apple (2005).
2 Benyon and Dunkerly (2000: 7–10) summarize different viewpoints on the history of globalization.
3 See Cvetkovich and Kellner (1997) in Benyon and Dunkerley (2000: 134) for a discussion.
4 We note Tickner's (2004) recent development of the trajectory of thought begun by Hooper (2000b). With a focus on women and the visible and invisible gendered frontiers of globalization, Tickner (2004) looks at the implications for policy reform.

Chapter 2 Place-based global ethnography

1 For example, despite the globalized complexities of their sites, Beaud and Pialoux (2001) and Auyero (2001) do not problematize their ethnographic methods in their respective studies of '[t]he contradictory inheritance of French workers in the postfordist factory' and '[n]eo-liberal violence(s) in the Argentine slum'.
2 We note that Poster (2002) links her study to the lines of thought put forward by Burawoy et al. (2000). However, her unusually broad definition of ethnography compounds the existing lack of a clear definition of global ethnography. Hence we will not pursue a discussion of her work.

Chapter 3 Reordering work

1 *The Man from Snowy River* is a famous nineteenth-century Australian bush ballad written by the poet A. B. (Banjo) Patterson and depicting a heroic underdog drover who triumphs over adversity. See H. Hestiltine, *The Penguin Book of Australian Verse* (1972: 78).
2 An earlier version of the first parts of this chapter was published as Kenway and Kraack (2004).
3 We acknowledge that this is a concept with a long and contested history and which involves many shifting meanings. A range of evocative positions on the debates is usefully illustrated in Eng and Kazanjian (2003).

4 In the mid-1990s, Morwell was recorded as the nation's largest provider of energy, supplying over 85 per cent of the State of Victoria's electricity (Morwell Local Government Board 1994).

5 For example, in October 1991 the Coober Pedy Courthouse was blown up (*Coober Pedy Times*, October 1991). Soon after that the Mines Department experienced the same treatment.

6 A Ute (short for Utility) is the colloquial Australian name given to a tray-back sedan; a hybrid of the family sedan and a pickup truck. Utes have two-seat cabs for the driver and a passenger and a rear tray for carrying loads.

7 According to the Australian Bureau of Statistics (2000a), Renmark contributes approximately $130 million per annum to the gross value of the horticultural industry in the Riverland.

Chapter 4   In and out of place

1 For valuable discussions of young people and friendship, see the special issue of *Discourse: Studies in the Cultural Politics of Education* 23 (2) 2002.

2 Halberstam's (2005) discussion of the small amount of existing literature on rural and small town queer life (p. 36) is an important intervention here. A contemporary film text which has similar cultural significance is Ang Lee's 2006 feature *Brokeback mountain*.

Chapter 5   Scapes of abjection

1 During the 1990s, significant numbers of local people suffered economic marginalization and state dependence in Eden and Morwell. Morwell had a particularly high unemployment rate, recorded as 17.4 per cent in 1999 (Gippsland Research and Information Service 2000). There was also a significant increase in the number of pension recipients in Morwell. For example, there was a 58.1 per cent increase in unemployment benefit recipients from 1991 to 1999 (CentreLink 2000). The most significant indicator of changed economic circumstances was the huge increase in the number of families receiving the maximum family payment, available to low-income earners, the number increased from 122 families in 1991 to 1073 families in 1999 (CentreLink 2000). This represented an increase of 780 per cent over the nine years of economic restructuring within the power industry.

2 ABS statistics for 2003 illustrate this point: 3.2 per cent of Aboriginal boys never went to school, as opposed to 0.9 per cent of non-Aboriginal boys. The percentage of Aboriginal boys who complete year 12 or equivalent is 16.5, whereas the proportion of non-Aboriginal boys who complete year 12 is 40.9 per cent (ABS 2003: 23). The ABS (p. 24) states that only 2.3 per cent of Aboriginal young men attain a university degree, whereas 13.2 per cent of non-Aboriginal young men will attain a degree (or an award that is higher than a degree).

Chapter 6   Everyday knowledges

1 The 'boy crisis' has strong links to the 'masculinity crisis'; both concepts promoted by the men's/boys' lobby and also fiercely contested by others (Kegan
Gardiner 2002; Lingard and Douglas 1999).
2 Titus (2004) offers a sophisticated analysis of the boys' debate, with one of
the best reading lists available on the topic.

Chapter 7   Wild and tame pleasures

1 A stovvie pole is a metal and concrete pole used to hold up power lines along
the sides of Australian roads.
2 P-Plates are signs that probationary drivers are required to show for the duration of their probationary period.
3 The commercialization and mediatization of sport has become an increasingly
popular area of research, highlighting what has been termed the 'sports nexus'
(Burstyn 1999: 17): the juncture of sport and 'its associations with mass
media, corporate sponsors, governments, medicine and biotechnology'. These
studies range from deconstructing advertising images to the political
economy of sports' corporate sponsors.

Bibliography

Adams, R. and Savran, D. (Eds), *The Masculinity Studies Reader* (Massachusetts: Blackwell, 2002).

Adkins, L. 'Reflexivity: Freedom or Habit of Gender?' Paper presented at *After Bourdieu: Feminists Evaluate Bourdieu* conference, University of Manchester, 11 October (2002a). Online URL: http://les.man.ac.uk/sociology/Seminar/afterbourdieu.shtm Accessed 19/12/04.

Adkins, L. *Revisions: Gender & Sexuality in Late Modernity* (Buckingham: Open University Press, 2002b).

Afshar, H. and Barrientos, S. (Eds), *Women, Globalization & Fragmentation in the Developing World* (Basingstoke: Macmillan Press – now Palgrave Macmillan, 1999).

Albrow, M. 'Traveling Beyond Local Cultures: Socioscapes in a Global City'. In J. Eade (Ed.), *Living in the Global City: Globalization as a Local Process* (London: Routledge, 1997), 20–36.

Amin, A. 'Post-Fordism: Models, Fantasies & Phantoms of Transition'. In A. Amin (Ed.), *Post-Fordism: A Reader* (London: Blackwell, 1994), 1–39.

Appadurai, A. *Modernity at Large: Cultural Dimensions of Globalization* (Minneapolis: University of Minnesota Press, 1996).

Appadurai, A. 'Disjuncture & Difference in the Global Cultural Economy'. In F. J. Lechner and J. Boli (Eds), *The Globalization Reader* (Oxford: Blackwell, 2000), 322–30.

Apple, M., Kenway, J. and Singh, M. *Globalizing Education: Policies, Pedagogies, & Politics* (New York: Peter Lang, 2005).

Arizona Rock Shop. Online URL: http://www.arizona-rockshop.com/shop/virgin.htm Accessed 08/06/04.

Australian Broadcasting Corporation. 'Magic & Mayhem: The Footballing World of the Krakouer Brothers'. *The Sports Factor*, ABC Radio, 13/05/05.

Australian Broadcasting Corporation. Radio National, Interview of Jonathon Nossiter by Julie Copeland, 04/09/2005.

Australian Bureau of Statistics. *A Regional Profile: Renmark Paringa (DC), South Australia* (Canberra: Australian Bureau of Statistics, 2000a).

Australian Bureau of Statistics. *A Regional Profile: Riverland Development Corporation Region, South Australia* (Canberra: Australian Bureau of Statistics, 2000b).

Australian Bureau of Statistics. *Updated Coober Pedy Stats 2001 Census*. Online URL: http://www.abs.gov.au/ Accessed 12/02/05. (2001a).

Australian Bureau of Statistics. *Updated Renmark Statistics 2001 Census*. Online URL: http://www.abs.gov.au/ Accessed 12/02/05. (2001b).

Australian Bureau of Statistics. *Updated Morwell Statistics 2001 Census*. Online URL: http://www.abs.gov.au/ Accessed 12/02/05. (2001c).

Australian Bureau of Statistics. *Updated Eden Statistics 2001 Census*. Online URL: http://www.abs.gov.au/ Accessed 12/02/05. (2001d).

Australian Bureau of Statistics. *The Health and Welfare of Australia's Aboriginal and Torres Straight Islander Peoples* 4704.0, 2003. Online URL: http://www.abs.gov.au/ Accessed 11/08/05.

Australian Dance Council. *Indigenous Dance: The Place, Not The Space*. Online URL: http://www.fuel4arts.com/touring/tips/pdf/aia_dance.pdf   Accessed 18/08/05.

Australian Rules. Goldman, P. (director), Goldman, P. (screenplay), Gwynne, P. (novel), (Australia: AFC/SBS/ SA Film Corp/AFA, 2002).

Auyero, J. *Poor People's Politics: Peronist Survival Networks & the Legacy of Evita* (Durham, NC: Duke University Press, 2001).

Bakker, I. (Ed.). *Rethinking Restructuring: Gender & Change in Canada* (Toronto: University of Toronto Press, 1996).

Barrett, J. 'The Organizational Construction of Hegemonic Masculinity: The Case of the US Navy'. In S. Whitehead and F. Barrett (Eds), *The Masculinities Reader* (Cambridge: Polity Press, 2001), 77–99.

Barthes, R. *The Pleasure & The Text*, trans. R. Miller (New York: Hill & Wang, 1975).

Bauman, Z. *Modernity & Ambivalence* (Cambridge: Polity Press, 1991).

Bauman, Z. *Globalization: The Human Consequences* (Cambridge: Polity, 1998a).

Bauman, Z. *Work, Consumerism & the New Poor* (Buckingham: Open University Press, 1998b).

Bauman, Z. *Liquid Modernity* (Cambridge: Polity Press, 2000).

Bauman, Z. *Society Under Siege* (Cambridge: Polity Press, 2002).

Beal, B. 'Alternative Masculinity & Its Effects on Gender Relations in the Subculture of Skateboarding', *Journal of Sport Behavior* 19(3) (1996), 204–20.

Beaud, S. and Pialoux, M. 'Between "Mate" & "Scab": The Contradictory Inheritance of French Workers in the Postfordist Factory', *Ethnography* 2(3) (2001), 323–55.

Beck, U. *Risk Society: Towards a New Modernity* (London: Sage, 1992).

Beck, U. *What is Globalization?*, trans. P. Camiller (Cambridge: Polity Press, 2000, reprinted 2001).

Beltran, M. C. 'The New Hollywood Racelessness: Only the Fast, Furious (& Multiracial) Will Survive', *Cinema Journal* 44(2) (2005), 50–67.

Bend it Like Beckham. Chada, G. (director), Chada, G. and P. Mayeda Berges (writers), (UK: Kintop Pictures/Bend It Films/Road Movies/Roc Media, 2002).

Benyon, J. and Dunkerly, D. *Globalization: The Reader* (London: The Athlone Press, 2000).

Beresford, Q. *Governments, Markets & Globalization: Australian Public Policy in Context* (St Leonards: Allen & Unwin, 2000).

Berg, L. D. and Longhurst, R. 'Placing Masculinities & Geography', *Gender, Place & Culture* 10(4) (2003), 351–60.

Bergson, H. *The Creative Mind: An Introduction to Metaphysics* (New York: Citadel Press, 1992).

Billy Elliot. Daldry, S. (director), Hall, L. (writer), (UK: Universal Studios, 2000).

Blackrock. Vidler, S. (director), Enright, N (writer), (Australia: Polygram, 1997).

Blum, J. 'Degradation without Deskilling: Twenty-five years in the San Francisco Shipyards'. In Burawoy et al. (Eds), *Global Ethnography: Forces, Connections & Imaginations in a Postmodern World* (California: University of California Press, 2000), 106–36.

Bochner, A. P. and Ellis, C. (Eds), *Ethnographically Speaking: Authoethnography, Literature & Aesthetics* (Walnut Creek, CA: Alta Mira Press, 2002).

Bochner, S. and Parkes, L. *The Psychological Effects of the Timber Industry in the Eden Region of New South Wales: A Critical Review of Social Impact Studies Con-*

ducted Between 1991–1995 (New South Wales: NSW Forest Products Association, 1998).

Bone R., Cheers, B. and Hil, R. 'Eden Lost-Young People's Experience of Rural Life in the Whitsunday Shire', *Rural Disadvantage in Australia, Australian Social Work* 43(1) (1990). James Cook University: Online URL: http://www.csu.edu.au/research/crsr/ruralsoc/v3n4p9.htm   Accessed 19/04/02.

Boys Don't Cry: The Brandon Teena Story Muska, S. and Olafsdottir, G. (directors) (1998).

Bourke, L. 'Rural Communities'. In S. Lockie and L. Bourke (Eds), *Rurality Bites: The Social & Environmental Transformation of Rural Australia* (Annandale, NSW: Pluto Press, 2001), 118–28.

Brennar, N. 'Beyond State-Centrism? Space, Territoriality & Geographical Scale in Globalization Studies', *Theory and Society* 28(1) (1999), reprinted in Gille and Ó Riain (Eds) (2002), 39–78.

Brokeback Mountain. Lee, A. (director), Proulx, A. E. and McMurtry, L. (writer), (Canada: Alberta Film Entertainment, 2006).

Broome, R. *Aboriginal Australians: Black Responses To White Dominance, 1788–2001*, 3rd edn (St Leonards, NSW: Allen & Unwin, 2001).

Browne, K. and Hamilton-Giachritis, C. 'The Influence of Violent Media on Children and Adolescents: A Public Health Approach', *The Lancet* Feb. 19–25 (2005), 702–10.

Bryant, L. 'A Job of One's Own'. In S. Lockie and L. Bourke (Eds), *Rurality Bites* (Australia: Pluto Press, 2001), 214–27.

Bullen, E. and Kenway, J. 'Subcultural Capital & the Female "Underclass"? A Feminist Response to an Underclass Discourse', *Journal of Youth Studies* 7(2) (2004), 141–53.

Bullen, E. and Kenway, J. 'Bourdieu, Subcultural Capital & Risky Girlhood', *Theory & Research in Education* 3(1) (2005), 47–61.

Bullen, E., Kenway, J. and Hey, V. 'New Labor, Social Exclusion & Educational Risk Management: The Case of 'Gymslip Mums', *British Educational Research Journal* 26(4) (2000), 441–56.

Bunnings Hardware. *About Bunnings.* Online URL: http://www.bunnings.com.au/site/awdepfour.asp?dealer=5709depnum=8569   Accessed 28/10/04.

Burawoy, M. 'Manufacturing the Global', *Ethnography* 2(2) (2001), 147–59.

Burawoy, M., Blum, J. A., George, S., Gille, Z., Gowan, T., Haney, L., Klawiter, M., Lopez, S. T., Riain, S. and Thayer, M. (Eds), *Global Ethnography: Forces, Connections, & Imaginations in a Postmodern World* (Berkeley: University of California Press, 2000. Reprinted 2001).

Burstyn, V. *The Rites of Men: Manhood, Politics & the Culture of Sport* (Toronto: University of Toronto Press, 1999).

Campbell, B. *Goliath: Britain's Dangerous Places* (London: Methuen, 1993).

Campbell, H. and Phillips E. 'Male Hegemony & Rural Leisure Sites: Evidence from New Zealand & Australia'. In P. Share (Ed.), *Communication & Culture in Rural Areas*, Key Papers No. 4 (New South Wales: Centre for Rural Social Research, Charles Sturt University, 1995).

Carrington, K. *Who Killed Leigh Leigh? A Story of Shame and Mateship in an Australian Town* (Sydney: Random House, 1998).

Carspecken, P. F. 'Critical Ethnographies from Houston: Distinctive Features & Directions'. In P. F. Carspecken and G. Walford (Eds), *Critical Ethnography &*

Education, Studies in Educational Ethnography, Vol. 5 (Oxford: JAI Press, 2001).

CBS News. *CBS Heads For Hills In Hick Hunt*. Online URL: http://www.cbsnews. com/stories/2002/08/29/entertainment/main520227.shtml Accessed 25/07/05.

Centre for Rural Strategies. *Rural Reality*. Online URL: http://www. ruralstrategies.org/campaign/ Accessed 21/05/05.

CentreLink. Online URL: http://www.centrelink.gov.au/ Accessed 19/01/00.

Cheers, B. and Luloff, A. E. 'Rural Community Development'. In S. Lockie and L. Bourke (Eds), *Rurality Bites: The Social & Environmental Transformation of Rural Australia* (Annandale: Pluto Press, 2001), 129–42.

Christison, B. 'The Trial of Jose Bove' *In Motion Magazine* (2000). Online URL: http://www.inmotionmagazine.com/bove.html Accessed 25/05/05.

Clemens Foundation, The. (2004). Online URL: http://www.free-4u.com/ the_clemens_foundation.htm Accessed 15/04/05.

Clifford, J. *Routes: Travel & Translation in the Late Twentieth Century* (Cambridge, MA: Harvard University Press, 1997).

Clifford, J. and Marcus, G. E. *Writing Culture: The Poetics & Politics of Ethnography* (Berkeley: University of California Press, 1986).

Cloke, P. 'Poor Country: Marginalization, Poverty and Rurality'. In P. Cloke and J. Little (Eds), *Contested Countryside Cultures: Otherness, Marginalization & Rurality* (London and New York: Routledge, 1997), 252–71.

Coca Cola. Online URL: http://www.cocacola.com Accessed 8/10/04.

Cohen, R. and Kennedy, P. *Global Sociology* (New York: New York University Press, 2000).

Collier S. J. and Ong A. 'Oikos/Anthropos: Rationality, Technology, Infrastructure', *Current Anthropology* 44(3) (2003), 421–31.

Collins, C. Kenway, J. and McLeod, J. *Factors Influencing the Educational Performance of Males & Females at School & their Initial Destinations after Leaving School* (Canberra: Department of Education, Training and Youth Affairs, 2000).

Collinson, D. and Hearn, J. ' "Men" and "Work": Multiple Masculinities/ Multiple Workplaces. In M. Mac an Ghaill (Ed.), *Understanding Masculinities* (Buckingham: Open University Press, 1997).

Collinson, D. and Hearn, J. 'Naming Men as Men: Implications for Work, Organization & Management'. In S. Whitehead and F. Barrett (Eds), *The Masculinities Reader* (Cambridge: Polity Press, 2001), 144–69.

Comaroff, J. and Comaroff, J. 'Ethnography on an Awkward Scale: Postcolonial Anthropology & the Violence of Abstraction', *Ethnography* 4(2) (2003), 147–79.

Common Dreams: Breaking News & Views for the Progressive Community. (2001). Online URL: http://www.commondreams.org/ Accessed 12/04/04.

Community Broadcasting Service. (2004) *Survivor*. Online URL: http://www.cbs. com/primetime/survivor/ Accessed 21/10/04.

Connell, R. W. *Masculinities* (Sydney: Allen & Unwin, 1995).

Connell, R. W. *The Men & The Boys* (NSW: Allen & Unwin, 2000a).

Connell, R. W. *Understanding Men: Gender Sociology & the New International Research on Masculinities*, Clark Lecture, Department of Sociology, University of Kansas (19 September 2000b).

Connell, R. W. 'Masculinity Politics on a Word Scale'. In S. M. Whitehead and F. J. Barrett (Eds), *The Masculinities Reader* (Cambridge: Polity, 2001), 369–74.

Connor, B. 'Good Buddha & Tzu: Middle-Class Wiggers from the Underside', *Youth Studies Australia* 22(2) (2003), 48–54.

Coober Pedy Tourist Centre. Telephone Correspondence 08/08/05.

Coober Pedy Times. 10 October 1991 (Coober Pedy, South Australia).

Coober Pedy Times. 19 April 1995 (Coober Pedy, South Australia).

Coober Pedy Times. 13 September 1999 (Coober Pedy, South Australia).

Cornwall, A. and Lindisfarne, N. *Dislocating Masculinity: Comparative Ethnographies* (London: Routledge, 1994).

Countryside Alliance. *Countryside Alliance News, 2002*. Online URL: http://www. countryside-alliance.org/news/ Accessed 19/04/04.

Cowlishaw, G. *Blackfellas Whitefellas and Hidden Injuries of Race* (Oxford: Blackwell Publishers, 2004).

Crang, M. 'Rhythms of the City: Temporalized Space and Motion', in J. May and N. Thrift (Eds), *Timespace: Geographies of Temporality* (London: Routledge, 2001), 187–207.

Creed, B. *Monstrous Feminine* (Routledge: London, 1993).

Crocodile Dundee. Faiman, P. (director), Cornell, J. and Hogan, P, (screenplay), (Australia: Paramount Pictures/Rimfire Films, 1986).

Cvetkovich, A. and Kellner, D. (Eds), *Articulating the Global & the Local* (Boulder: Westview Press, 1997).

Cvetkovich, A. and Kellner, D. 'The Intersection of the Local and the Global'. In J. Benyon and D. Dunkerly (Eds), *Globalization: The Reader* (London: The Athlone Press, 2000), 134–5.

Daly, K. 'Re-Placing Theory in Ethnography: A Postmodern View', *Qualitative Inquiry* 3(2) (1997), 343–65.

Davidson, A. P. 'Farming Women & the Masculinization of Farming Practices'. In S. Lockie and L. Bourke (Eds), *Rurality Bites: The Changes Sweeping Rural Australia & Dividing the Nation* (Sydney: Pluto Press, 2001), 204–13.

Davies, C. A. *Reflexive Ethnography: a Guide to Researching; Selves & Others* (London: Routledge, 1999).

De Certeau, M. *The Practice of Everyday Life* (Berkley: University of California Press, 1984).

Deleuze, G. and Guattari, F. *A Thousand Plateaus: Capitalism & Schizophrenia* (Minneapolis: University of Minnesota Press, 1987).

Deleuze, G. and Guattari, F. *Anti-Oedipus: Capitalism & Schizophrenia* (Minneapolis: University of Minnesota Press, 1983).

Deliverance. Boorman, J. (director), Dickey, J. (writer), (United States: Warner Pictures, 1972).

Denzin, N. K. and Lincoln, Y. S. *Handbook of Qualitative Research* (Thousand Oaks: Sage Publications, 1994).

Dery, M. (Ed.), *Flame Wars: The Discourse by Cyberculture* (Durham, NC: Duke University Press, 1994).

Dimitriadis, G. *Friendship, Cliques, & Gangs: Young Black Men Coming of Age in Urban America* (New York: Teachers College Press, 2003).

Dimitriadis, G. *Performing Identity/Performing Culture: Hip Hop as Text, Pedagogy & Lived Practice* (New York: Peter Lang, 2001).

Discourse: Studies in the Cultural Politics of Education 23(2) (London: Taylor & Francis, 2002).

District Council of Coober Pedy. Online URL: http://www.opalcapitalofthe-world.com.au/history.asp   Accessed 09/07/05.

Dowler, L. 'Till Death Do Us Part: Masculinity, Friendship & Nationalism in Belfast, Northern Ireland', *Environment & Planning D: Society & Space* 19 (2001), 53–71.

Du Gay, P. 'Making up Managers: Bureaucracy, Enterprise & the Liberal Art of Separation', *British Journal of Sociology* 45(4) (1994), 655–74.

Eden Council, *Eden Business Challenge* (Eden, NSW: Eden Council).

Education Reporter (2003), 204, January. Online URL: http://www.eagleforum.org/educate/2003/jan03/logging-foundation.shtml   Accessed 15/04/05.

Endless Summer. Brown, B. (director), Brown, B. (writer/narrator), (United States: Columbia Pictures, 1966).

Eng, D. L. and Kazanjian, D. (Eds), *Loss: The Politics of Mourning* (Berkeley: University of California Press, 2003).

Escobar, A. 'Culture Sits in Places: Reflections on Globalism & Subaltern Strategies of Localization', *Political Geography* 20 (2001), 139–74.

Evers, C. 'Men Who Surf', *The Cultural Studies Review.* Online URL: http://www.csreview.unimelb.edu.au/docs/csr10-1_evers.pdf.   Accessed 08/09/04.

Fairfax Digital. 'Coober Pedy' *Walkabout Australian Travel Guide.* Online URL: http://walkabout.fairfax.com.au/theage/locations/SACooberPedy.shtml   Accessed 08/07/05.

Falk, R. *Predatory Globalization: A Critique* (Cambridge: Polity Press, 1999).

Featherstone, M. *Consumer Culture & Postmodernism* (London: Sage Publications, 1992).

Federal Australian Government. Online URL: http://www.fed.gov.au/   Accessed 12/09/04.

Feitas, E, de. 'Pre-Service Teachers & the Re-Inscription of Whiteness: Disrupting Dominant Cultural Codes Through Textual Analysis', *Teaching Education* 16(2) (14) (2005), 151–64.

Film Inside Out. Online URL: http://www.iofilm.co.uk/fm/c/cupcup_r2_1998.shtml   Accessed 08/09/04.

Finkelstein, J. and Bourke, L. 'The Rural as Urban Myth: Snack Foods and Country Life', in S. Lockie and L. Bourke (Eds), *Rurality Bites: The Social and Environmental Transformation of Rural Australia* (Annandale, NSW: Pluto Press, 2001), 45–52.

Fitzclarence, L. 'Sports Frankenstein: Character, Commerce and Cloning', *Arena Magazine* 78 (2005), 14–15.

Flaccus, G. 'Loss of Logging Leaves Few Options in Oregon Timber Town', *Montana Forum*, Sunday 31 September 2003. Online URL: http://www.montanaforum.com/rednews/2003/08/31/build/forests/roseburg.php?nnn=5   Accessed 30/10/03.

Foley, D. 'Critical Ethnography: The Reflexive Turn', *International Journal of Qualitative Studies in Education* 15(4), (July 2002), 469.

Fox, C. *Fighting Back–The Politics of the Unemployed in Victoria in the Great Depression* (Australia: Melbourne University Press, 2000).

Fox Studios. *The Simple Life.* Online URL: http://www.fox.com/simplelife/   Accessed 21/10/04.

Fraser, N. *Justice Interruptus: Critical Reflections on the 'Postsocialist' Condition* (New York: Routledge, 1997).

Freeman, C. *High Tech & High Heels in The Global Economy: Women, Work, & Pink-Collar Identities in the Caribbean* (Durham, NC: Duke University Press, 2000).

Freud, S. 'Mourning & Melancholia'. In A. Richards (Ed.), *The Pelican Freud Library*, Vol. 11, *On Metapsychology*, trans J. Strachey (Middlesex: Penguin, 1917, republished 1984), 245–68.

Friend, T. 'He's Been Everywhere, Man', *The Good Weekend, The Age Magazine* 13 August 2005, 20–4.

Gagen, E. A. 'Playing the Part: Performing Gender in America's Playgrounds'. In S. L. Holloway and G. Valentine (Eds), *Children's Geographies: Playing, Living, Learning* (London: Routledge, 2000), 213–29.

Geertz, C. *Works & Lives: The Anthropologist as Author* (California: Stanford University Press, 1983).

George, S. '"Dirty" Nurses & "Men Who Play": Gender & Class in Transnational Migration'. In M. Buroway et al. (Eds), *Global Ethnography: Forces, Connections & Imaginations in a Postmodern World* (California: University of California Press, 2000), 144–74.

Gibbs, A. 'Contagious Feelings: Pauline Hanson & the Epidemiology of Affect', *Australian Humanities Review* (2001). Online URL: http://www.lib.latrobe.edu.au/AHR/archive/Issue-December-2001 Accessed 08/07/05.

Giddens, A. *The Consequences of Modernity* (Cambridge: Polity Press, 1990).

Giddens, A. *Modernity & Self Identity: Self & Society in the Late Modern Age* (Cambridge: Polity Press, 1991).

Giddens, A. *Beyond Left & Right; The Future of Radical Politics* (California: Stanford University Press, 1994).

Giddens, A. *BBC Reith Lectures: Runaway World* (1999). Online URL: http://news.bbc.co.uk/ Accessed 12/03/04.

Gille, Z. 'Critical Ethnography in the Time of Globalization: Toward a New Concept of Site', *Cultural Studies: Critical Methodologies* 1(3) (2001), 319–34.

Gille, Z. and Ó Riain, S. 'Review Essay: Ethnography After Locality', *Ethnography* 2(2) (2001), 301–20.

Gille, Z. and Ó Riain, S. 'Global Ethnography', *Annual Review of Sociology* 28 (2002), 271–95.

Gippsland Research and Information Service. *Statistical Profile: Latrobe City* (Taralgon, Victoria: Latrobe City Council, 2000).

Giroux, H. 'Mis/Education & Zero Tolerance: Disposable Youth & the Politics of Domestic Militarization', *boundary 2* 28(3) (2001), 61–80.

Gorman, S. 'Magic & Mayhem: The Footballing World of the Krakouer Brothers', *The Sports Factor*, ABC Radio, 13 May 2005.

Gowan, T. 'Excavating "Globalization" from Street Level: Homeless Men Recycle Their Pasts'. In M. Buroway et al. (Eds), *Global Ethnography: Forces, Connections & Imaginations in a Postmodern World* (California: University of California Press, 2000), 74–105.

Grace, D. J. and Tobin, J. 'Carnival in the Classroom: Elementary Students Making Videos'. In J. Tobin (Ed.), *Making a Place For Pleasure in Early Childhood Education* (New Haven, CT: Yale University Press, 1997).

Grewal I. and Kaplan C. (Eds), *Scattered Hegemonies: Postmodernity & Transnational Feminist Practices* (Minneapolis: University of Minnesota Press, 1994).

Grosz, E. *Sexual Subversions: Three French Feminists* (Sydney: Allen & Unwin, 1989).

Grosz, E. *Space, Time & Perversion* (London: Allen & Unwin, 1995).

Grosz, E. *Architecture from the Outside* (Massachusetts: MIT Press, 2001).

Grosz-Ngate, M. and Kokole, H. O. (Eds), *Gendered Encounters: Challenging Cultural Boundaries & Social Hierarchies in Africa* (New York: Routledge, 1997).

Gubrium, J. and Holstein, J. *The New Language of Qualitative Method* (New York: Oxford University Press, 1997).

Gutteridge, Haskins and Davey. 'Flinders Outback Tourism Strategy', *South Australian Tourism Commission, Haskin and Davey Pty, Ltd (GHD)* (South Australia, 1997), 10.

Haebich, A. *Broken Circles: Fragmenting Indigenous Families 1800–2000* (Fremantle: FACP, 2001).

Halberstam, J. *In a Queer Time & Place* (New York: New York Univeristy Press, 2005).

Hall, J. with Wood, L. *An Oregon Logging Pioneer, George Shroyer's Life, Work, and Humor* (United States: Webb Research Group, 1998).

Hall, S. 'Introduction: Who Needs Identity?'. In S. Hall and P. du Gay (Eds), *Questions of Cultural Identity* (Sage: London, 1996).

Hammersley, M. and Atkinson, P. *Ethnography: Principles in Practice* (London and New York: Routledge, 1995).

Hannerz, U. 'Scenarios for Peripheral Cultures'. In A. King (Ed.), *Culture, Globalization & the World-System* (Binghamton: State University of New York, 1991).

Haraway, D. *Simians, Cyborgs, & Women: The Reinvention of Nature* (London: Free Association Books, 1991).

Hartig, L. and Dunn, K. 'Roadside Memorials: Interpreting New Deathscapes in Newcastle, New South Wales', *Australian Geographical Studies* (Institute of Australian Geographers, 1998), 5–20.

Harvey, D. *Spaces of Hope* (Edinburgh: Edinburgh University Press, 2000).

Haywood, C. and Mac an Ghaill, M. *Men & Masculinities* (Buckingham: Open University Press, 2003).

Healy, C. and Mueke, S. (Eds), *The Cultural Studies Review* http://www.csreview.unimelb.edu.au/docs/csr10-1_editorial.pdf Accessed 08/09/04.

Hebdige, D. *Hiding in the Light: On Images & Things* (London: Routledge-Comedia, 1988).

Held, D. and McGrew, A. *Globalization/Anti-Globalization* (Cambridge: Polity Press, 2002a).

Held, D. and McGrew, A. *Governing Globalization: Power, Authority & Global Governance* (Massachusetts: Polity Press, 2002b).

Held, D., Mc Grew, A. Goldblatt, D. and Perraton, J. (1999). In J. Benyon and D. Dunkerley (Eds), *Globalization: The Reader* (London: Athlone Press, 2000).

Hestiltine, H. *The Penguin Book of Australian Verse* (Australia: Penguin Books, 1972), 78.

Hickey, C., Fitzclarence, L. and Matthews, R. *Where the Boys Are: Masculinity, Sport & Education* (Geelong: Deakin University Press, 2000).

Hinkson, M. 'Encounters with Aboriginal Sites in Metropolitan Sydney: Broadening a Horizon for Cultural Tourism?', *Journal of Sustainable Tourism* 11(4) (2003), 295–306.

Homan, S. 'Geographies of Noise: Youth, Live Music and Urban Leisure', *Youth Studies Australia* 22(2) (2003), 12–18.

Hooper, C. 'Masculinities in Transition: The Case of Globalization'. In M. Marchand and A. Runyan (Eds), *Gender & Global Restructuring: Sightings, Sites & Resistances* (London and New York: Routledge, 2000a), 59–73.

Hooper, C. Manly States (New York: Columbia University Press, 2000b).

Hooton, A. 'Dude, Where's my Wave?', *The Age Magazine*, 28 May 2005, 36–40.

Iocco, M. 'Whom Do You Fight?: The Limits & Excesses of Masculinity in *Fight Club*', *M/C: A Journal of Media & Culture* 6(1) (2003). Online URL: http://www.media-culture.org.au/0302/08-whodoyou.html   Accessed 08/07/04.

Iocco, M. 'Addicted to Affliction: Masculinity & Perversity'. In *Crash & Fight Club: Gothic Studies* (Manchester: Manchester University Press, 2005).

Jackson, P. 'The Cultural Politics of Masculinities: Towards a Social Geography', *Transactions, Institute of British Geographers* 16 (1991), 199–213.

Jones, C. and Novak, T. *Poverty, Welfare and the Disciplinary State* (London and New York: Routledge, 1999).

Jones, G. W. *Babes in the Bush: Youth, Gender & Identity Among Young Rural Women*, unpublished PhD thesis (Melbourne: Department of Educational Policy and Management, University of Melbourne, 1999).

Karsten, L. and Pel, E. 'Skateboarders Exploring Urban Public Space: Ollies, Obstacles & Conflicts', *Journal of Housing & the Built Environment* 15 (2001), 327–40.

Kazakevitch, G., Foster, B. and Stone, S. *The Effects of Economic Restructuring on Population Movements in the Latrobe Valley* (Canberra: Department of Immigration and Multicultural Affairs, 1997).

Kearns, G. and Philo, C. *Selling Places: The City as Cultural Capital, Past & Present*. (Oxford: Pergamon, 1993).

Kegan Gardiner, J. (Ed.), *Masculinity Studies & Feminist Theory* (New York: Columbia University Press, 2002).

Kennicott, P. '"Amish in The City": Hollywood's Urban Desert', *Washington Post*. Thursday 29 July 2004. Online URL: http://www.washingtonpost.com/wp-dyn/articles/A23547-2004Jul29.html   Accessed 21/10/04.

Kenway, J. and Bullen, E. *Consuming Children: Education, Entertainment, Advertising* (Buckingham: Open University Press, 2001).

Kenway, J. and Kraack, A. 'Reordering Work & Destabilizing Masculinity', In N. Dolby, G. Dimiriadis, with P. Willis (Eds), *Learning to Labor in New Times* (London: Routledge/Falmer, 2004).

Kenway, V. 'Dodos, Dinosaurs & Men: Representations of Melancholy Masculinities in *Brassed Off, Billy Elliot & The Full Monty*', Honours Dissertation (Australia: Department of English with Cultural Studies, Melbourne University, 2001).

Klein, N. *No Logo* (London: Flamingo/Harper Collins, 2000).

Knopp, L. 'Ontologies of Place, Placelessness, & Movement: Queer Quests for Identity & Their Impacts on Contemporary Geographic Thought' *Gender, Place & Culture* 11(1) (2004), 121–34.

Kofman, E. 'Beyond a Reductionist Analysis of Female Migrants in Global European Cities: The Unskilled, Deskilled & Professional'. In M. Marchand and A. Runyan (Eds), *Gender & Global Restructuring: Sightings, Sites & Resistances* (London and New York: Routledge, 2000).

Kraidy, M. M. 'The Global, the Local, & the Hybrid: A Native Ethnography of Glocalization', *Critical Studies in Mass Communication* 16(4) (1999), 456–76.

Kristeva, J. *Powers of Horror* (New York: Columbia University Press, 1982).

Lash, S. 'Reflexive Modernization: The Aesthetic Dimension', *Theory, Culture & Society* 10(1) (1993), 1–23.

Lash, S. and Urry, J. *Economies of Signs & Space* (London: Sage Publications, 1994).

Latour, B. *Science in Action.* (Cambridge, MA: Harvard University Press, 1987).

Lawrence, G. *Capitalism & the Countryside: The Rural Crisis in Australia* (Sydney and London: Pluto Press, 1987).

Lincoln, Y. S. 'Emerging Criteria for Qualitative & Interpretive Research', *Qualitative Inquiry* 3 (1995), 275–89.

Lingard, B. and Douglas P. *Men Engaging Feminisms: Pro-Feminism, Backlashes & Schooling* (Buckingham and Philadelphia: Open University Press, 1999).

Lippard, L. *The Lure of the Local: Senses of Place in a Multicentered Society* (New York: The New Press, 1997).

Lister, R. (Ed.), *Charles Murray and the Underclass* (London: IEA Health and Welfare Unit, 1996).

Little, J. 'Rural Geography: Rural Gender Identity & the Performance of Masculinity & Femininity in the Countryside', *Progress in Human Geography* 26(5) (2002), 665–70.

Little, J. and Panelli R. 'Gender Research in Rural Geography', *Gender, Place & Culture* 10(3) (2003), 281–9.

Lowther, S. In 'Timber-r-r-r-r: Logging Foundation Topples Scholarship Programme', *The Education Reporter* No. 204, (January 2003). Online URL: http://www.eagleforum.org/educate/2003/jan03/logging-foundation.shtml Accessed 15/04/05.

Local Government Board. *A Vision for Gippsland: Gippsland Area Review*, Interim Report (Victoria: Local Government Board, 1994).

Lockie, S. and Bourke, L. *Rurality Bites: The Social & Environmental Transformation of Rural Australia* (Victoria: Pluto Press, 2001).

London, *The Militant* (2001). Online URL: http://www.themilitant.com/ Accessed 16/05/03.

Luke, T. and Ó Tuathail, G. 'Global Flowmations, Local Fundamentalisms, & Fast Geopolitics: "America" in an accelerating world order'. In A. Herod G. Ó Tuathail and S. M. Roberts (Eds), *An Unruly World? Globalization, Governance & Geography* (London and New York: Routledge, 1998), 72–94.

MacCannell, D. *The Tourist: A New Theory of the Leisure Class* (Berkeley: University of California Press, 1999).

MacDonald, R. 'Dangerous Youth & the Dangerous Classes'. In R. MacDonald (Ed.), *Youth, the 'Underclass' & Social Exclusion* (London and New York: Routledge, 1997a), 1–25.

MacDonald, R. (Ed.), *Youth, the 'Underclass' & Social Exclusion* (London: Routledge, 1997b).

Mac an Ghaill, M. *The Making of Men: Masculinities, Sexualities & Schooling* (Buckingham and Philadelphia: Open University Press, 1994).

Mac an Ghaill, M. (Ed.), *Understanding Masculinities: Social Relations & Cultural Arenas* (Buckingham and Philadelphia: Open University Press, 1996).

Mad Max 3. Miller, G. and Ogilvie, G. (directors), Hayes, T. and Miller, G. (writers), (Australia: Warner, 1985). Online URL: http://www.imdb.com/title/tt0089530/ Accessed 19/02/04.

Maira, S. and Soep, E. (Eds), *Youthscapes: The Popular, the National, the Global* (Philadelphia: University of Pennsylvania Press, 2005).

Majors, R. 'Cool Pose: Black Masculinity and Sports'. In S. Whitehead and F. Barrett (Eds), *The Masculinities Reader* (Cambridge: Polity Press, 2001), 209–18.

Marcus, G. E. *Ethnography Through Thick & Thin* (Princeton: Princeton University Press, 1998).

Marcus, G. E. (Ed.), *Critical Anthropology Now: Unexpected Contexts, Shifting Constituencies, Changing Agendas* (Santa Fe, NM: School of American Research, 1999).

Marcus, G. E. and Fischer, M. J. *Anthropology as Cultural Critique: An Experimental Moment in the Human Sciences* (Chicago: The University of Chicago Press, 1986).

Martino, W. 'We Just Get Really Fired Up': Indigenous Boys, Masculinities & Schooling', *Discourse: Studies in the Cultural Politics of Education* (Hants: Carfax Publishing Group) 24(2) (August 2003), 159–74.

Massey, D. 'Power-Geometry' & A Progressive Sense of Place'. In J. Bird, B. Curtis, G. Robertson and L. Tricker (Eds), *Mapping the Futures: Local Culture, Global Change* (London: Routledge, 1993).

Massey, D. *Space, Place & Gender* (Cambridge: Polity Press, 1994).

Massey, D. *Spatial Divisions of Labour: Social Structures of the Geography of Production* (Basingstoke: Macmillan, 1995).

Massey, D. *For Space* (London: Sage, 2005).

Matthews, H., Limb, M. and Taylor, M. 'The "Street as Third Space"'. In S. Holloway and J. Valentine (Eds), *Children's Geographies: Playing, Living, Learning* (London and New York: Routledge, 2000), 63–79.

Matthews, H., Taylor, M., Percy-Smith, B. and Limb, M. 'The Unacceptable Flaneur: The Shopping Mall as a Teenage Hangout', *Childhood: Global Journal of Child Research* 7(3) (2000), 279–94.

May, C. *The Information Society: A Sceptical View* (Cambridge: Polity, 2002).

May, J. and Thrift, N. *Timespace: Geographies of Temporality* (London and New York: Routledge, 2001).

McClintock, A. *Imperial Leather: Race, Gender & Sexuality in the Colonial Contest* (New York: Routledge, 1995).

McDonnell, K. *Kid Culture: Children, Adults & Popular Culture* (Toronto: Second Storey Press, 1994).

McDowell, L. *Redundant Masculinities? Employment Change & White Working Class Youth* (Oxford: Blackwell, 2003).

McDowell, L. *Capital Culture: Gender at Work in the City* (Oxford: Blackwell, 1997).

McDowell, L. *Gender, Identity & Place* (Minneapolis: University of Minnesota Press, 1999).

McMichael, P. and Lawrence, G. 'Globalizing Agriculture: Structures of Constraint for Australian Farming'. In S. Lockie and L. Bourke (Eds), *Rurality Bites: The Social & Environmental Transformation of Rural Australia* (Sydney: Pluto Press, 2001), 153–64.

McNamee, S. 'The Home: Youth, Gender and Video Games'. In T. Skelton and G. Valentine (Eds), *Cool Places: Geographies of Youth Cultures* (London: Routledge, 1997, republished 1998), 195–206.

Mendes, P. *Australia's Welfare Wars: The Players, the Politics and the Ideologies* (Sydney: UNSW Press, 2003).

Mercer, K. *Welcome to the Jungle* (New York: Routledge, 1994).

Miller, D. (Ed.), *Worlds Apart: Modernity Through the Prism of the Local* (London: Routledge, 1995).

Mirande, A. 'And Ar'n't I a Man?': Toward a Chicano/Latino Men's Studies'. In S. Whitehead and F. Barrett (Eds), *The Masculinities Reader* (Cambridge: Polity Press, 2001), 341–50.

Mol, A. and Law, J. 'Regions, Networks and Fluids: Anemia and Social Topology', *Social Studies of Science* 26 (1994), 641–71.

Mondovino, Nossiter, J. (director), Nossiter, J. (writer), (Australia: Goatwork Film and Films de la Goisade, 2004).

Moore, M. *Roger & Me* (United States: Dog Eat Dog Films, 1989).

Morwell Local Government Board (Morwell: Local Government, 1994).

Morris, M. 'Things to Do with Shopping Centers'. In S. During (Ed.), *Cultural Studies Reader* (London: Routledge, 1993, reprinted 1994).

Murray, C. *The Emerging British Underclass*. (London: IEA Health and Welfare Unit, 1990).

Murray, C. *Underclass: The Crisis Deepens*. (London: IEA Health and Welfare Unit/Sunday Times, 1994).

Murray, C. *Income Inequality and IQ* (Washington, DC: The AEI Press, 1998).

Murray, C. *The Underclass Revisited* (Washington, DC: AEI Online, 1999). http://www.aei.org/docLib/20021130_71317.pdf Accessed 10/9/03.

Nagar, R., Lawson, V., McDowell, L. and Hanson, S. 'Locating Globalization: Feminist (Re)Readings of the Subjects and Spaces of Globalization'. Paper presented at *Geographies of Global Economic Change* conference, Graduate School of Geography, Clark University, 2001.

National Aboriginal and Torres Straight Islander Health Council (NATSIHC). *National Strategic Framework for Aboriginal and Torres Straight Islander Health: Framework for Action by Governments* (Canberra: NATSIHC, 2003).

National Literacy Trust (UK) (2000). Online URL: http://www.literacytrust.org.uk/ Accessed 12/03/2000.

Nespor, J. 'Anonymity and Place in Qualitative Inquiry', *Qualitative Inquiry* 6(4) (2000a), 546–60.

Nespor, J. 'Topologies of Masculinity: Gendered Spatialities of Preadolescent Boys'. In N. Lesko (Ed.), *Masculinities at School* (Thousand Oaks: Sage Publications, 2000b).

Newitz, A. and Wray, M. (Eds), *White Trash: Race and Class in America* (New York: Routledge, 1996).

Nicholls, M. *Scorsese's Men: Melancholia & The Mob* (Australia: Pluto Press, 2004).

Nintendo. Online URL: http://www.nintendo.com/gamelist Accessed 08/10/04.

O'Donnell, M. and Sharpe, S. *Uncertain Masculinities: Youth, Ethnicity & Class in Contemporary Britain* (London and New York: Routledge, 2000).

O'Regan. 'Magic and Mayhem: The Footballing World of the Krakouer Brothers', *The Sports Factor*, ABC Radio, 13 October 2005.

Ong, A, *Flexible Citizenship: The Cultural Logics of Transnationality* (Durham, NC: Duke University Press, 1999a).

Ong, A. *Critical Ethnography of Globalizing Asian Cities, Unexpected Contexts, Shifting Constituencies, Changing Agendas* (Berkeley: University of California, 1999b).

Online Dictionary. Online URL: http://dictionary.reference.com/ Accessed 19/04/04.

Ontario Job Futures. *Ontario Job Futures*. Online URL: http://www1.on.hrdc-drhc.gc.ca/ojf/ojf.jsp?lang=esection=Profilenoc=8251 Accessed 08/06/04.

Paris Texas. Wenders, S. (writer), Shepard, S. (screenplay), Carson, K. (adaptation) (United States: Argos Films/Road Movies Filmproduktion, 1984).

Patterson, A. B 'The Man From Snowy River'. In H. Hesiltine (Ed.), *The Penguin Book of Australian Verse* (Australia: Penguin Books, 1972), 78.

Peel, M. *The Lowest Rung: Voices of Australian Poverty* (Australia: Cambridge University Press, 2003).

Phillips, R. 'Racism and Small Town Bigotry: Australian Rules, directed by Paul Goldman' *World Socialist Website*. Online URL: http://www.wsws.org/articles/2002/sep2002/arul-s19.shtml   Accessed 19/09/02.

Philomath Chamber. Online URL: http://www.philomathchamber.org/ Accessed 15/04/05.

Pillow, W. and St Pierre, E. (Eds), *Working the Ruins: Feminist Poststructural Theory & Methods in Education* (New York: Routledge, 2000).

Pittsburgh Post Gazette (2003). Online URL: http://www.post-gazette.com/ Accessed 19/12/04.

Poster, W. 'Racism, Sexuality, and Masculinity: Gendering "Global Ethnography" of the Workplace', *Social Politics* (Spring 2002), 126–58.

Potter, G. *Deeper than Debt: Economic Globalization & the Poor* (London: Latin America Bureau, 2000).

Power Works. Online URL: http://www.powerworks.com.au/   Accessed 13/05/04.

Poynting, S., Noble, G. and Tabar, P. 'Protest Masculinity and Lebanese-Australian Youth in Western Sydney: An Ethnographic Study'. In S. Tomsen and M. Donaldson (Eds), *Male Trouble: Looking at Australian Masculinities* (Australia: Pluto Press, 2003).

Probert, B. (2001) 'Holding Together: Class in the Year 2001', The Barton Lectures, Part 6. Online URL: http://www.abc.net.au/rn/sunspect/stories/s261974.htm   Accessed date 20/08/02.

Public Broadcasting Service. '6/29/01 Ann' *Store Wars: When Wal-Mart Comes to Town Talkback* (2001). Online URL: http://www.pbs.org/itvs/storewars/talkback5.html   Accessed 06/10/04.

Quiksilver Company History. Online URL: http://www.quiksilver.com/ ?pageID=70   Accessed 24/06/04.

Rabaté, J. M. 'Roland Barthes', *The John Hopkins Guide to Literary Theory & Criticism* (1997). Online URL: http://press.jhu.edu/books/hopkins_guide_to_literary_theory/rol& _barthes.html   Accessed 25/06/04.

Rantanen, T. *The Media & Globalization* (London: Sage, 2005).

Ratsch, G. *Facing the Riverland's Future Today: A Report into the Needs, Wants, Issues & Perceptions of Young People in the Riverland & Surrounding Districts* (Berri, South Australia: Murray Institute Youth Strategy for the Riverland Youth Network, 1995).

Ray, L. and Sayer, A. (Eds), *Culture & Economy After the Cultural Turn* (London: Sage, 1999).

Red Planet. Hoffman, A. (director), Pfarrer, C. and Lemkin, J. (writers), (Australia: Mars Production/NPV Entertainment/Village Roadshow, 2000).

Resource Centre of the Americas (2005). Online URL: http://www.americas.org/ Accessed 12/09/04.

Reynolds, H. *Why Weren't We Told?: A Personal Search for the Truth About Our History* (Ringwood, Victoria: Penguin, 1999).

Reville, G. 'Reading *Rosehill*: Community, Identity and Inner-City Derby'. In M. Keith and S. Pile (Eds), *Place & the Politics of Identity* (London: Routledge, 1993), 117–40.

Rip Curl. Online URL: http://www.ripcurl.com/ Accessed 19/05/04.

Robertson, R. *Globalization: Social Theory & Global Culture*, (London: Sage Publications, 1992).

Roeper, P. J. and Voas, R. B. 'Underage Drivers are Separating Drinking from Driving', *American Journal of Public Health* 89(5) (May 1999), 755–7.

Rouvalis, C. 'Pittsburgh Post Gazette', 20 January 2003. In *The Centre for Rural Strategies, Rural Reality: What's the Buzz?* Online URL: http://www. ruralstrategies.org/campaign/buzz.html Accessed 12/09/04.

Royal Peacock Mining. Online URL: http://www.royalpeacock.com/ Accessed 19/04/05.

Sampath, N. 'Crabs in a Bucket': Reforming Male Identities in Trinidad'. In S. Whitehead and F. Barrett (Eds), *The Masculinities Reader* (Cambridge: Polity Press, 2001), 330–40.

Sassen, S. *Globalization & Its Discontents: Essays on the New Mobility of People and Money* (New York: The New Press, 1998).

Sassen, S. *Losing Control? Sovereignty in an Age of Globalization* (New York: Columbia University Press, 1999).

Sassen, S. 'Spatialities and Temporalities of the Global'. In A. Appadurai (Ed.), *Globalization* (Durham, NC, and London: Duke University Press, 2001), 260–78.

Scholte, J. A. *Globalization: A Critical Introduction* (New York: St. Martin's, 2000).

Scorsese, M. (director). *Taxi Driver*. Schrader, P. (writer), (United States: Columbia Pictures/Italo/Urdeo Productions/ Bill Phillips, 1976).

Scorsese, M. (director). *Raging Bull*. La Moffa, J. Carter, J. Savage, P. Schrader, P. and Martin, M. (writers), (United States: Chartoff-Winkler Productions, 1980).

Scorsese, M. (director). *Good Fellas*. Pileggi, N. (screenplay), (United States: Warner Bros, 1990).

Scorsese, M. (director). *Cape Fear*. Webb, J. R. and Strick, W. (screenplay), (United States: Amblin Ent./Cappa Films/Tribeca Prod/Universal Pictures, 1991)

Scorsese, M. (director). *The Age of Innocence*. Cocks, J. (screenplay), (United States: Cappa Productions/Columbia Pictures, 1993).

Sea Change, ABC TV. Cox, D. with Knight, A. (creators), Masters, S. (Executive producer). Online URL: http://www.australiantelevision.net/seachange/ seachange.html Accessed 19/04/04.

Segal, A. 'Masculinity, School, and Self in Sweden and the Netherlands'. In S. Whitehead and F. Barratt (Eds), *The Masculinities Reader* (Cambridge: Polity Press, 2001), 184–208.

Shaw, J. '"Winning Territory"': Changing Place to Change Pace'. In J. May and N. Thrift, *Timespace: Geographies of Temporality* (London: Routledge, 2001), 120–32.

Shilling, C. *The Body and Social Theory* (Sage: London, 1993).

Shire, C. 'Men Don't Go to the Moon: Language, Space and Masculinities in Zimbabwe', In A. Cornwall and N. Lindisfarne (Eds), *Dislocating Masculinity: Comparative Ethnographies* (New York: Routledge, 1994).

Shroyer, G. (2005). Online URL: http://gallery.bcentral.com/ GID4953142P2169097-Gardens/Greengable-Gardens-Tickets.aspx Accessed 19/03/05.

Siam Sunset. Polson, J. (director), Dann, M. and Knight, A. (writers), (Australia: Bac Films, UIP, 1999).

Sibley, D. *Geographies of Exclusion: Society & Difference in the West* (London: Routledge, 1995).

Silver, S. (writer) *8 Mile* Hanson, C. (director), (United States: Imagine Entertainment/Mikona Productions/Universal, 2002).

Simon, R. and Dippo, D. 'On Critical Ethnographic Work', *Anthropology & Education Quarterly*, 17(4) (1986), 195–222.

Simpson, M. 'Active Sports: The Anus and Its Goal-Posts'. In M. Simpson (Ed.), *Male Impersonators* (London and New York: Cassell, 1994), 69–93.

Singh, M., Kenway, J. and Apple, M. 'Globalizing Education: Perspectives for Above and Below'. In M. Apple, J. Kenway and M. Singh (Eds), *Globalizing Public Education: Policies, Pedagogies and Politics* (New York: Peter Lang, 2005), 1–29.

Soja, E. *Thirdspace: Journeys to Los Angeles & Other Real & Imagined Places* (Oxford: Blackwell Publishers, 1996).

Sommers, C. H. *The War Against Boys: How Misguided Feminism Is Harming Our Young Men* (New York: Simon & Schuster, 2000).

South Australian Tourism Commission. *Tourism Research: International Visitors to South Australia by Places Visited* (Adelaide: South Australian Tourism Incorporated, 1999).

South Australian Tourism Commission. *South Australia: Arts and Culture*. Online URL: http://www.southaustralia.com/product.asp?product_id=9002779   Accessed 08/07/05.

South East New South Wales Area Consultative Committee. *Regional Employment Profiles for South East NSW* (Bega, NSW: South East New South Wales Area Consultative Committee, 1999).

Spicer, A. and Jones, C. 'The Sublime Object of Entrepreneurship', *Organization* 12(2) (2003), 223–46.

Spriggs, K. 'Road Trip to Manhood: Understanding Young Rural Men, Risk Driving and the Community'. Honours Dissertation (Adelaide: University of South Australia, 2000).

Stacey, J. 'Ethnography Confronts the Global Village: A New Home for a New Century?', *Journal of Contemporary Ethnography* 28(6) (1999), 687–97.

Stehlik, D. 'The Rural as Urban Myth: Snack Foods and Country Life'. In S. Lockie and L. Bourke (Eds), *Rurality Bites: The Social and Environmental Transformation of Rural Australia* (Annandale: Pluto Press, 2001).

Stewart, K. *Space on the Side of the Road; Cultural Poetics in an 'other' America* (Princeton: Princeton University Press, 1996).

Stiglitz, J. *Globalization & Its Discontents* (New York: W. W. Norton, 2002).

Stilwell, F. *Understanding Cities & Regions: Spatial Political Economy* (Australia: Pluto Press, 1992).

Stoller, P. 'Back to the Ethnographic Future', *Journal of Contemporary Ethnography* 28(6) (1999), 698–704.

Store Wars: When Wal-Mart Comes to Town. Pele, Micha X. (director). Distributed by Bullfrog Films (United States: Teddy Bear Films with the Independent Television Service, 2001).

Sunder Rajan, R. *Real and Imagined Women: Gender, Culture and Postcolonialism* (London: Routledge, 1993).

Sunder Rajan, R. (Ed.), *The Lie of the Land: English Literary Studies in India* (Delhi: Oxford University Press, 1993).

Suroor, H. 'Pro-Hunters Stage Protest', *The Hindu Times* 16 September 2004. Online URL: http://www.hindu.com/2004/09/16/stories/2004091602331302. htm Accessed 29/05/05.

Tea and Coffee Net. Online URL: http://www.tea & coffee.net/0202/special.htm Accessed 07/10/04.

The Adventures of Priscilla, Queen of the Desert. Elliot, S. (director), (Australia: PolyGram Video, 1994).

The Archers. BBC Radio 4. Online URL: http://www.bbc.co.uk/radio4/archers/ Accessed 19/04/05.

The Australian Newspaper. 'The Trouble with Boys', 19 June 2000. Online URL: http://www.theaustralian.news.com.au/ Accessed 12/05/05.

The Centre for Rural Strategies. *Rural Reality vs. Reality TV: Anatomy of a Public Awareness Campaign* (Whitesburg: The Centre for Rural Strategies, 2003) Online URL: http://www.ruralstrategies.org/campaign/report/ Accessed 27/05/04.

The Countryside Alliance (2002). *Liberty & Livelihood March*. Online URL: http://www.countryside-alliance.org/news/02/020422aam.htm Accessed 19/04/05.

The Cup/Phorpa. Norbu, K. (director), Norbu, K. (writer), (India: Bhutan, 1998).

The District Council of Coober Pedy. Online URL: http://www.opalcapitalofthe-world.com.au/history.asp Accessed 09/07/05.

The Education Reporter: The Newspaper of Education Rights. 'Timber-r-r-r-r: Logging Foundation Topples Scholarship Programme', No. 204, January 2003. Online URL: http://www.eagleforum.org/educate/2003/jan03/logging-foundation.shtml Accessed 15/04/05.

The Full Monty. Cattaneo, P. (director), Beaufou, S. (writer), (UK: Twentieth Century Fox, 1997).

The *Guardian*. 'Girls Beat Boys at Reading – Worldwide', 2 July 2003. Online URL: http://www.guardian.co.uk/gender/story/0,11812,989338,00.html.

The *Guardian*. 'Crisis in the Countryside' Online URL: http://www.guardian.co. uk/country/flash/0,6189,191473,00.html Accessed 29/10/04.

The *Guardian*. Online URL: http://www.guardian.co.uk/print/0,3858,5030682-110878,00.html Accessed 4/10/04.

The Lonely Planet (2005a). *Journeys to Authentic Australia*. Online URL: http://www.lonleyplanet.com Accessed 08/07/05.

The Lonely Planet (2005b). *Guide to Aboriginal Australia*. Online URL: http://www.lonleyplanet.com Accessed 08/07/05.

The South Australian Tourist Commission (STAC). Online URL: http://www.southaustralia.com Accessed 08/07/05.

The *Sydney Morning Herald*. 'The Trouble with Boys', 17 June 2000. Online URL: http://smh.com.au/ Accessed 12/05/05.

The Weekend Australian September 26–7 1998. Online URL: http://www. theaustralian.news.com.au/ Accessed 12/05/05.

Thomas, J. *Doing Critical Ethnography* (London: Sage, 1993).

Tickner, A. J. 'The Gendered Frontiers of Globalization', *Globalizations* 1(1) (2004), 15–23.

Titus, J. J. 'Boy Trouble: Rhetorical Framing of Boys' Underachievement', *Discourse: Studies in the Cultural Politics of Education* 25(2) (2004), 145–69.

Tomlinson, J. *Globalization & Culture* (Cambridge: Polity Press, 1999).

Tsing, A. 'The Global Situation', *Cultural Anthropology* 15(3) (2000), 327–61.

Tyler, R. 'Polish Farmers Blockade Borders', *World Socialist Website*, 8 June 1999. Online URL: http://www.wsws.org/articles/1999/feb1999/pol1-f10.shtml Accessed 21/04/05.

Tyler, R. 'Dioxin Contamination Scandal Hits Belgium', *World Socialist Website*, 10 February 1999. Online URL: http://www.wsws.org/ Accessed 21/04/05.

UPN. *Ahmish in the City.* Online URL: http://www.upn.com/shows/amish_in_the_city/ Accessed 21/10/04.

Urry, J. *The Tourist Gaze* (London: Sage, 1990).

Urry, J. *Consuming Places* (London and New York: Routledge, 1995).

Urry, J. *Sociology Beyond Societies: Mobilities for the Twenty-First Century* (New York: Routledge, 2000).

Victorian Tourist Information Bureau (2005). Online URL: http://www.tourismvictoria.com.au/ Accessed 24/05/05.

Walby, S. *Gender Transformations* (London and New York: Routledge, 1997).

Walker, J. C. *Louts & Legends: Male Youth in Inner City Schools* (Sydney: Allen & Unwin, 1988).

Walker, L. 'Car Culture, Technological Dominance and Young Men of the Working Class'. In M. Donaldson and S. Tomsen (Eds), *Male Trouble: Looking at Australian Masculinities* (North Melbourne: Pluto Press, 2003), 40–68.

Walker, L., Butland, D. and Connell, R. W. 'Boys on the Road: Masculinities, Car Culture and Road Safety Education', *The Journal of Men's Studies* 8(2) (2000), 153–69.

Walkerdine, V. 'Children in Cyberspace: A New Frontier'. In K. Lesnik Oberstein (Ed.), *Children in Culture* (Basingstoke: Macmillan – now Palgrave Macmillan, 1998).

Wal-Mart: The High Cost of Low Price. Greenwald, R. (director), (Australia: Brave New Films, 2005).

Waters, M. *Globalization* (London and New York: Routledge, 1995).

Wheaton, B. ' "Just do it": Consumption, Commitment, and Identity in the Windsurfing Subculture', *Sociology of Sport* 17(3) (2000), 254–75.

Whitehead, S. *Men & Masculinities: Key Themes & New Directions* (Cambridge: Polity Press, 2002).

Whitehead, S. and Barrett, F. (Eds), *The Masculinities Reader* (Cambridge: Polity Press, 2001).

Williams. R. *The Sociology of Culture* (New York: Schlocken Books, 1982).

Willis, P. *Learning to Labor: How Working-Class Kids Get Working-Class Jobs* (Hampshire: Gower Publishing, 1977, reprinted 1983).

Willis, P. *The Ethnographic Imagination* (Cambridge: Polity Press, 2000).

Willis, P. and Trondman, M. 'Manifesto for Ethnography', *Ethnography* 1(1) (2000), 5–16.

Wolf, D. L. *Feminist Dilemmas in Fieldwork* (Colorado: Westview Press, 1996).

Wood, K. and Jewkes, R. 'Violence, Rape and Sexual Coercion: Everyday Love in a South African Township'. In S. Whitehead and F. Barrett (Eds), *The Masculinities Reader* (Cambridge: Polity, 2001), 133–40.

Woodward, R. '"It's a Man's Life!": Soldiers, Masculinity and the Countryside', *Gender, Place & Culture: A Journal of Feminist Geography* 5(3) (1998), 277–300.

Youdell, D. 'Identity Traps or How Black Students Fail: The Interactions between Biographical, Sub-Cultural, and Learner Identities', *British Journal of Sociology of Education* 1(24) (2003), 3–20.

Yuen, E., Rose, D. and Katsiaficas, G. *The Battle of Seattle: The New Challenge to Capitalist Globalization* (New York: Soft Skull Press, 2001).

Index